THE PUNISHER

VERY SPECIAL HOLIDAYS

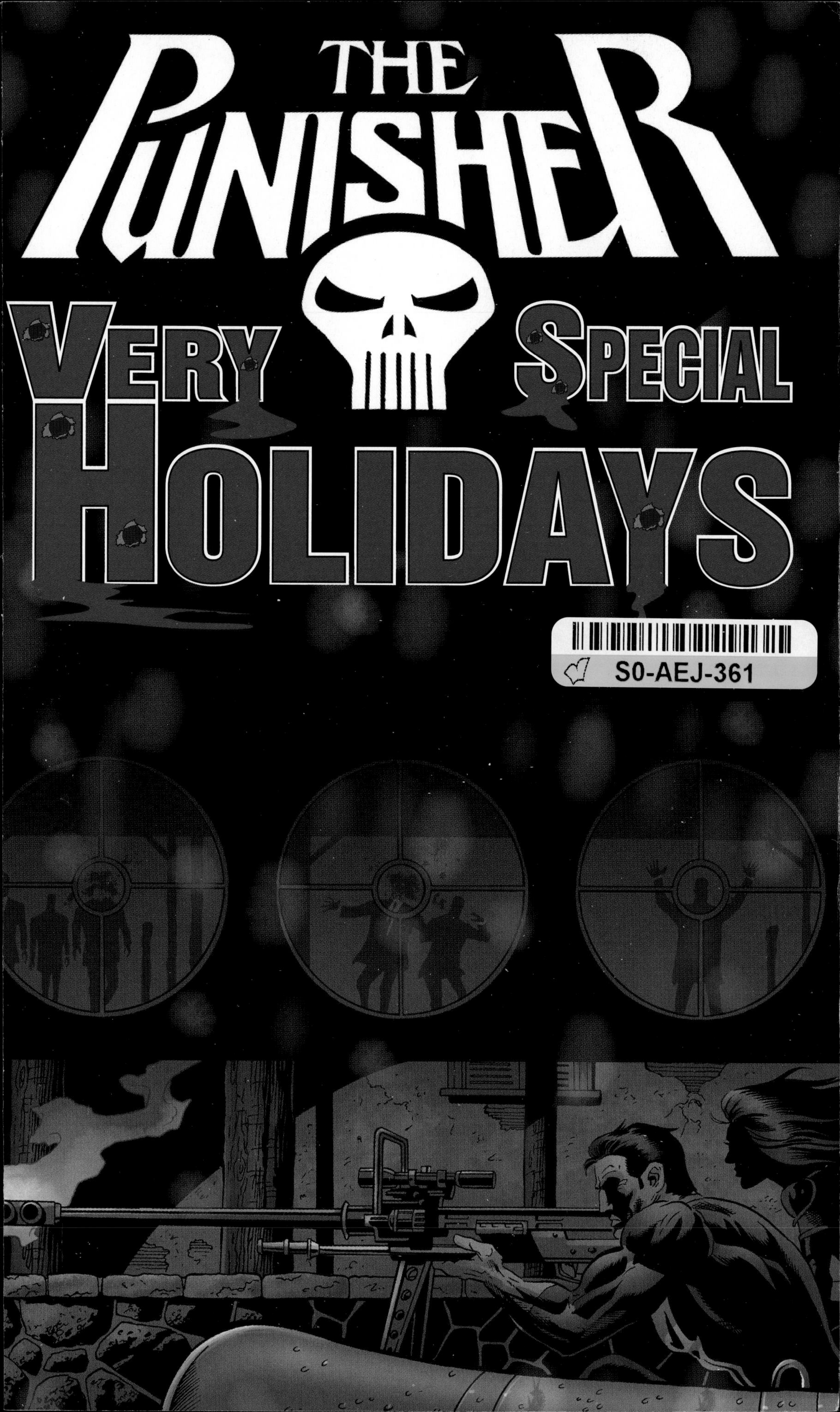

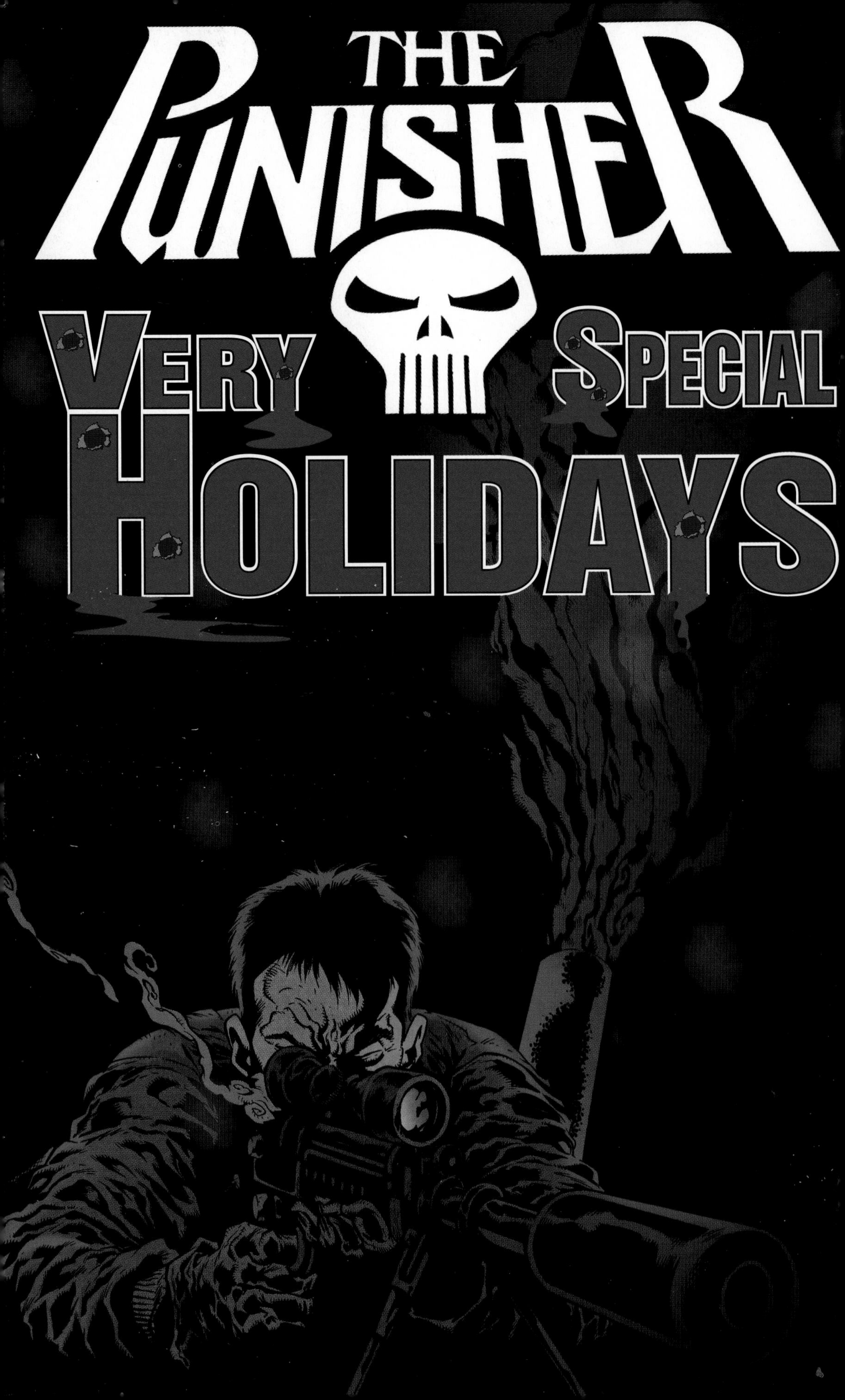
THE PUNISHER
VERY SPECIAL HOLIDAYS

Red X-Mas
Writers: Jimmy Palmiotti & Justin Gray
Pencils: Mark Texeira
Inks: Jimmy Palmiotti
Colors: Raul Treviño

Bloody Valentine
Writers: Jimmy Palmiotti & Justin Gray
Pencils: Paul Gulacy
Inks: Jimmy Palmiotti
Colors: Paul Mounts

Silent Night
Writer: Andy Diggle
Artist: Kyle Hotz
Colors: Jose Villarrubia
Cover Art: Mike Deodato .Jr

Letters: Virtual Calligraphy's Randy Gentile
Associate Editor: Cory Sedlmeier
Editor: Axel Alonso

Collection Editor: Jennifer Grünwald
Assistant Editor: Michael Short
Associate Editor: Mark D. Beazley
Senior Editor, Special Projects: Jeff Youngquist
Vice President of Sales: David Gabriel
Book Designer: Ryan Lewis
Vice President of Creative: Tom Marvelli

Editor in Chief: Joe Quesada
Publisher: Dan Buckley

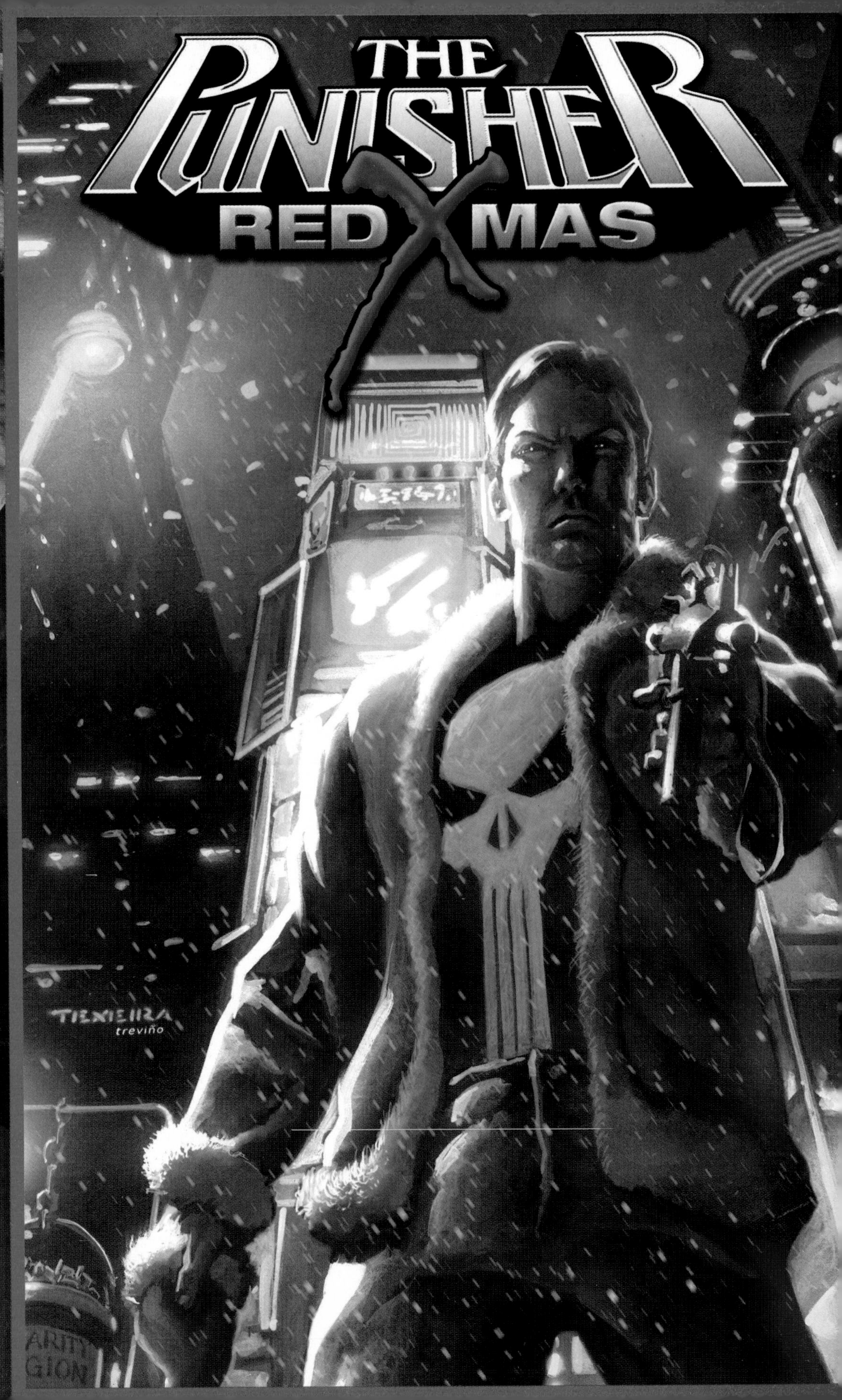
THE PUNISHER
RED X MAS
TEIXEIRA
treviño

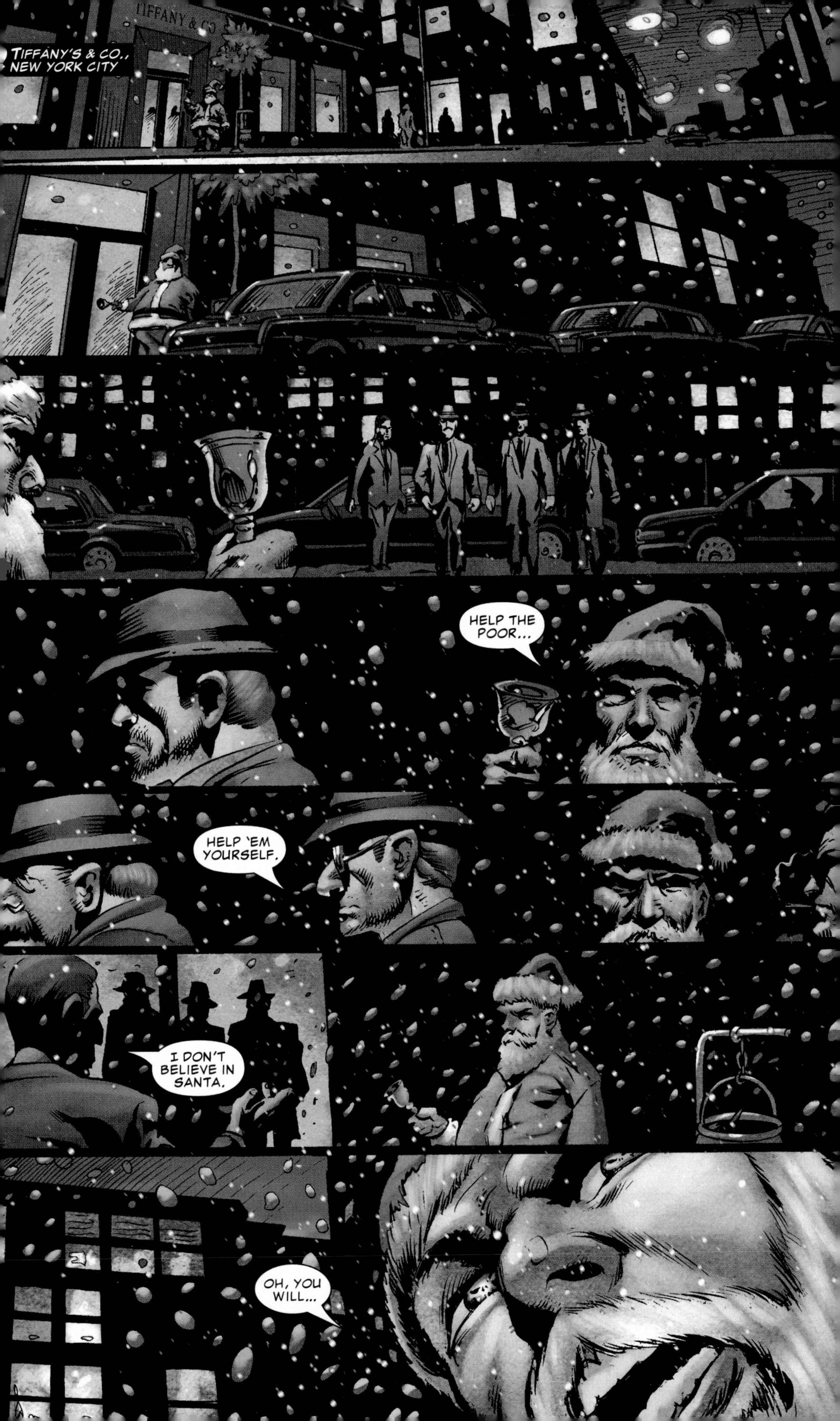
TIFFANY & CO.
TIFFANY'S & CO., NEW YORK CITY
HELP THE POOR...
HELP 'EM YOURSELF.
I DON'T BELIEVE IN SANTA.
OH, YOU WILL...

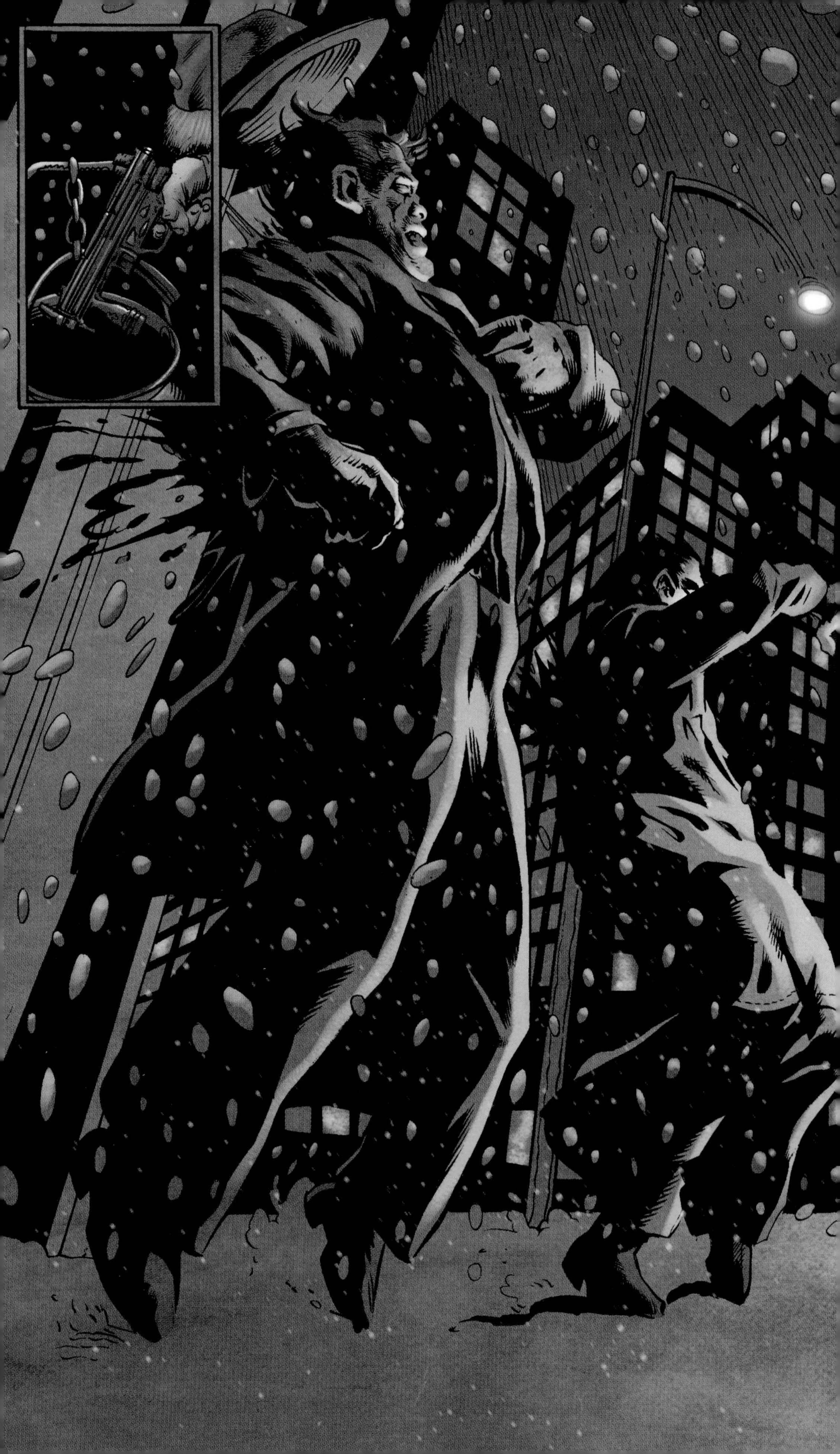

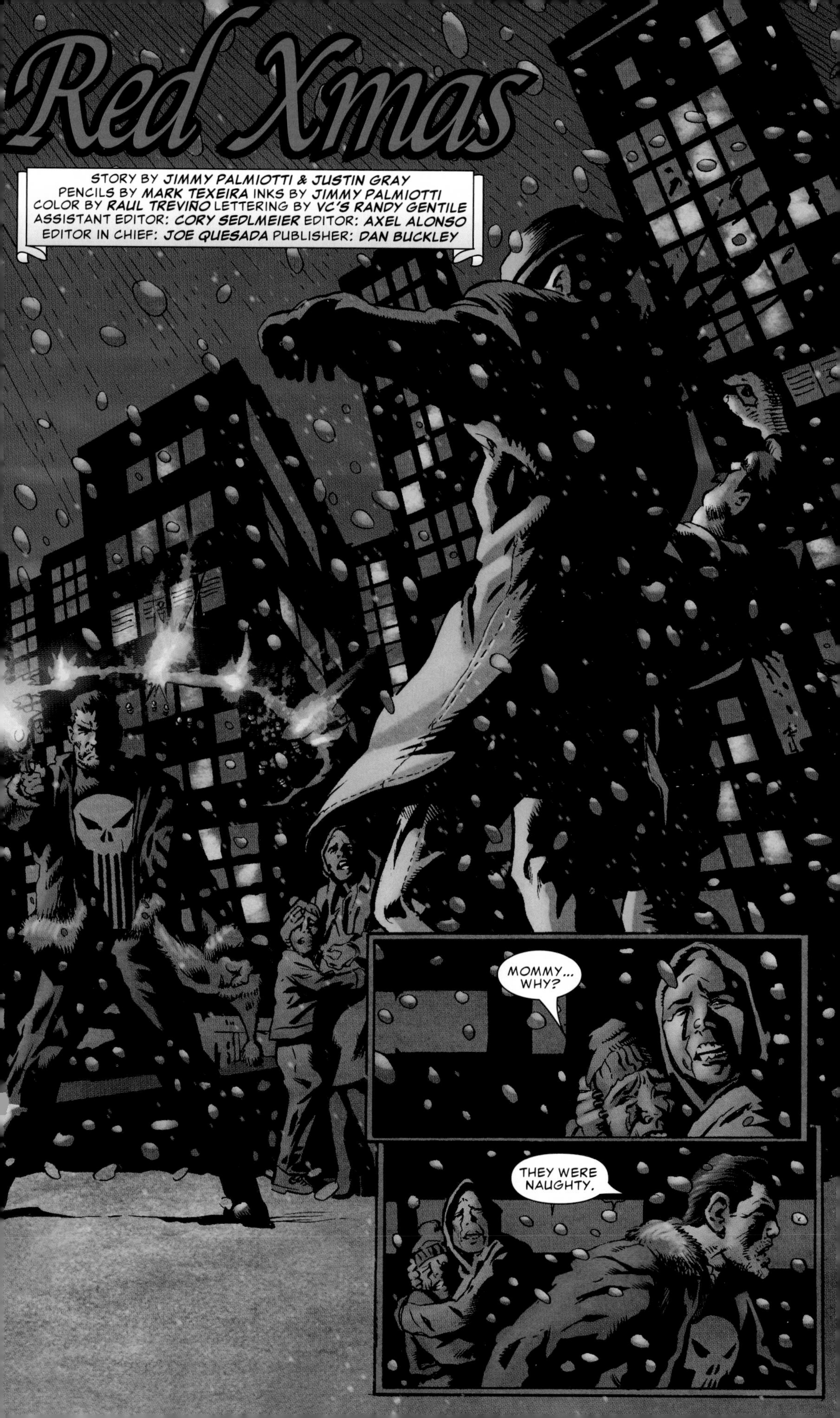
Red Xmas
STORY BY JIMMY PALMIOTTI & JUSTIN GRAY
PENCILS BY MARK TEXEIRA INKS BY JIMMY PALMIOTTI
COLOR BY RAUL TREVIÑO LETTERING BY VC'S RANDY GENTILE
ASSISTANT EDITOR: CORY SEDLMEIER EDITOR: AXEL ALONSO
EDITOR IN CHIEF: JOE QUESADA PUBLISHER: DAN BUCKLEY
MOMMY... WHY?
THEY WERE NAUGHTY.

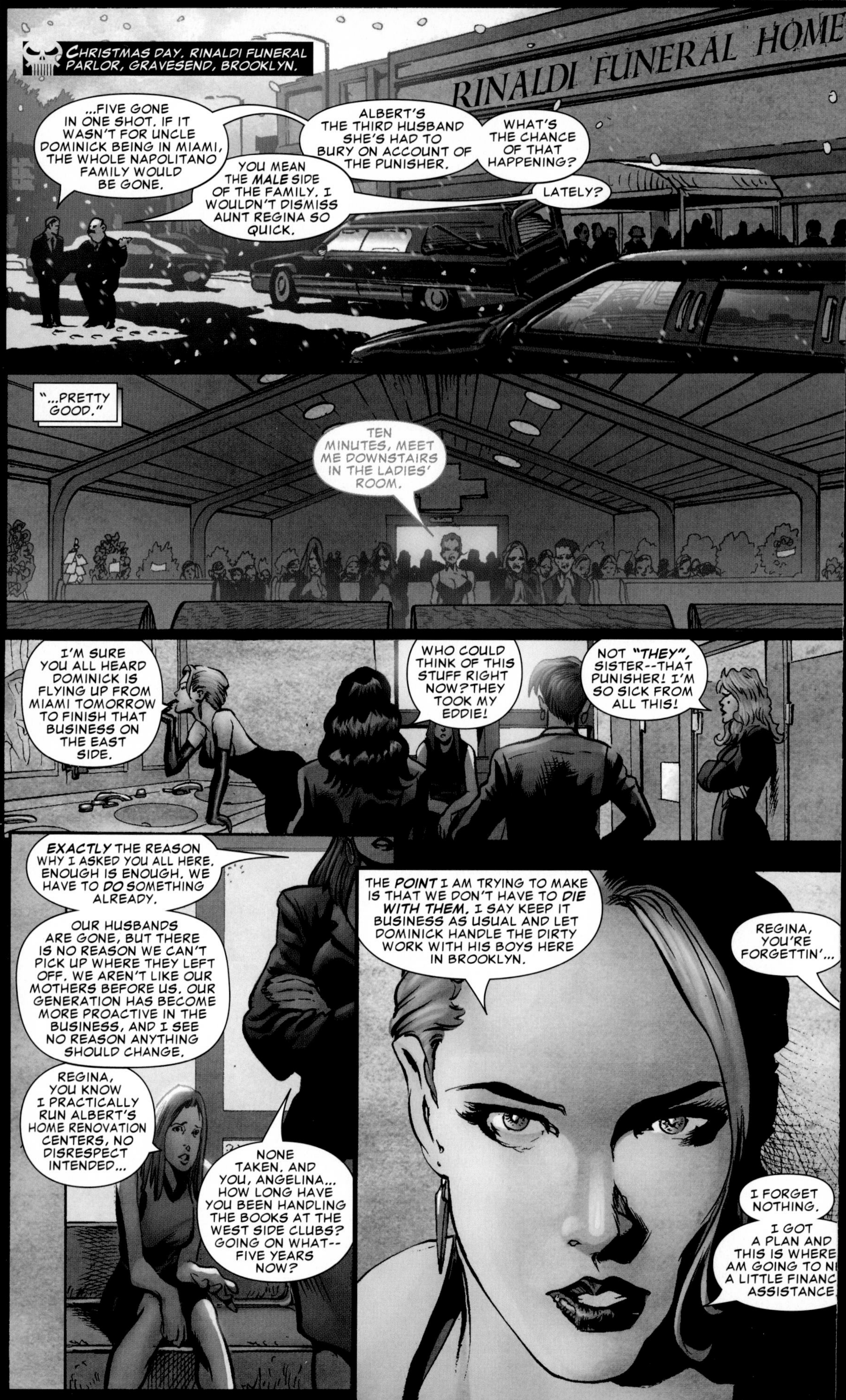
CHRISTMAS DAY, RINALDI FUNERAL PARLOR, GRAVESEND, BROOKLYN.
RINALDI FUNERAL HOME
...FIVE GONE IN ONE SHOT. IF IT WASN'T FOR UNCLE DOMINICK BEING IN MIAMI, THE WHOLE NAPOLITANO FAMILY WOULD BE GONE.
YOU MEAN THE MALE SIDE OF THE FAMILY. I WOULDN'T DISMISS AUNT REGINA SO QUICK.
ALBERT'S THE THIRD HUSBAND SHE'S HAD TO BURY ON ACCOUNT OF THE PUNISHER.
WHAT'S THE CHANCE OF THAT HAPPENING?
LATELY?
"...PRETTY GOOD."
TEN MINUTES, MEET ME DOWNSTAIRS IN THE LADIES' ROOM.
I'M SURE YOU ALL HEARD DOMINICK IS FLYING UP FROM MIAMI TOMORROW TO FINISH THAT BUSINESS ON THE EAST SIDE.
WHO COULD THINK OF THIS STUFF RIGHT NOW? THEY TOOK MY EDDIE!
NOT "THEY", SISTER--THAT PUNISHER! I'M SO SICK FROM ALL THIS!
EXACTLY THE REASON WHY I ASKED YOU ALL HERE. ENOUGH IS ENOUGH. WE HAVE TO DO SOMETHING ALREADY.
OUR HUSBANDS ARE GONE, BUT THERE IS NO REASON WE CAN'T PICK UP WHERE THEY LEFT OFF. WE AREN'T LIKE OUR MOTHERS BEFORE US. OUR GENERATION HAS BECOME MORE PROACTIVE IN THE BUSINESS, AND I SEE NO REASON ANYTHING SHOULD CHANGE.
REGINA, YOU KNOW I PRACTICALLY RUN ALBERT'S HOME RENOVATION CENTERS, NO DISRESPECT INTENDED...
NONE TAKEN, AND YOU, ANGELINA... HOW LONG HAVE YOU BEEN HANDLING THE BOOKS AT THE WEST SIDE CLUBS? GOING ON WHAT--FIVE YEARS NOW?
THE POINT I AM TRYING TO MAKE IS THAT WE DON'T HAVE TO DIE WITH THEM. I SAY KEEP IT BUSINESS AS USUAL AND LET DOMINICK HANDLE THE DIRTY WORK WITH HIS BOYS HERE IN BROOKLYN.
REGINA, YOU'RE FORGETTIN'...
I FORGET NOTHING.
I GOT A PLAN AND THIS IS WHERE

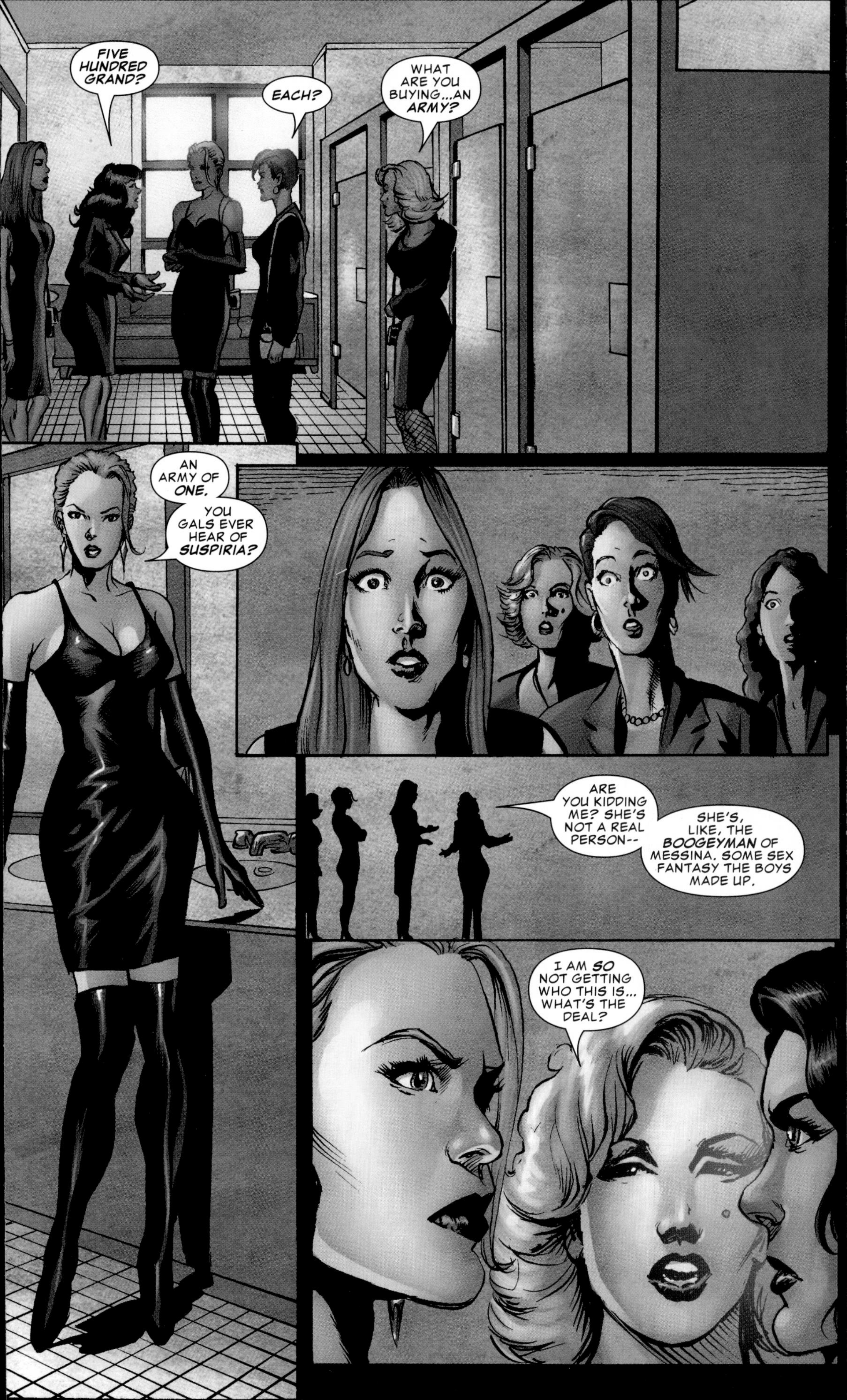
FIVE HUNDRED GRAND?
EACH?
WHAT ARE YOU BUYING...AN ARMY?
AN ARMY OF ONE.
YOU GALS EVER HEAR OF SUSPIRIA?
ARE YOU KIDDING ME? SHE'S NOT A REAL PERSON--
SHE'S, LIKE, THE BOOGEYMAN OF MESSINA. SOME SEX FANTASY THE BOYS MADE UP.
I AM SO NOT GETTING WHO THIS IS... WHAT'S THE DEAL?

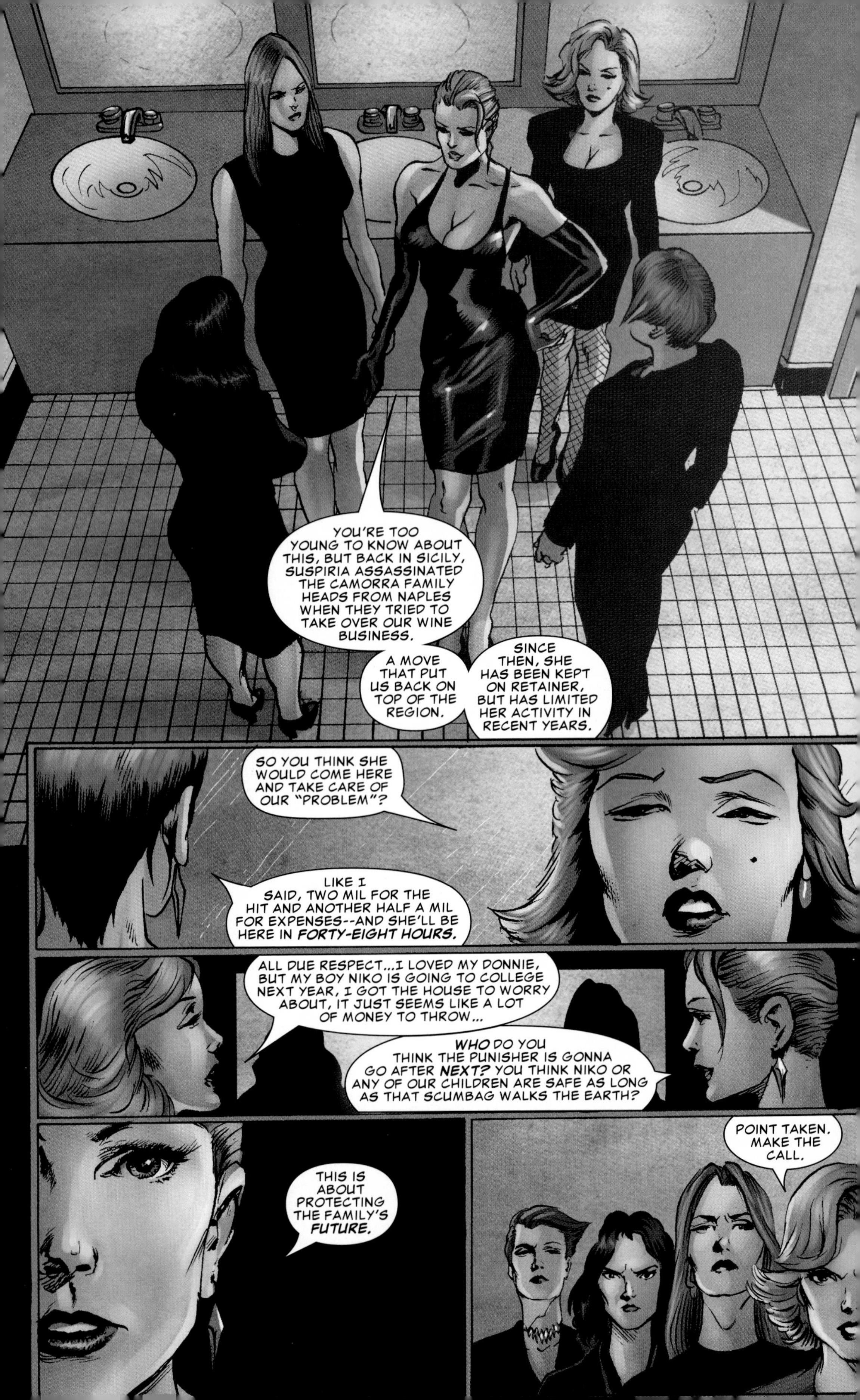
YOU'RE TOO YOUNG TO KNOW ABOUT THIS, BUT BACK IN SICILY, SUSPIRIA ASSASSINATED THE CAMORRA FAMILY HEADS FROM NAPLES WHEN THEY TRIED TO TAKE OVER OUR WINE BUSINESS.
A MOVE THAT PUT US BACK ON TOP OF THE REGION.
SINCE THEN, SHE HAS BEEN KEPT ON RETAINER, BUT HAS LIMITED HER ACTIVITY IN RECENT YEARS.
SO YOU THINK SHE WOULD COME HERE AND TAKE CARE OF OUR "PROBLEM"?
LIKE I SAID, TWO MIL FOR THE HIT AND ANOTHER HALF A MIL FOR EXPENSES--AND SHE'LL BE HERE IN ***FORTY-EIGHT HOURS.***
ALL DUE RESPECT...I LOVED MY DONNIE, BUT MY BOY NIKO IS GOING TO COLLEGE NEXT YEAR, I GOT THE HOUSE TO WORRY ABOUT, IT JUST SEEMS LIKE A LOT OF MONEY TO THROW...
WHO DO YOU THINK THE PUNISHER IS GONNA GO AFTER ***NEXT?*** YOU THINK NIKO OR ANY OF OUR CHILDREN ARE SAFE AS LONG AS THAT SCUMBAG WALKS THE EARTH?
THIS IS ABOUT PROTECTING THE FAMILY'S ***FUTURE.***
POINT TAKEN. MAKE THE CALL.

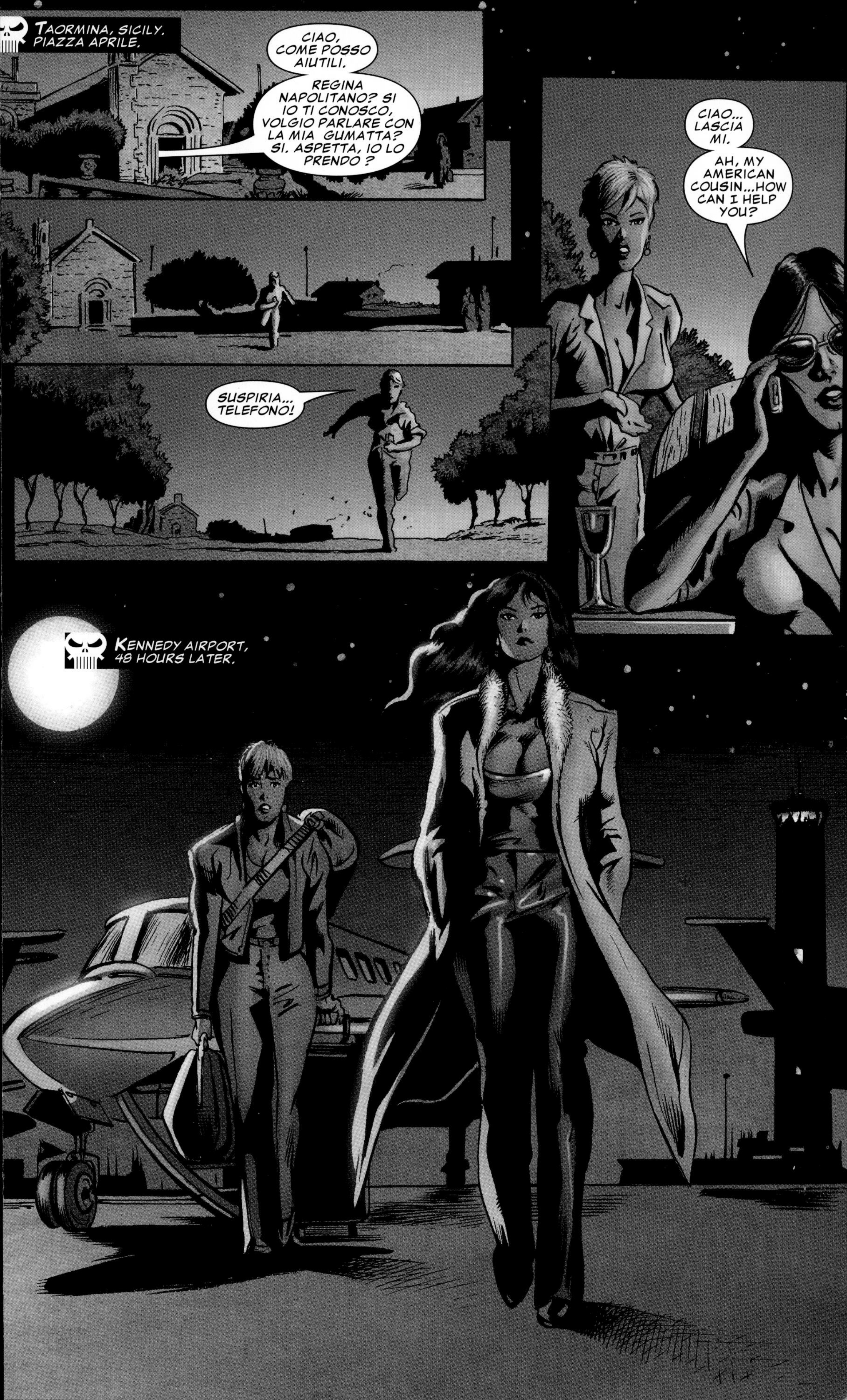
TAORMINA, SICILY. PIAZZA APRILE.
CIAO, COME POSSO AIUTILI.
REGINA NAPOLITANO? SI IO TI CONOSCO, VOLGIO PARLARE CON LA MIA GUMATTA? SI. ASPETTA, IO LO PRENDO ?
SUSPIRIA... TELEFONO!
CIAO... LASCIA MI.
AH, MY AMERICAN COUSIN...HOW CAN I HELP YOU?
KENNEDY AIRPORT, 48 HOURS LATER.

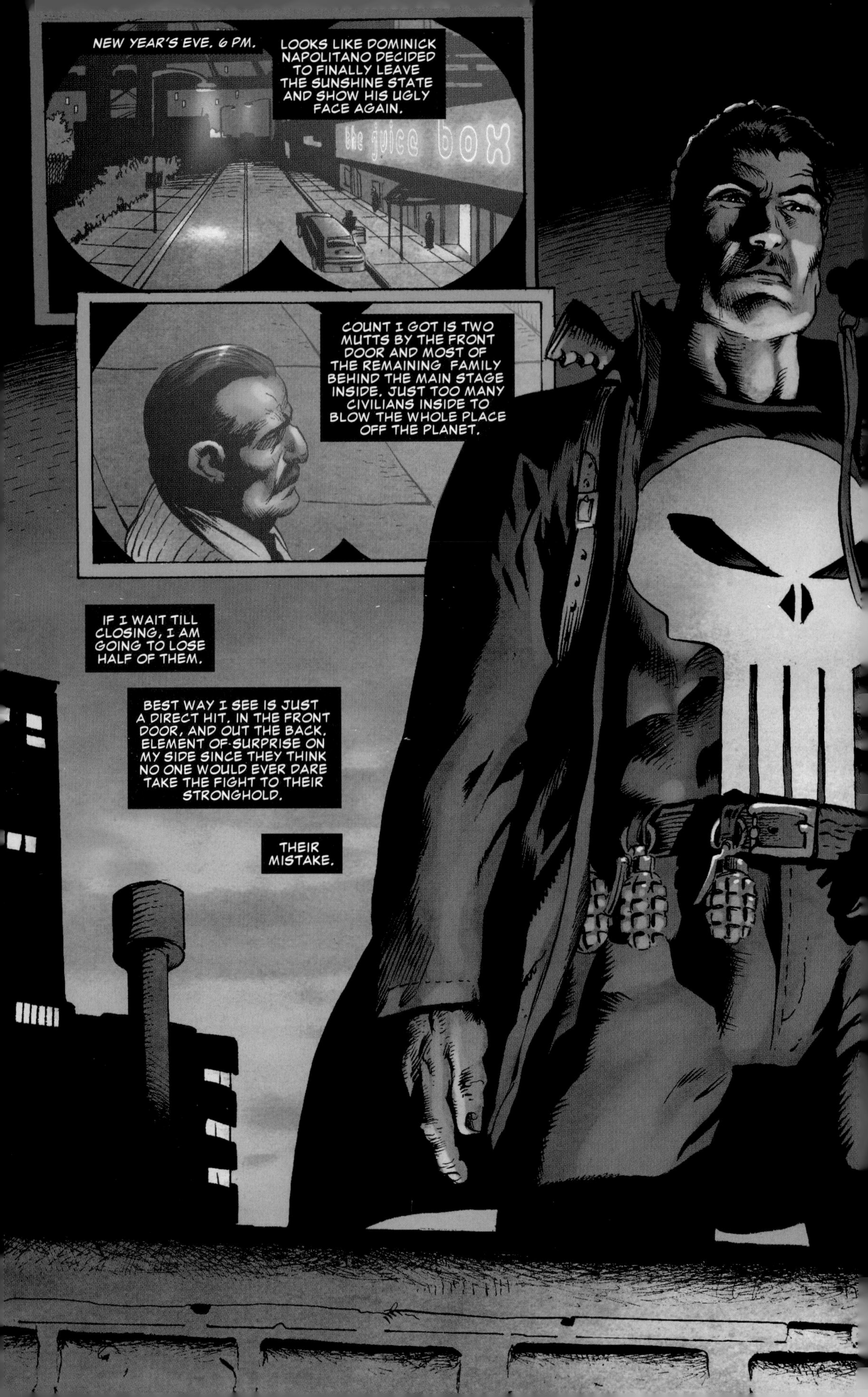
NEW YEAR'S EVE. 6 PM.
LOOKS LIKE DOMINICK NAPOLITANO DECIDED TO FINALLY LEAVE THE SUNSHINE STATE AND SHOW HIS UGLY FACE AGAIN.
the juice box
COUNT I GOT IS TWO MUTTS BY THE FRONT DOOR AND MOST OF THE REMAINING FAMILY BEHIND THE MAIN STAGE INSIDE. JUST TOO MANY CIVILIANS INSIDE TO BLOW THE WHOLE PLACE OFF THE PLANET.
IF I WAIT TILL CLOSING, I AM GOING TO LOSE HALF OF THEM.
BEST WAY I SEE IS JUST A DIRECT HIT. IN THE FRONT DOOR, AND OUT THE BACK. ELEMENT OF SURPRISE ON MY SIDE SINCE THEY THINK NO ONE WOULD EVER DARE TAKE THE FIGHT TO THEIR STRONGHOLD.
THEIR MISTAKE.

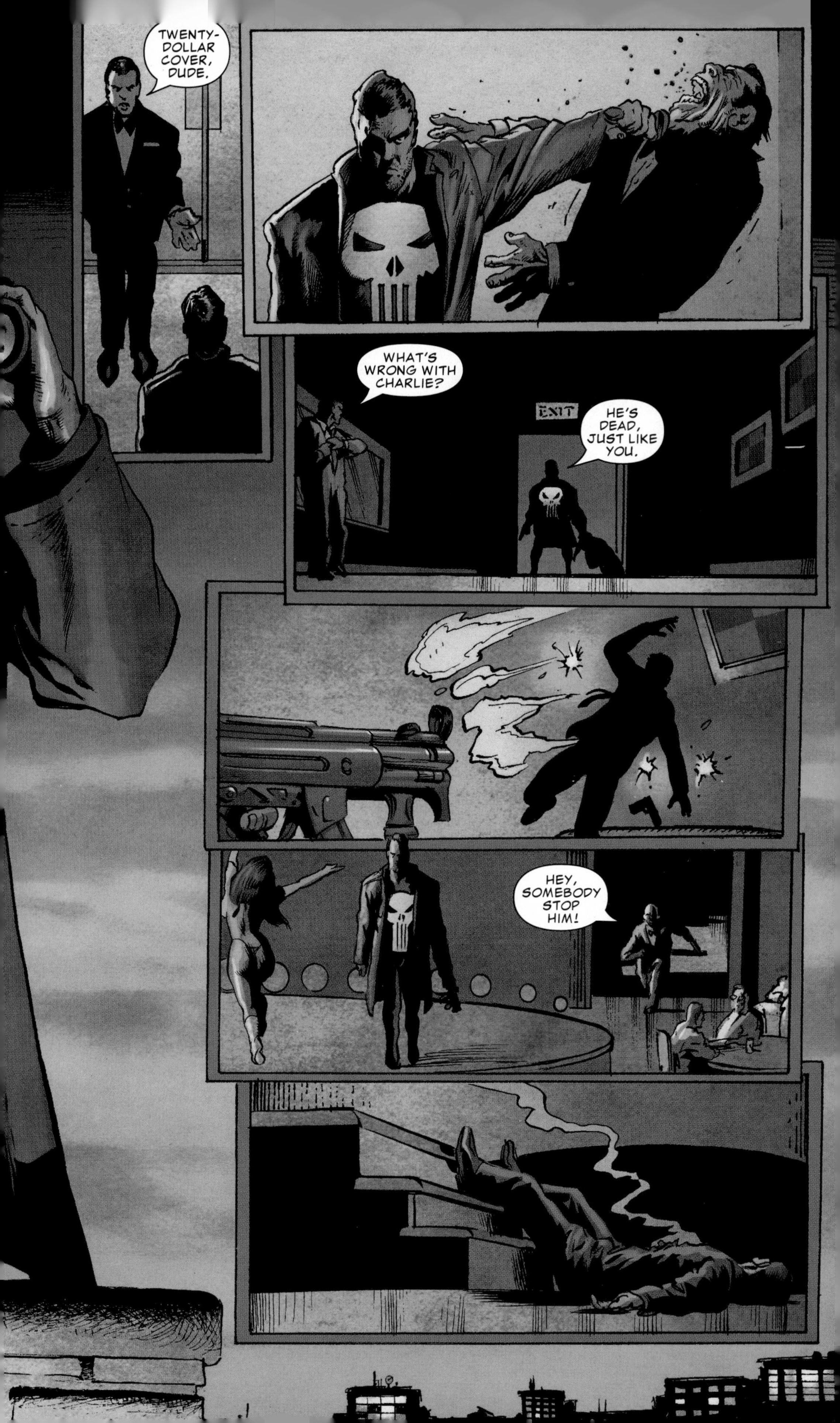
TWENTY-DOLLAR COVER, DUDE.
WHAT'S WRONG WITH CHARLIE?
EXIT
HE'S DEAD, JUST LIKE YOU.
HEY, SOMEBODY STOP HIM!

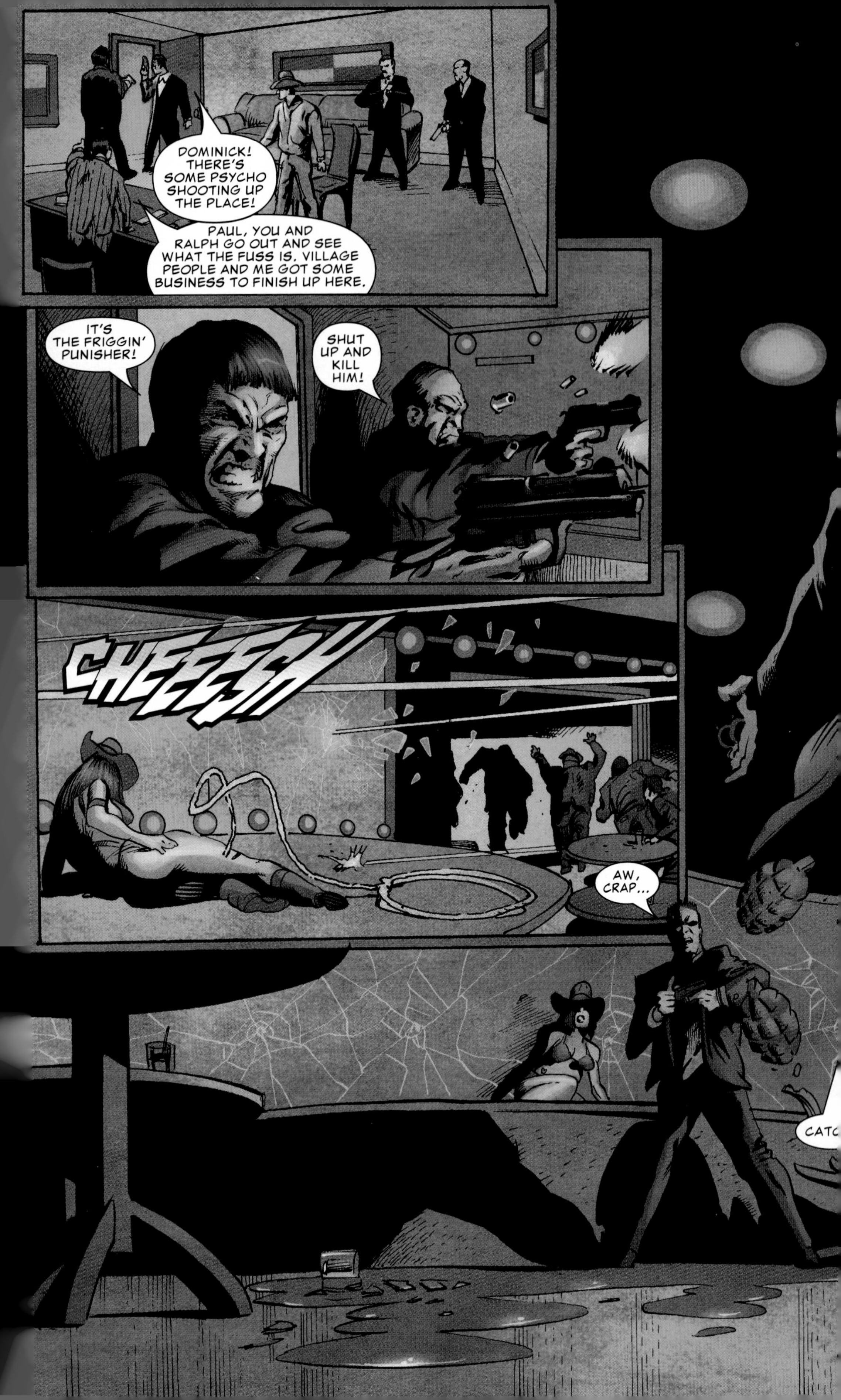
DOMINICK! THERE'S SOME PSYCHO SHOOTING UP THE PLACE!
PAUL, YOU AND RALPH GO OUT AND SEE WHAT THE FUSS IS. VILLAGE PEOPLE AND ME GOT SOME BUSINESS TO FINISH UP HERE.
IT'S THE FRIGGIN' PUNISHER!
SHUT UP AND KILL HIM!
CHEEESH
AW, CRAP...
CATC

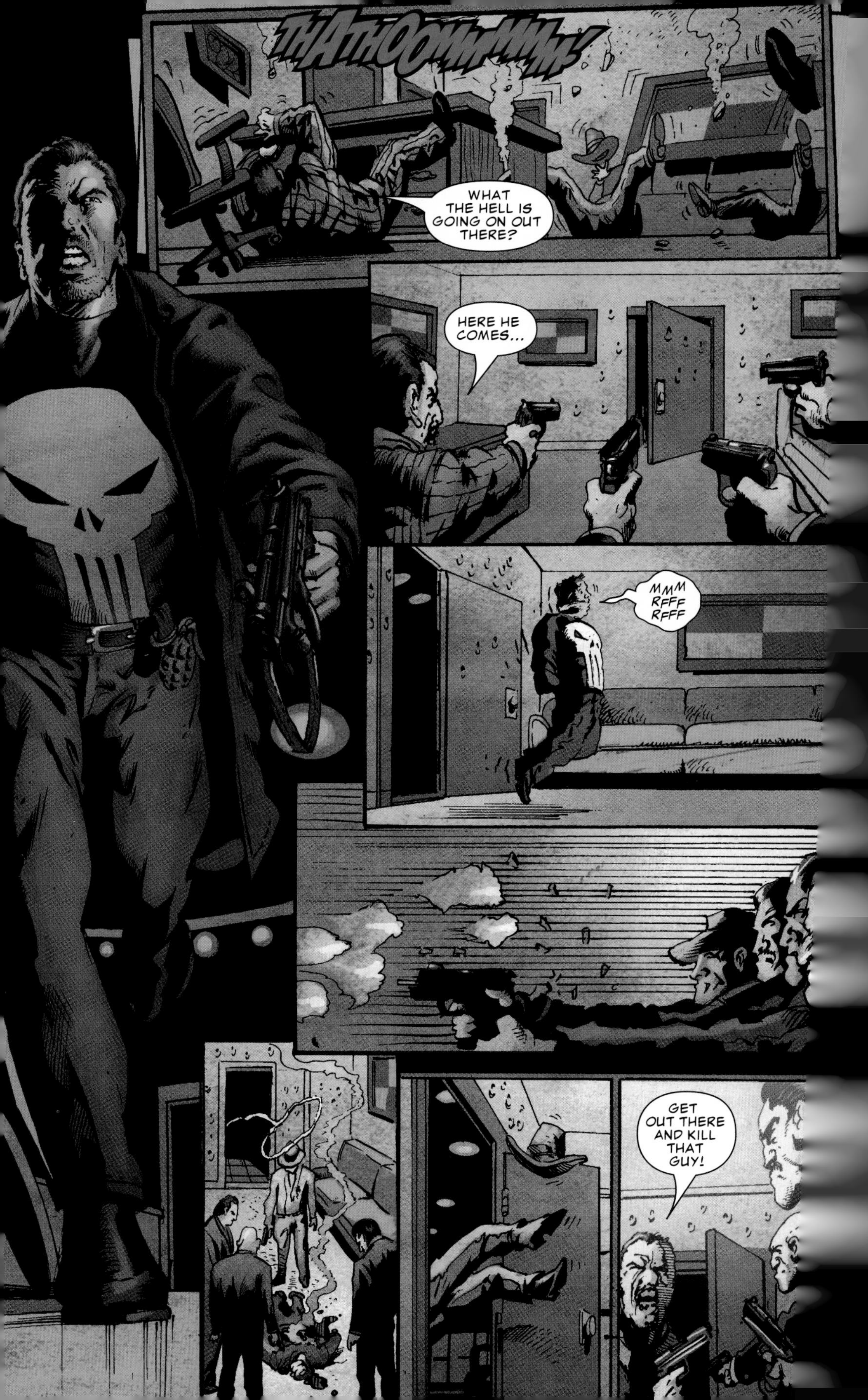
THATHOOMMMMM!
WHAT THE HELL IS GOING ON OUT THERE?
HERE HE COMES...
MMM RFFF RFFF
GET OUT THERE AND KILL THAT GUY!

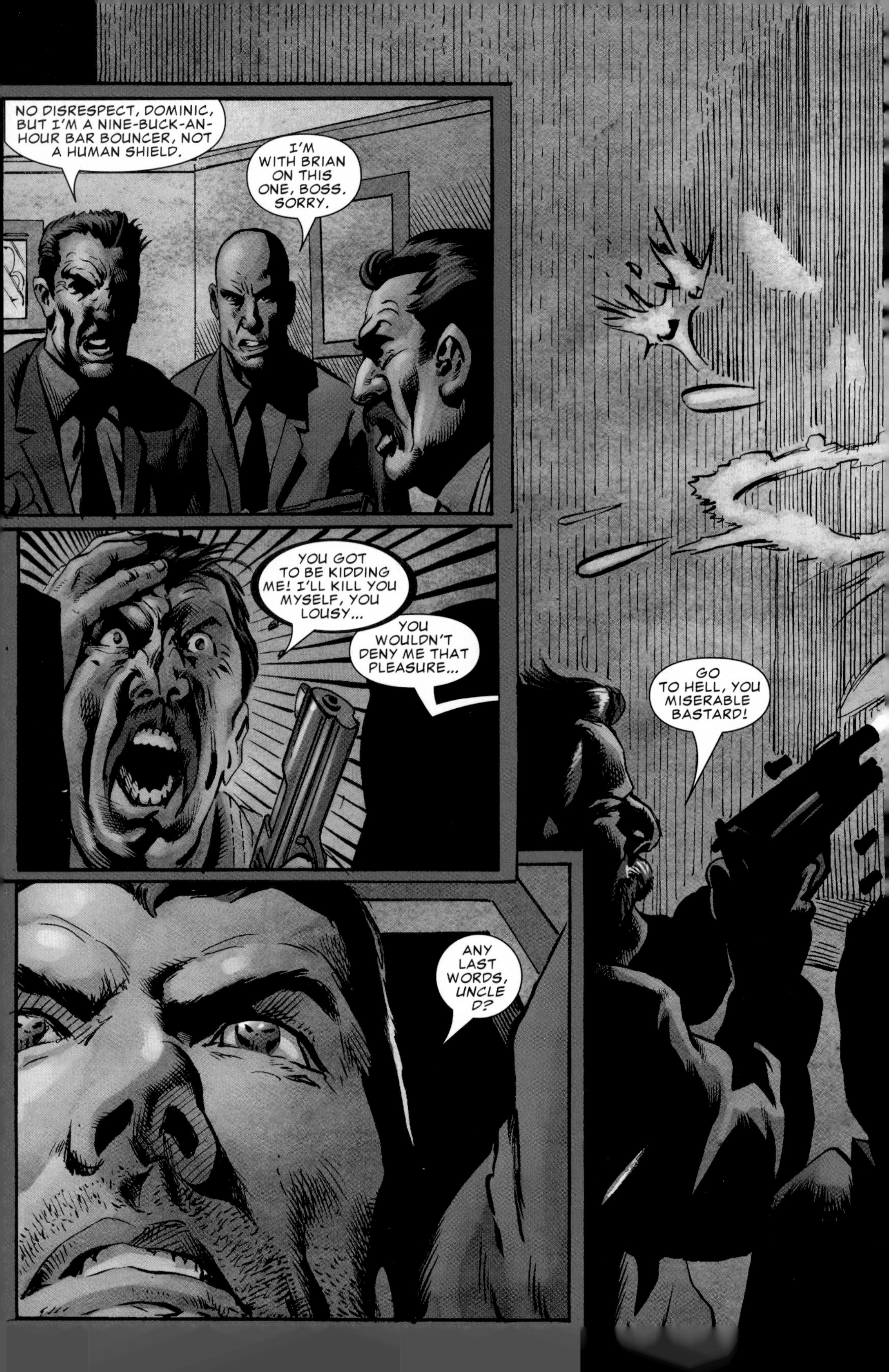
NO DISRESPECT, DOMINIC, BUT I'M A NINE-BUCK-AN-HOUR BAR BOUNCER, NOT A HUMAN SHIELD.
I'M WITH BRIAN ON THIS ONE, BOSS. SORRY.
YOU GOT TO BE KIDDING ME! I'LL KILL YOU MYSELF, YOU LOUSY...
YOU WOULDN'T DENY ME THAT PLEASURE...
ANY LAST WORDS, UNCLE D?
GO TO HELL, YOU MISERABLE BASTARD!

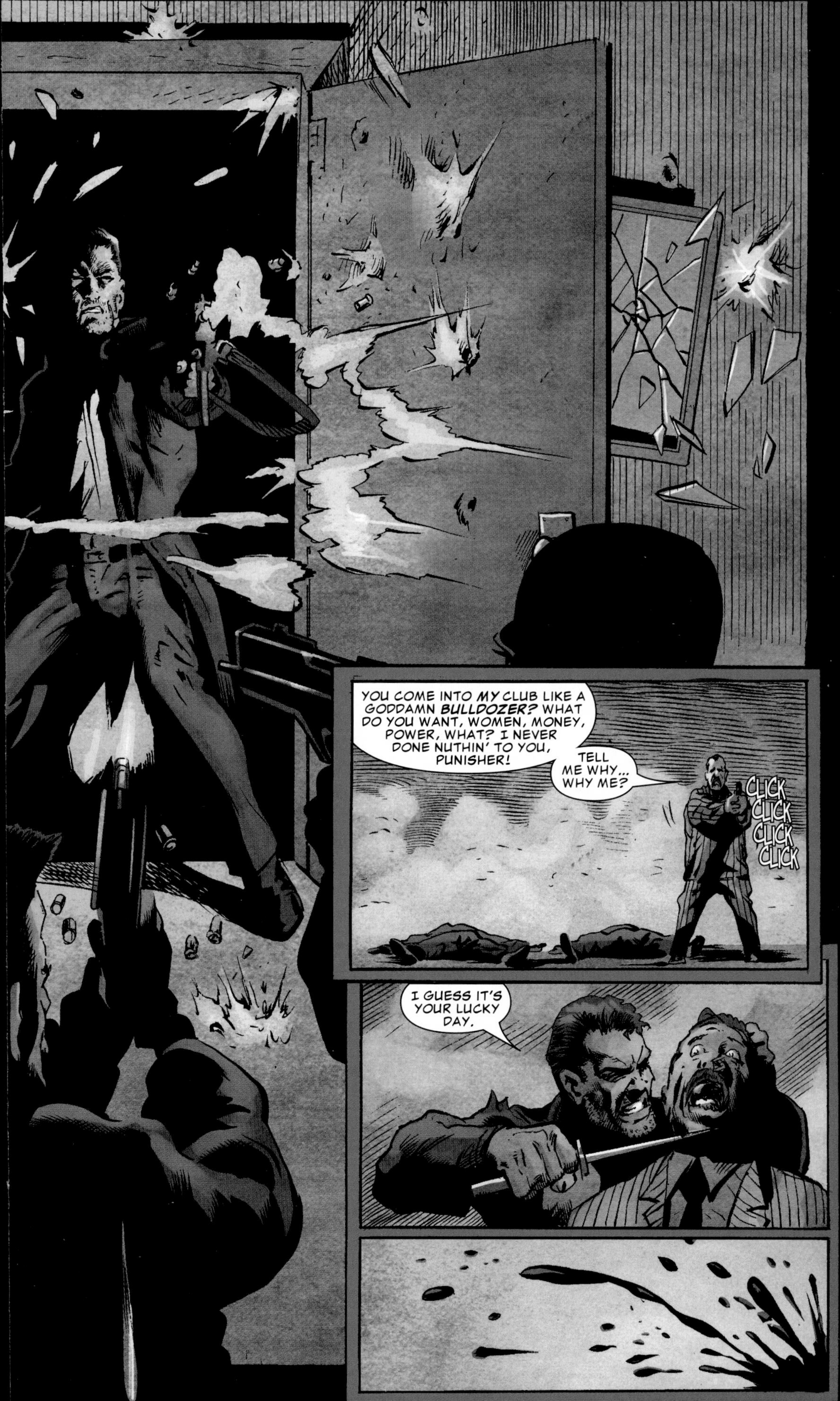
YOU COME INTO MY CLUB LIKE A GODDAMN BULLDOZER? WHAT DO YOU WANT, WOMEN, MONEY, POWER, WHAT? I NEVER DONE NUTHIN' TO YOU, PUNISHER!
TELL ME WHY... WHY ME?
CLICK
CLICK
CLICK
CLICK
I GUESS IT'S YOUR LUCKY DAY.

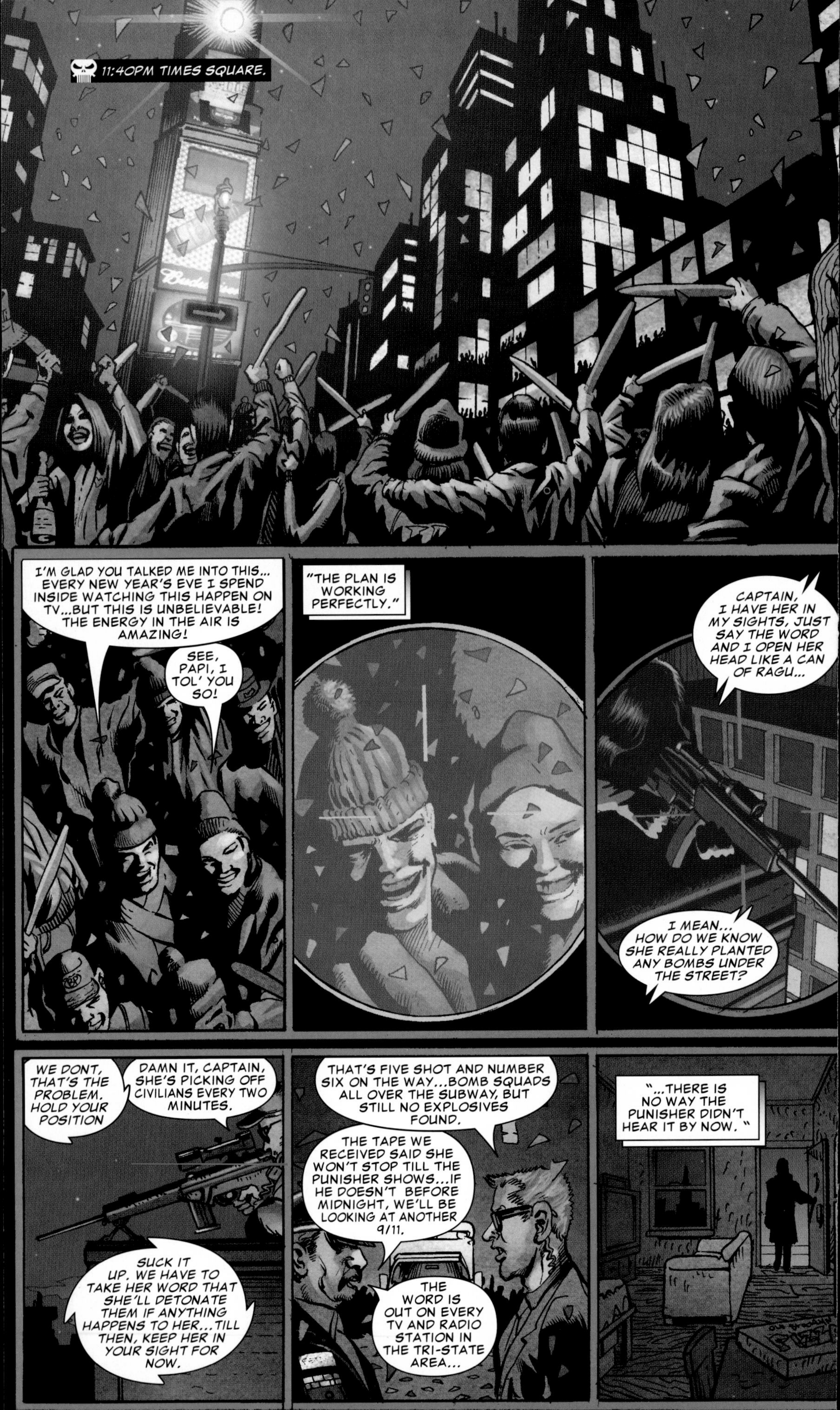
11:40PM TIMES SQUARE.
I'M GLAD YOU TALKED ME INTO THIS... EVERY NEW YEAR'S EVE I SPEND INSIDE WATCHING THIS HAPPEN ON TV...BUT THIS IS UNBELIEVABLE! THE ENERGY IN THE AIR IS AMAZING!
SEE, PAPI, I TOL' YOU SO!
"THE PLAN IS WORKING PERFECTLY."
CAPTAIN, I HAVE HER IN MY SIGHTS, JUST SAY THE WORD AND I OPEN HER HEAD LIKE A CAN OF RAGU...
I MEAN... HOW DO WE KNOW SHE REALLY PLANTED ANY BOMBS UNDER THE STREET?
WE DONT, THAT'S THE PROBLEM. HOLD YOUR POSITION
DAMN IT, CAPTAIN, SHE'S PICKING OFF CIVILIANS EVERY TWO MINUTES.
SUCK IT UP. WE HAVE TO TAKE HER WORD THAT SHE'LL DETONATE THEM IF ANYTHING HAPPENS TO HER...TILL THEN, KEEP HER IN YOUR SIGHT FOR NOW.
THAT'S FIVE SHOT AND NUMBER SIX ON THE WAY...BOMB SQUADS ALL OVER THE SUBWAY, BUT STILL NO EXPLOSIVES FOUND.
THE TAPE WE RECEIVED SAID SHE WON'T STOP TILL THE PUNISHER SHOWS...IF HE DOESN'T BEFORE MIDNIGHT, WE'LL BE LOOKING AT ANOTHER 9/11.
THE WORD IS OUT ON EVERY TV AND RADIO STATION IN THE TRI-STATE AREA...
"...THERE IS NO WAY THE PUNISHER DIDN'T HEAR IT BY NOW."

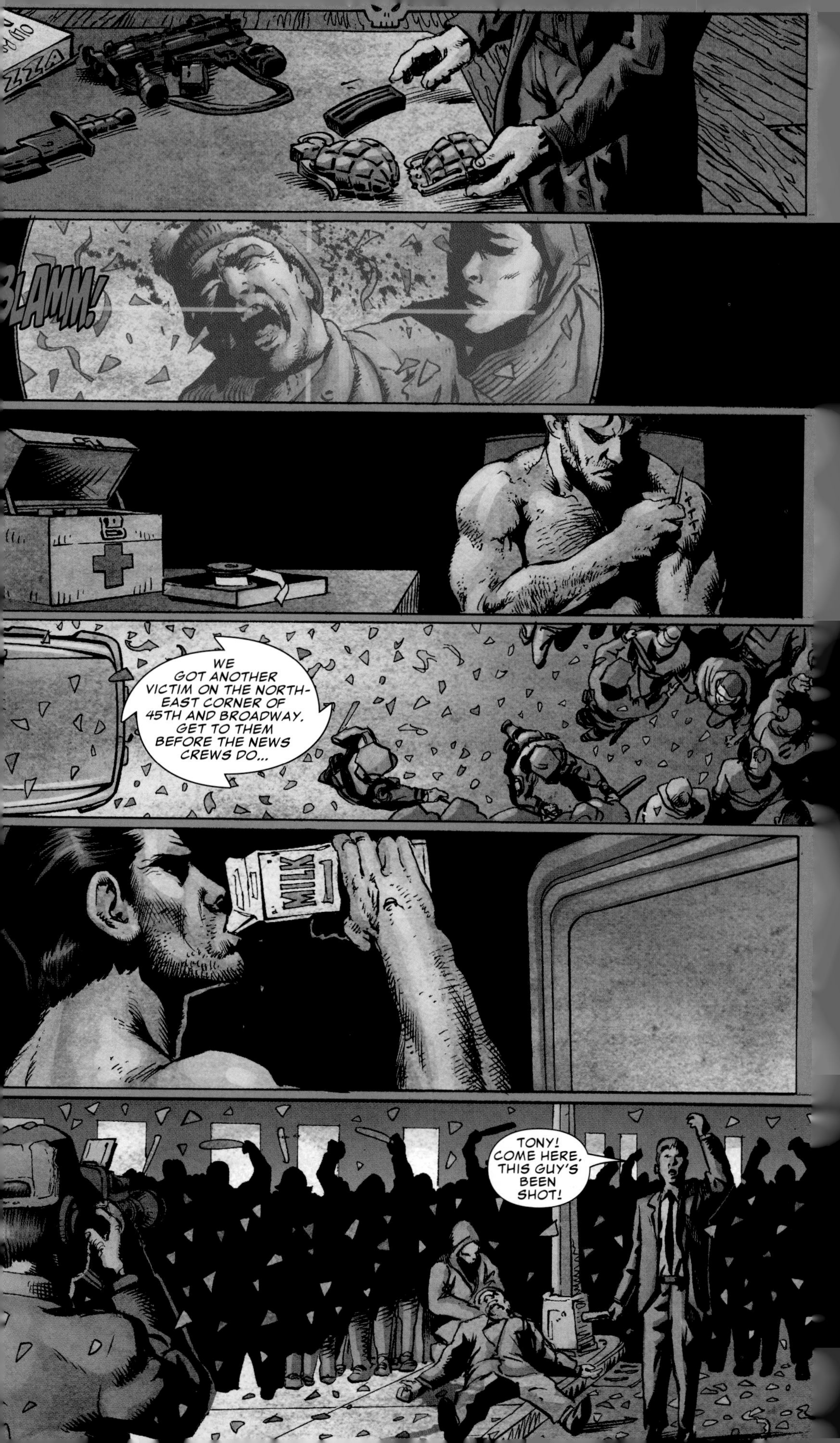

BLAMM!
WE GOT ANOTHER VICTIM ON THE NORTH-EAST CORNER OF 45TH AND BROADWAY. GET TO THEM BEFORE THE NEWS CREWS DO...
MILK
TONY! COME HERE. THIS GUY'S BEEN SHOT!

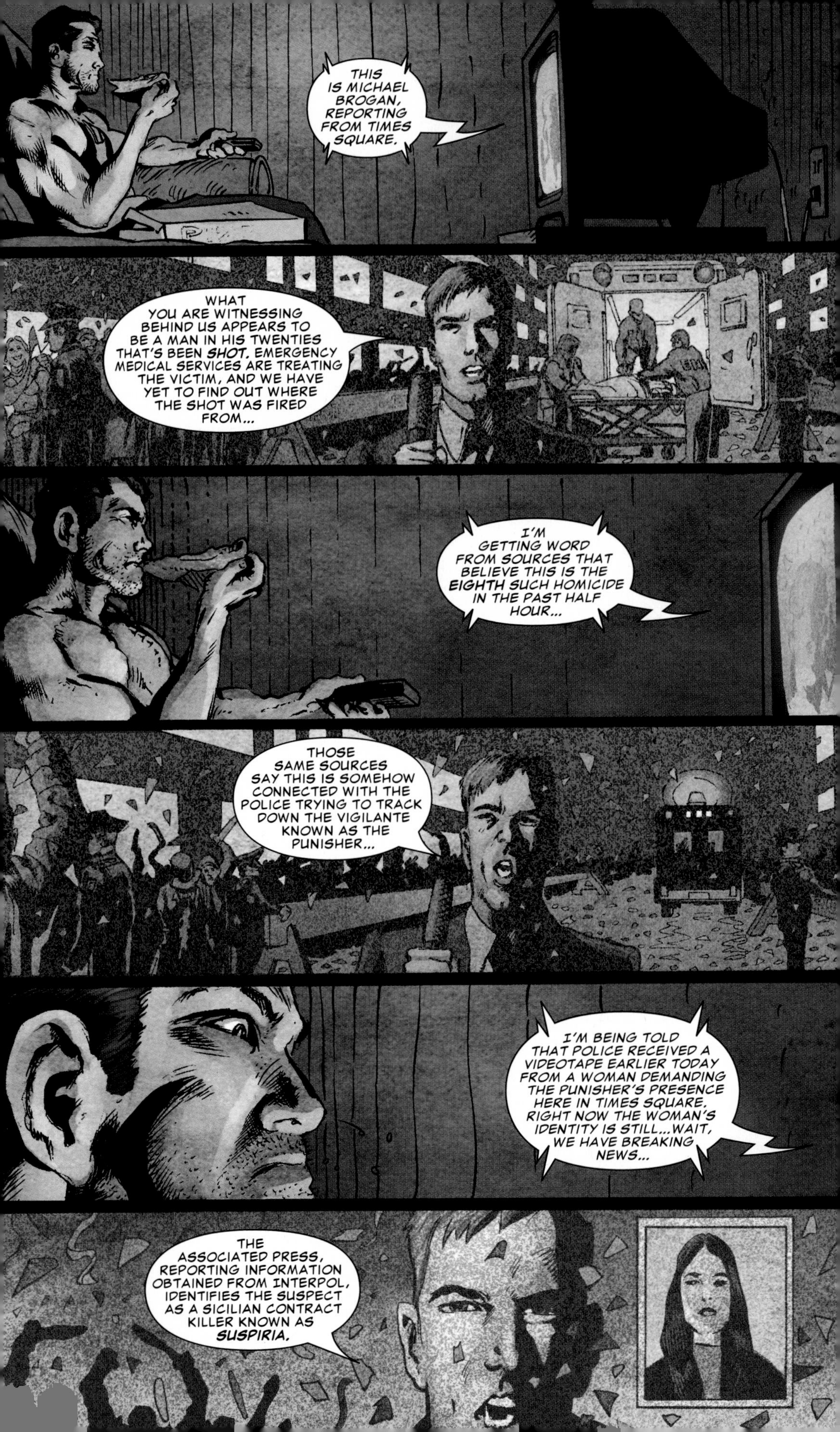
THIS IS MICHAEL BROGAN, REPORTING FROM TIMES SQUARE.
WHAT YOU ARE WITNESSING BEHIND US APPEARS TO BE A MAN IN HIS TWENTIES THAT'S BEEN SHOT. EMERGENCY MEDICAL SERVICES ARE TREATING THE VICTIM, AND WE HAVE YET TO FIND OUT WHERE THE SHOT WAS FIRED FROM...
I'M GETTING WORD FROM SOURCES THAT BELIEVE THIS IS THE EIGHTH SUCH HOMICIDE IN THE PAST HALF HOUR...
THOSE SAME SOURCES SAY THIS IS SOMEHOW CONNECTED WITH THE POLICE TRYING TO TRACK DOWN THE VIGILANTE KNOWN AS THE PUNISHER...
I'M BEING TOLD THAT POLICE RECEIVED A VIDEOTAPE EARLIER TODAY FROM A WOMAN DEMANDING THE PUNISHER'S PRESENCE HERE IN TIMES SQUARE. RIGHT NOW THE WOMAN'S IDENTITY IS STILL...WAIT, WE HAVE BREAKING NEWS...
THE ASSOCIATED PRESS, REPORTING INFORMATION OBTAINED FROM INTERPOL, IDENTIFIES THE SUSPECT AS A SICILIAN CONTRACT KILLER KNOWN AS SUSPIRIA.

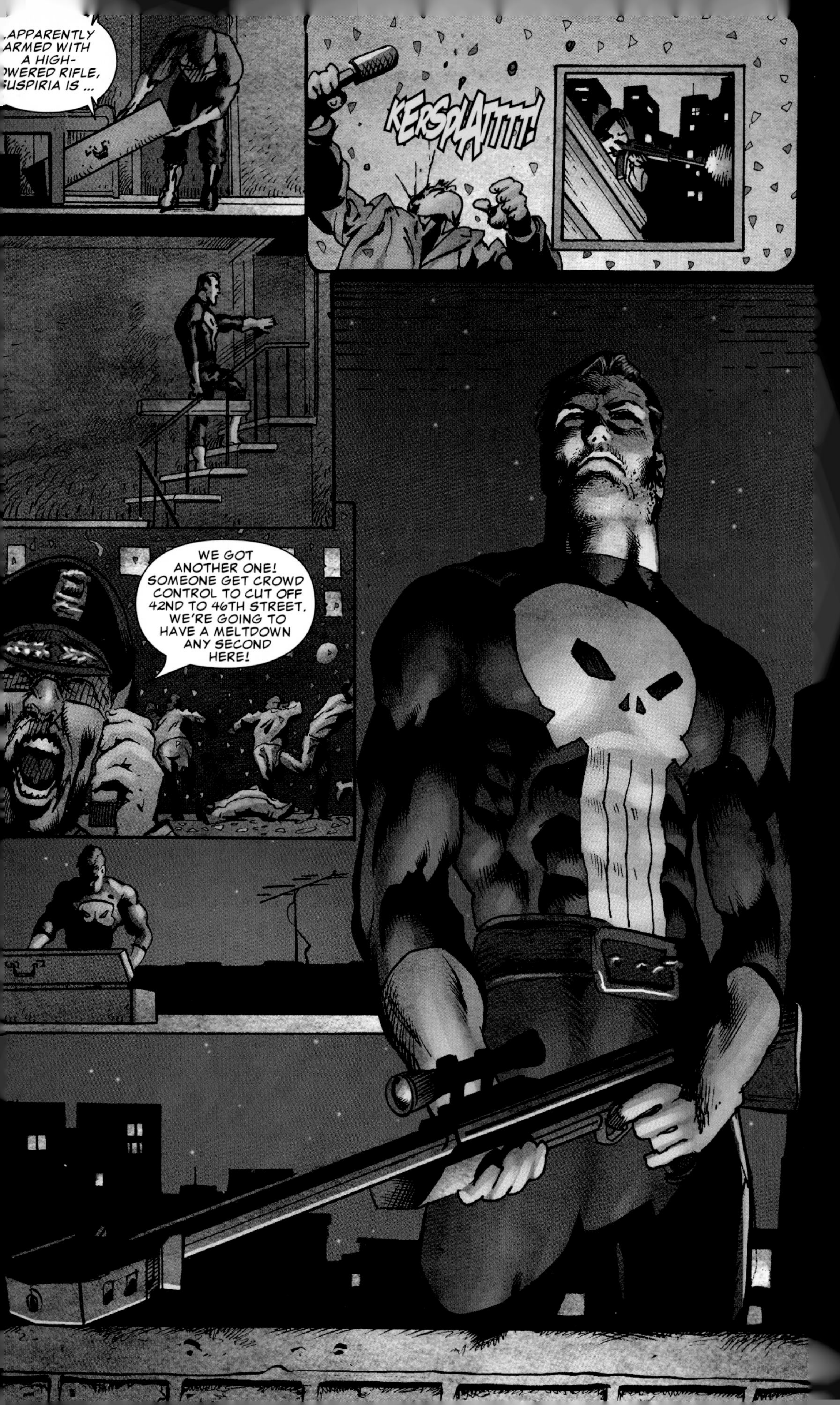
...APPARENTLY ARMED WITH A HIGH-POWERED RIFLE, SUSPIRIA IS ...
KERSPLATTTT!
WE GOT ANOTHER ONE! SOMEONE GET CROWD CONTROL TO CUT OFF 42ND TO 46TH STREET. WE'RE GOING TO HAVE A MELTDOWN ANY SECOND HERE!

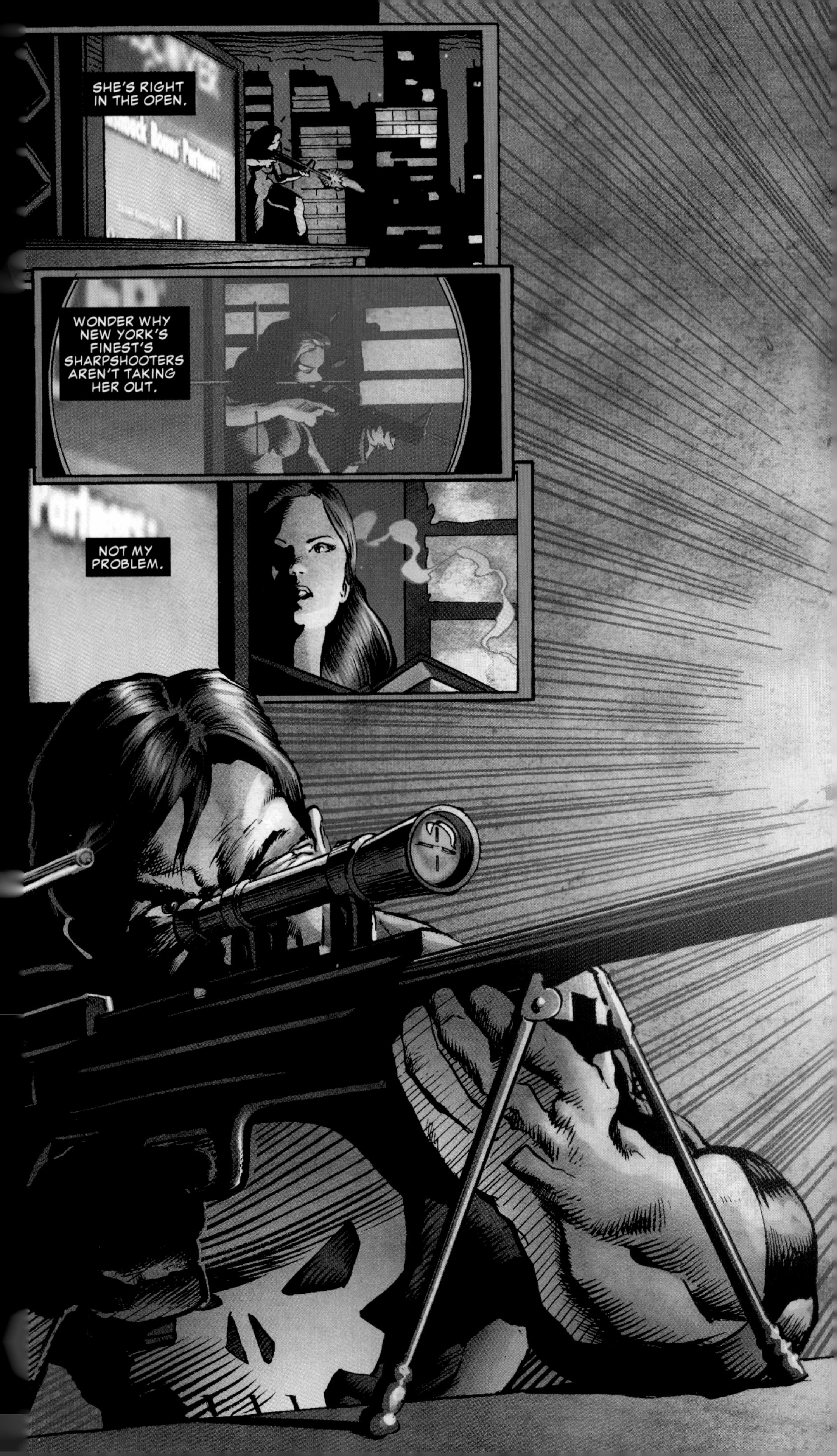
SHE'S RIGHT IN THE OPEN.
WONDER WHY NEW YORK'S FINEST'S SHARPSHOOTERS AREN'T TAKING HER OUT.
NOT MY PROBLEM.

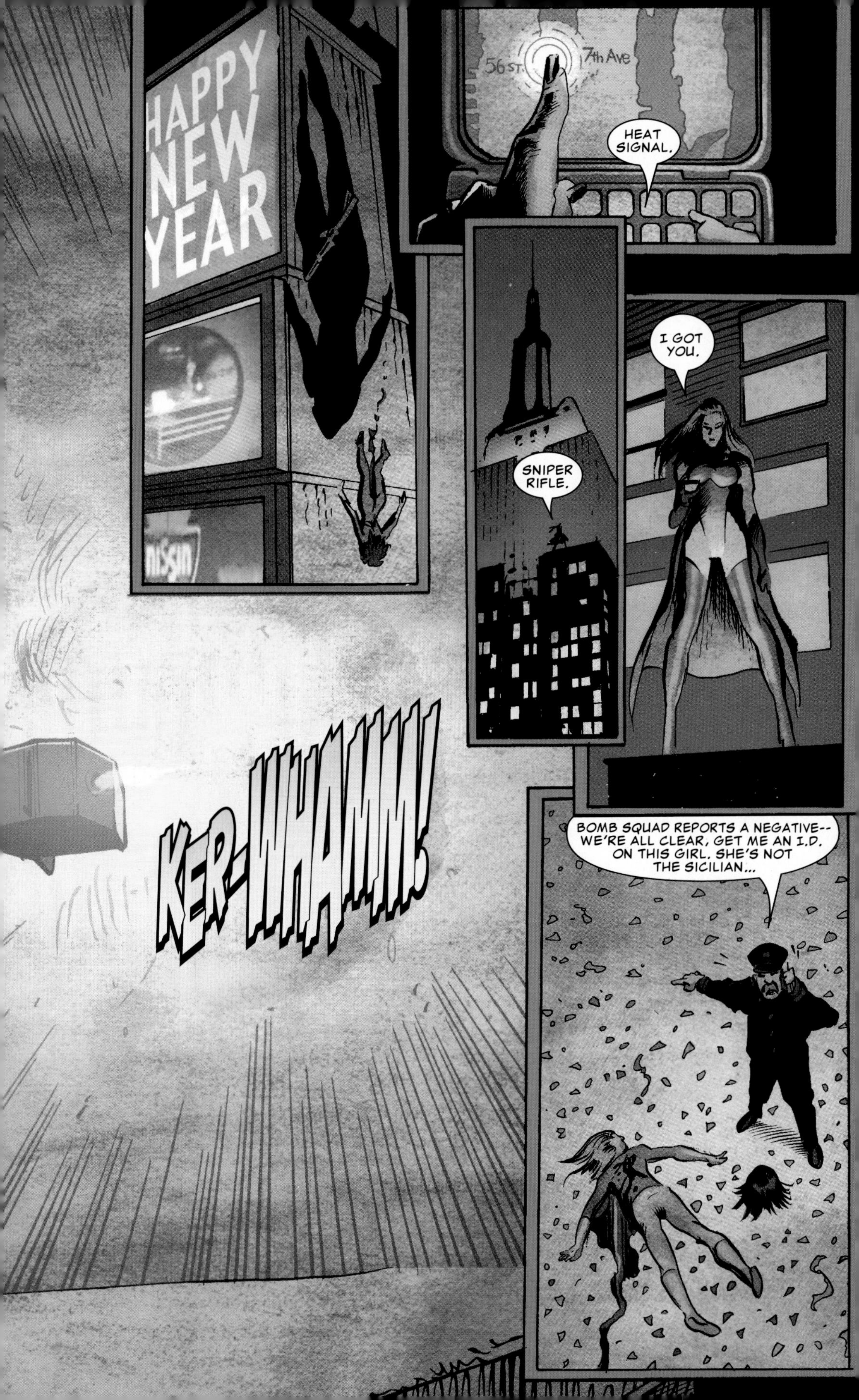
HAPPY NEW YEAR
56 ST.
7th Ave
HEAT SIGNAL.
SNIPER RIFLE.
I GOT YOU.
KER-WHAMM!
BOMB SQUAD REPORTS A NEGATIVE-- WE'RE ALL CLEAR, GET ME AN I.D. ON THIS GIRL. SHE'S NOT THE SICILIAN...

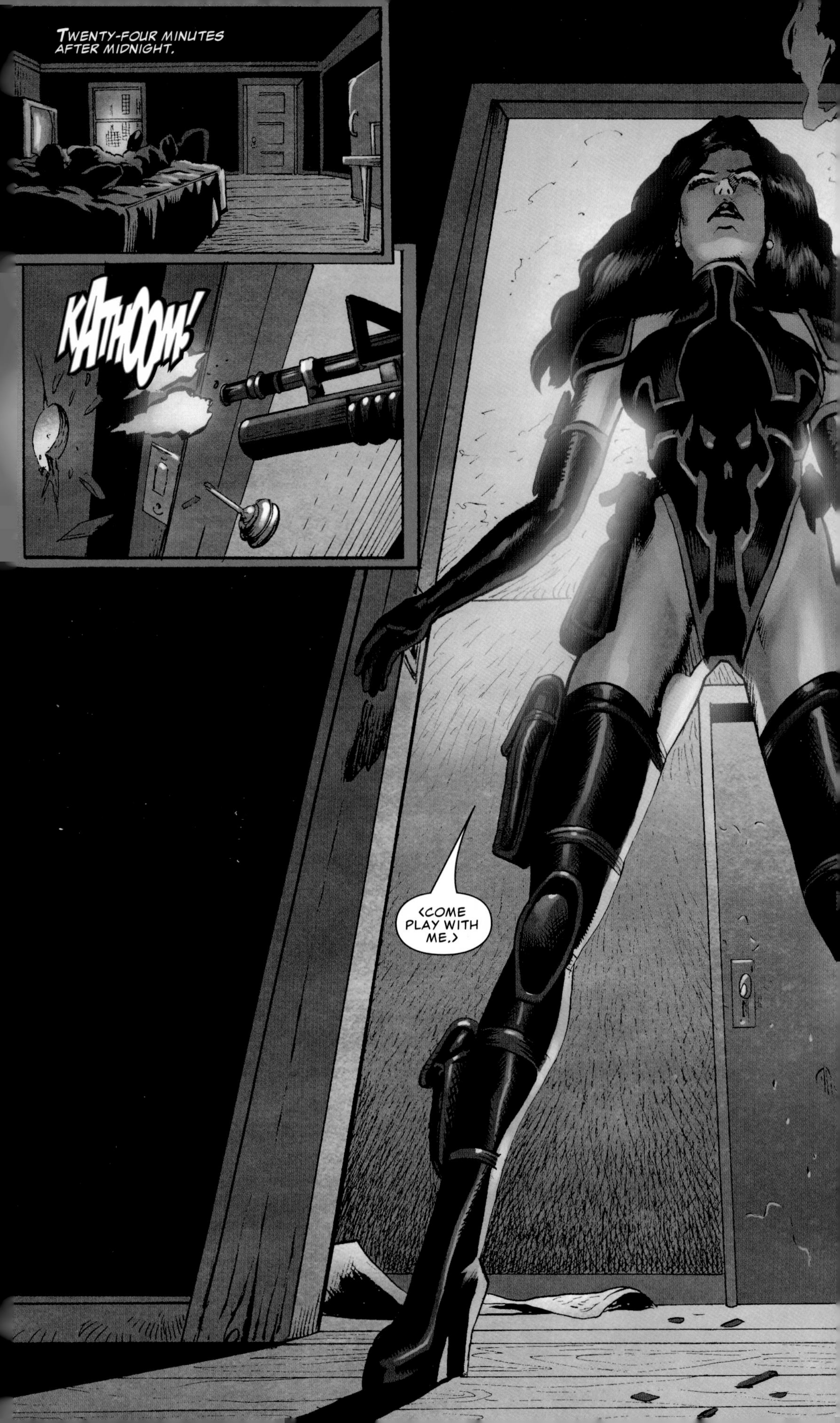
TWENTY-FOUR MINUTES AFTER MIDNIGHT.
KATHOOM!
<COME PLAY WITH ME.>

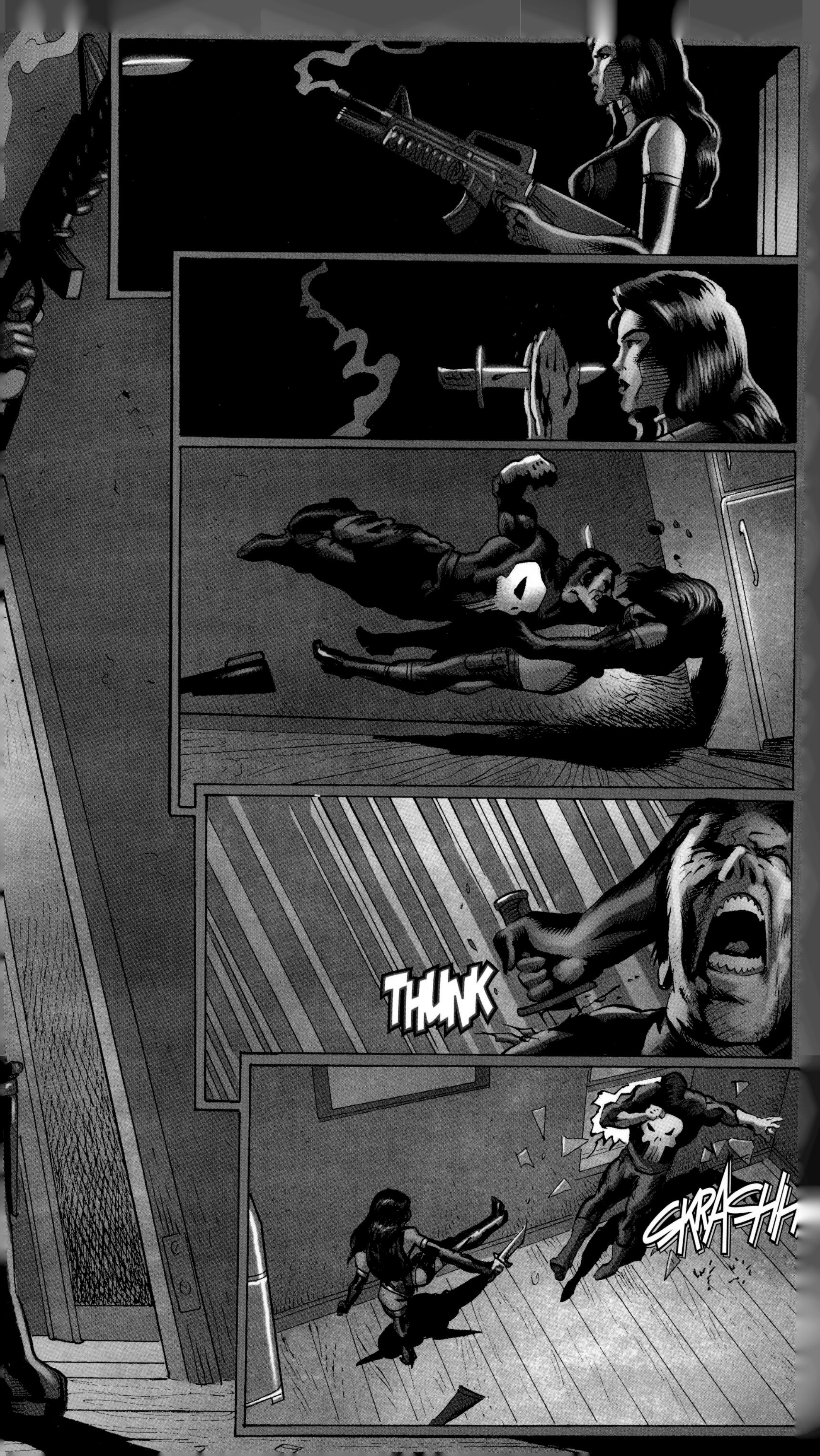

THUNK
SKRASHH

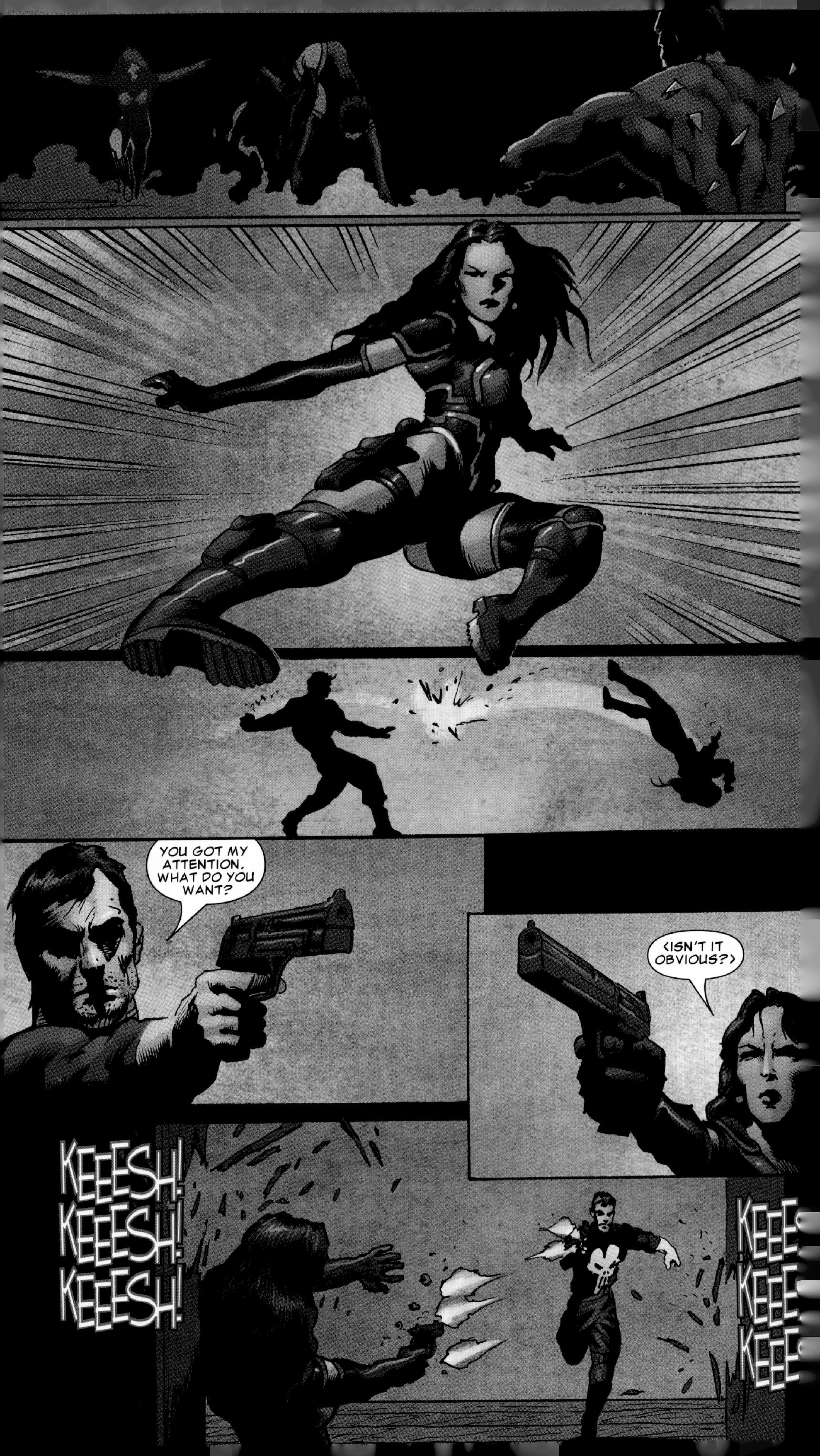
YOU GOT MY ATTENTION. WHAT DO YOU WANT?
<ISN'T IT OBVIOUS?>
KEEESH! KEEESH! KEEESH!

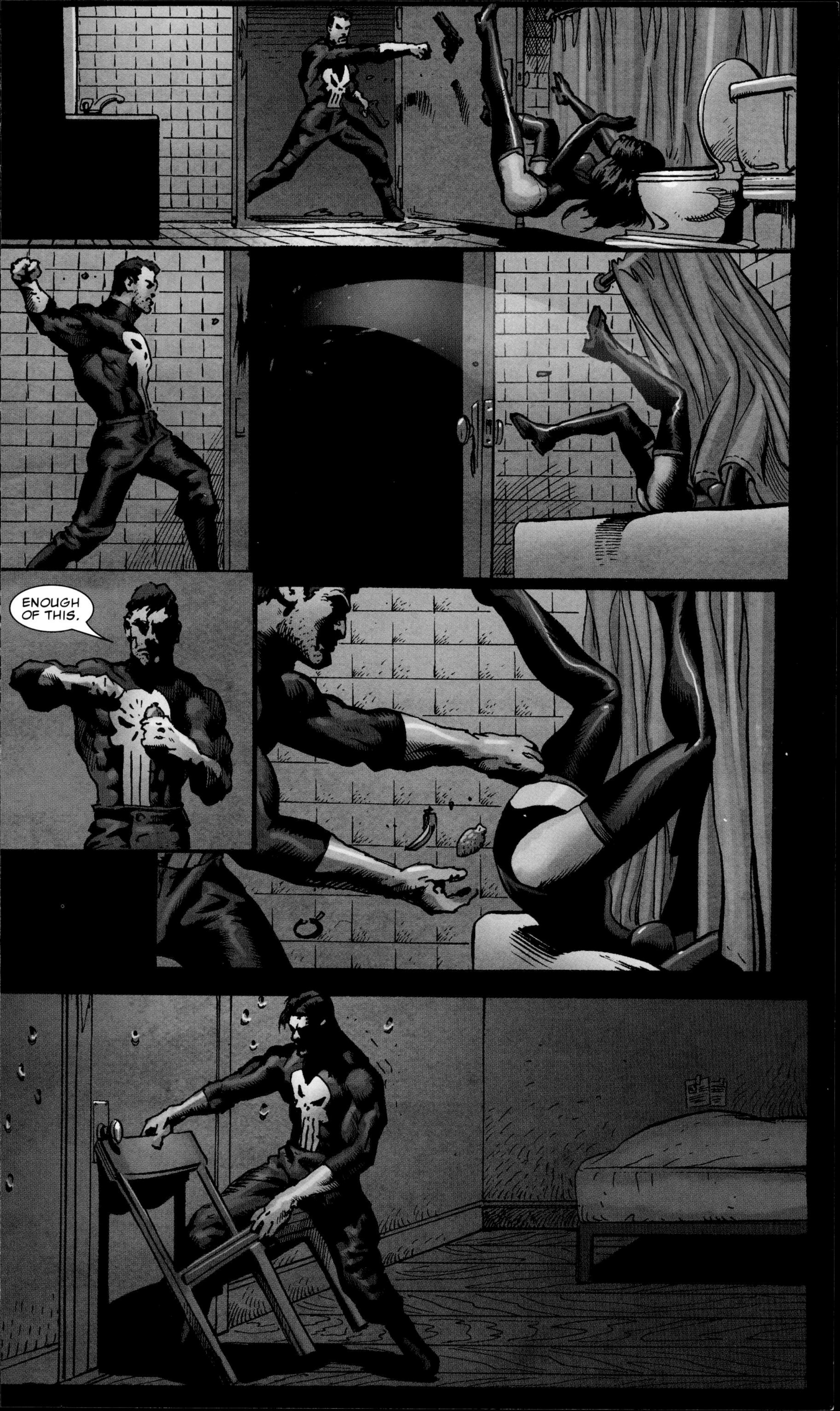
ENOUGH OF THIS.

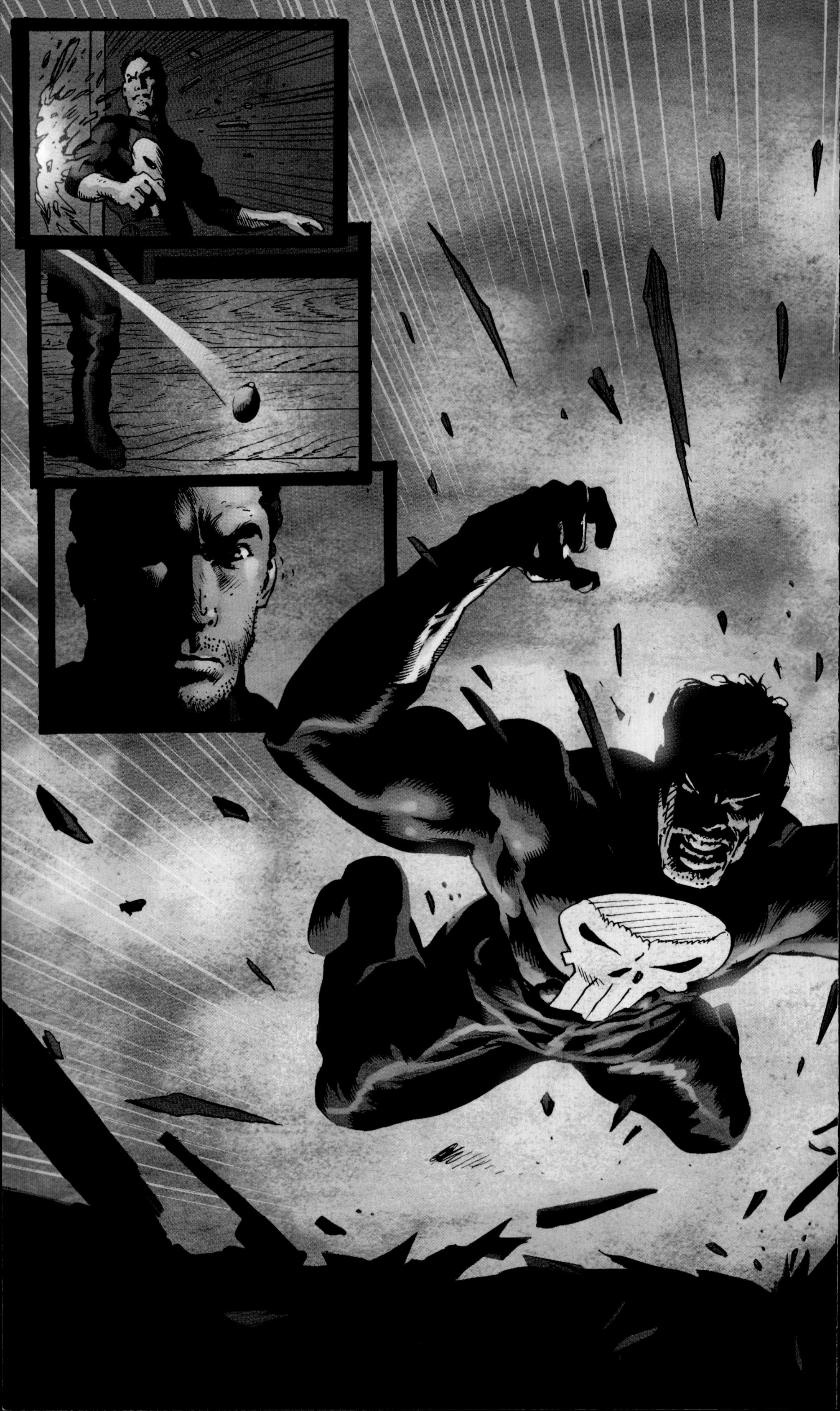

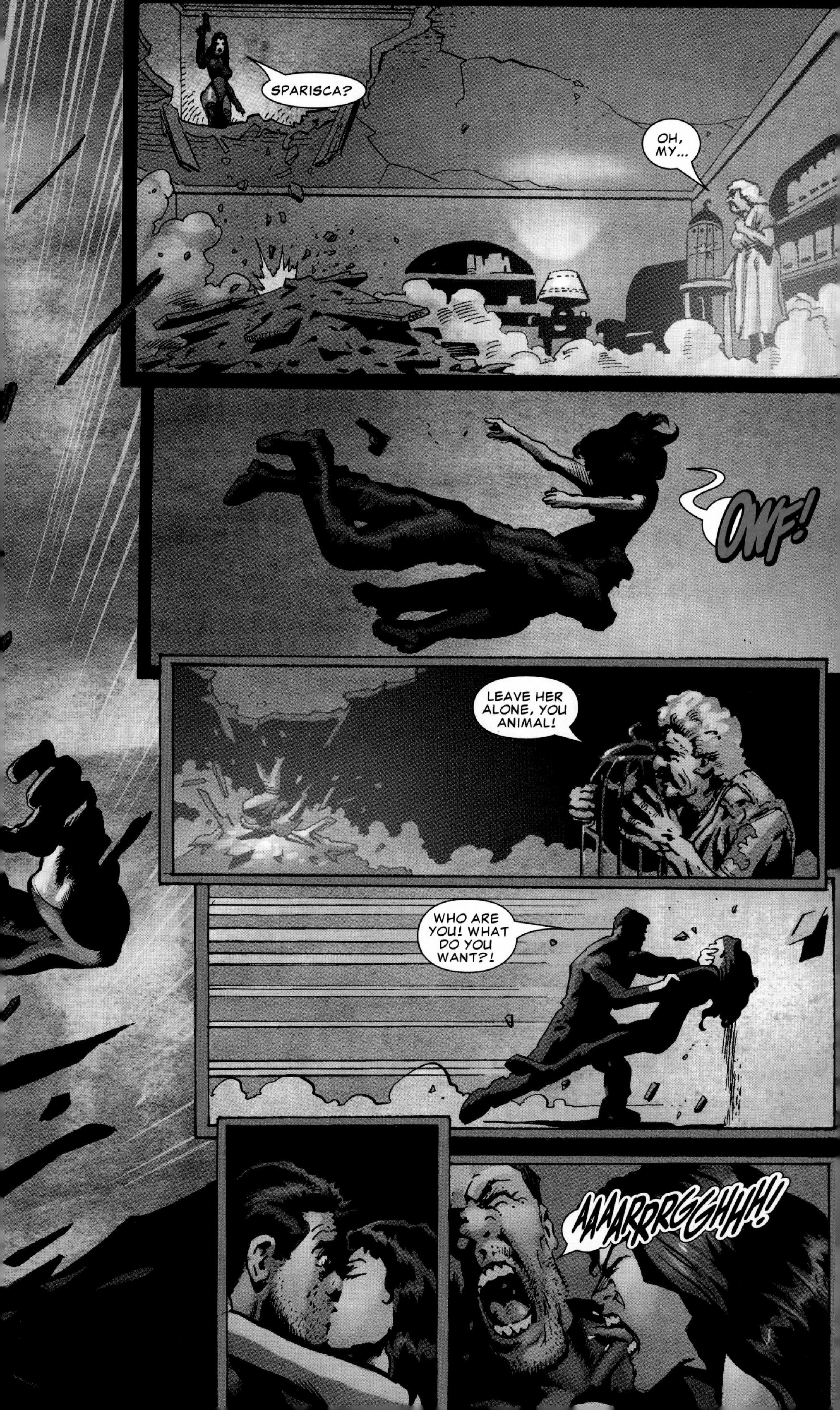
SPARISCA?
OH, MY...
OWF!
LEAVE HER ALONE, YOU ANIMAL!
WHO ARE YOU! WHAT DO YOU WANT?!
AAAARRRGGHHH!

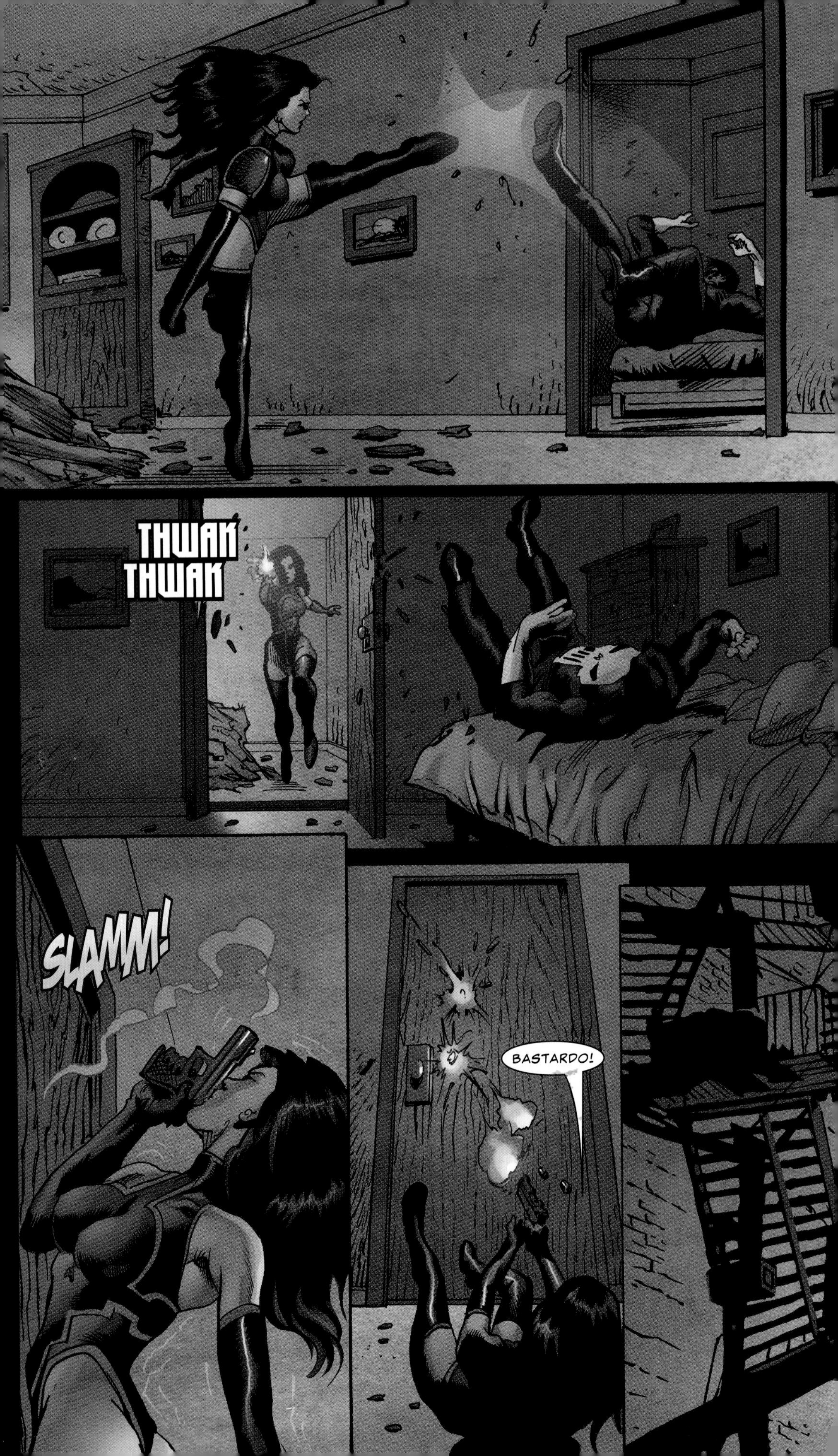
THWAK
THWAK
SLAMM!
BASTARDO!

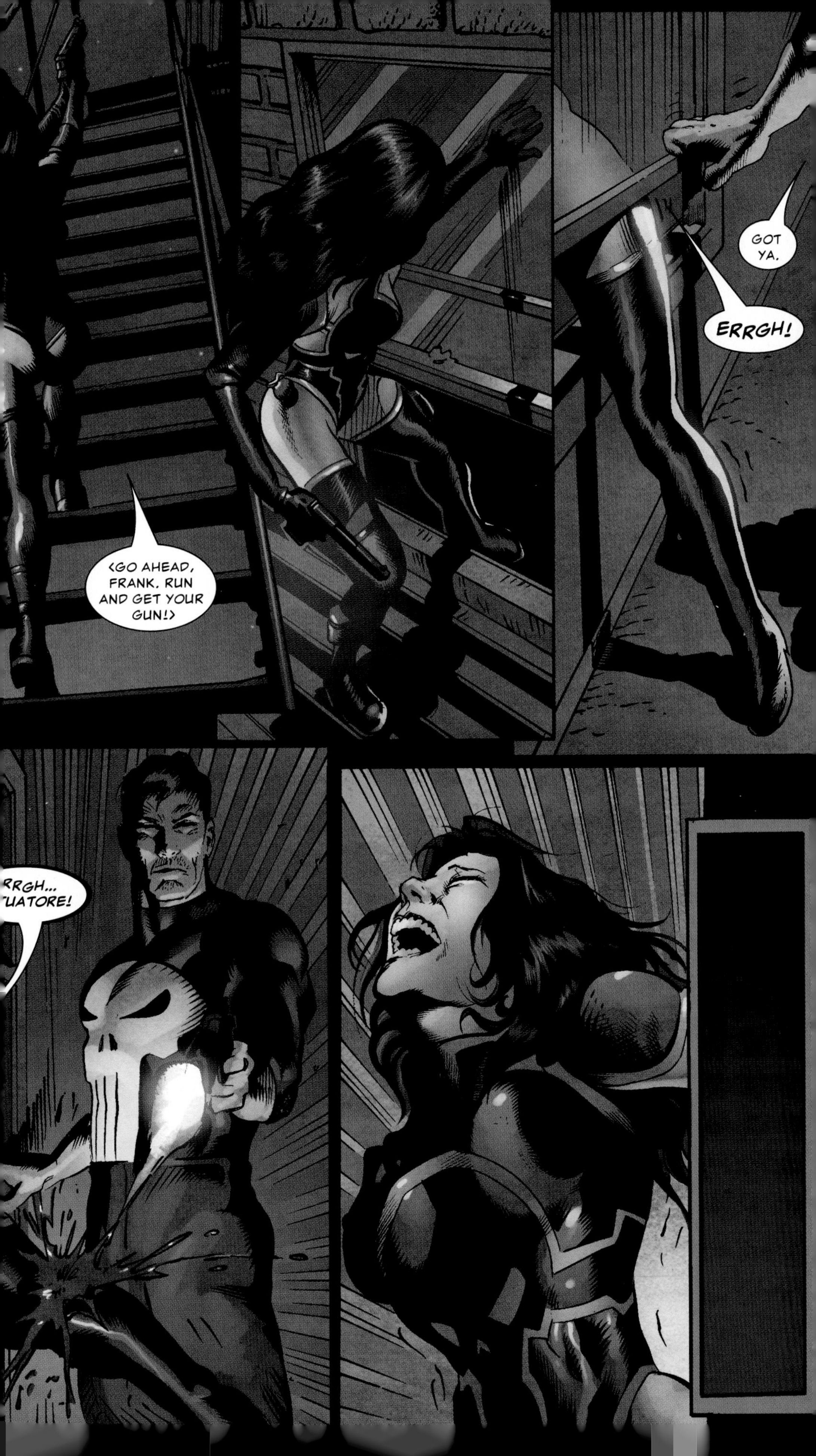
<GO AHEAD, FRANK. RUN AND GET YOUR GUN!>
GOT YA.
ERRGH!
RRGH... UATORE!

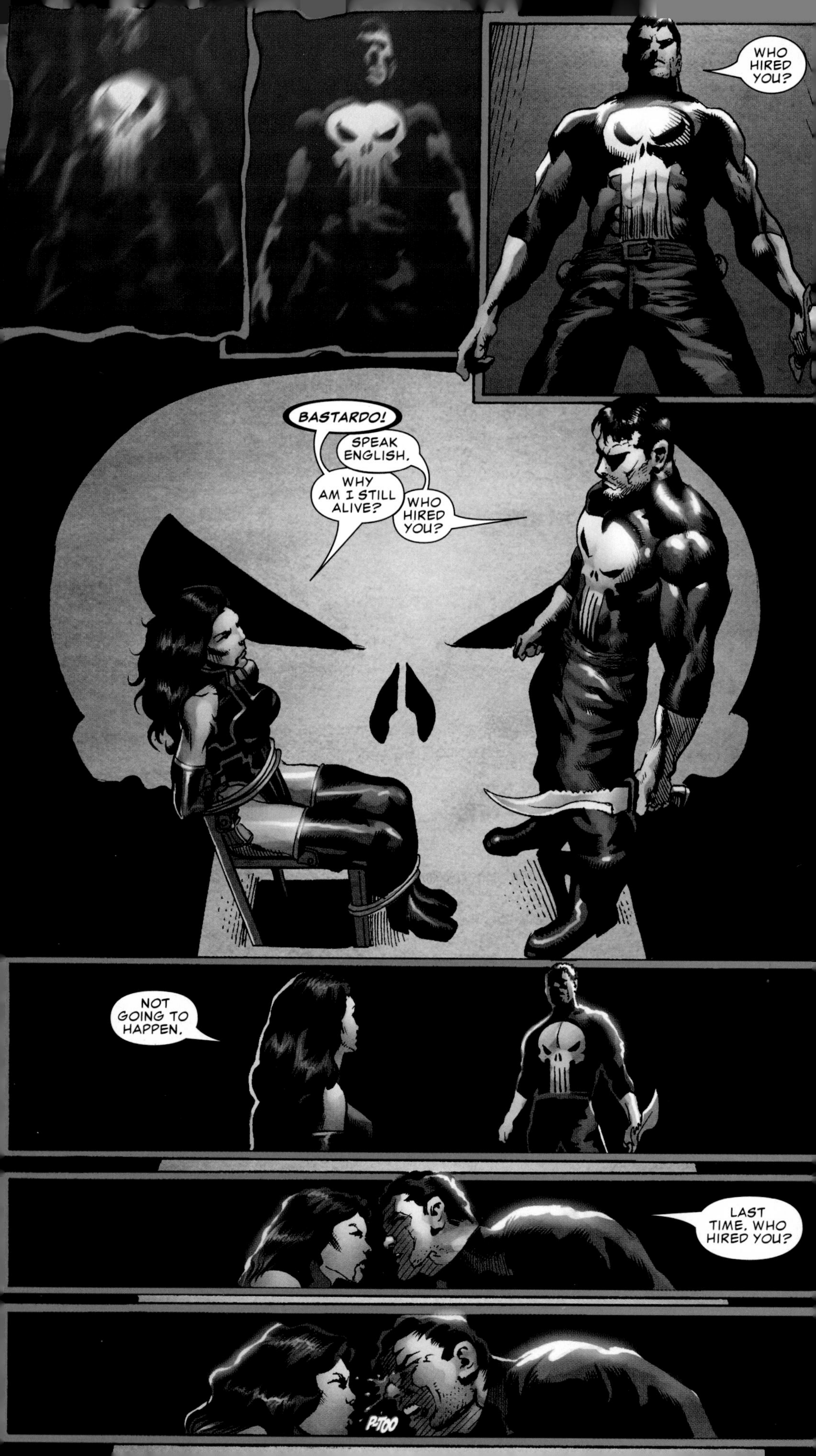
WHO HIRED YOU?
BASTARDO!
SPEAK ENGLISH.
WHY AM I STILL ALIVE?
WHO HIRED YOU?
NOT GOING TO HAPPEN.
LAST TIME. WHO HIRED YOU?
P-TOO

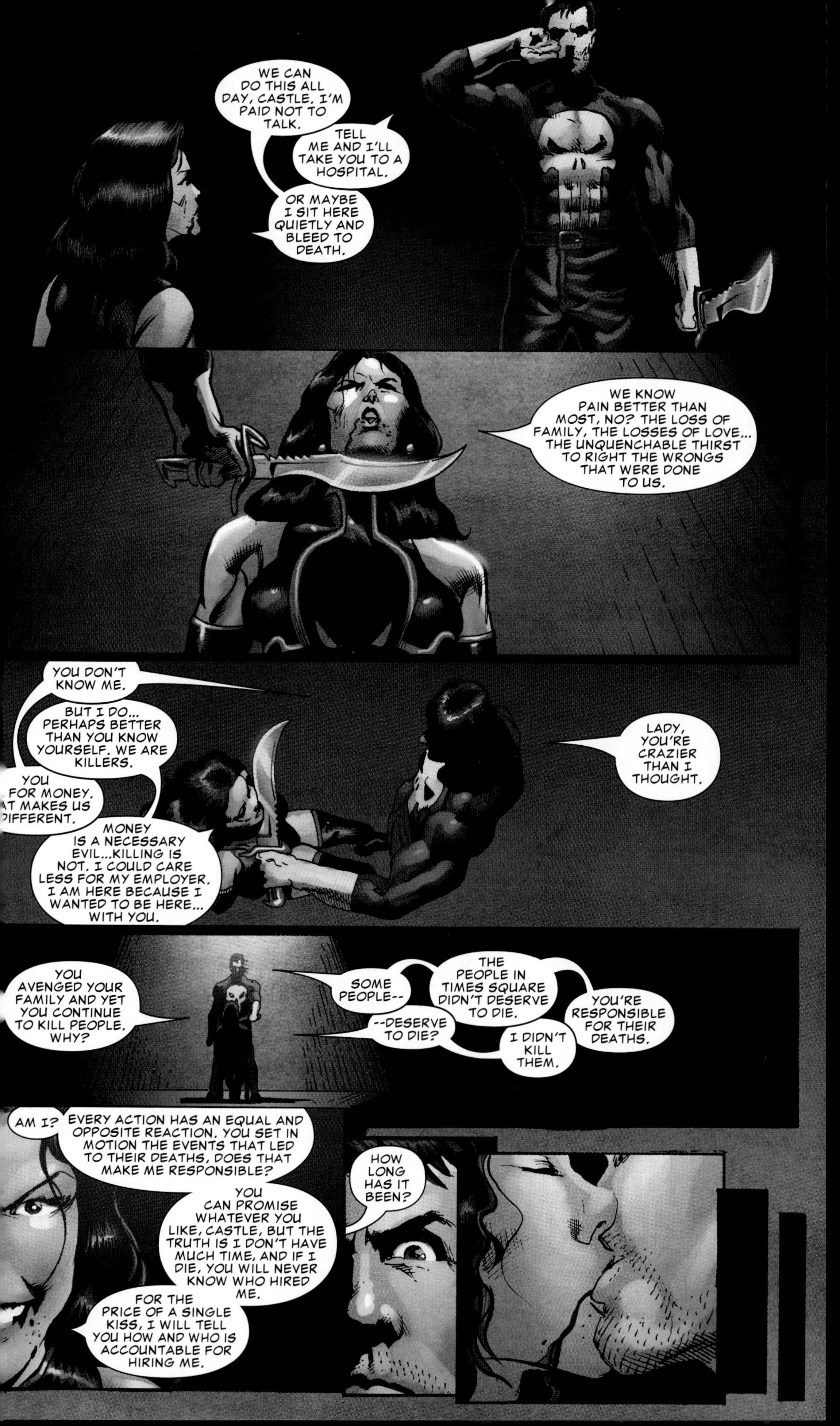

WE CAN DO THIS ALL DAY, CASTLE. I'M PAID NOT TO TALK.
TELL ME AND I'LL TAKE YOU TO A HOSPITAL.
OR MAYBE I SIT HERE QUIETLY AND BLEED TO DEATH.
WE KNOW PAIN BETTER THAN MOST, NO? THE LOSS OF FAMILY, THE LOSSES OF LOVE... THE UNQUENCHABLE THIRST TO RIGHT THE WRONGS THAT WERE DONE TO US.
YOU DON'T KNOW ME.
BUT I DO... PERHAPS BETTER THAN YOU KNOW YOURSELF. WE ARE KILLERS.
YOU FOR MONEY. AT MAKES US IFFERENT.
MONEY IS A NECESSARY EVIL...KILLING IS NOT. I COULD CARE LESS FOR MY EMPLOYER. I AM HERE BECAUSE I WANTED TO BE HERE... WITH YOU.
LADY, YOU'RE CRAZIER THAN I THOUGHT.
YOU AVENGED YOUR FAMILY AND YET YOU CONTINUE TO KILL PEOPLE. WHY?
SOME PEOPLE--
--DESERVE TO DIE?
THE PEOPLE IN TIMES SQUARE DIDN'T DESERVE TO DIE.
I DIDN'T KILL THEM.
YOU'RE RESPONSIBLE FOR THEIR DEATHS.
AM I?
EVERY ACTION HAS AN EQUAL AND OPPOSITE REACTION. YOU SET IN MOTION THE EVENTS THAT LED TO THEIR DEATHS, DOES THAT MAKE ME RESPONSIBLE?
YOU CAN PROMISE WHATEVER YOU LIKE, CASTLE, BUT THE TRUTH IS I DON'T HAVE MUCH TIME, AND IF I DIE, YOU WILL NEVER KNOW WHO HIRED ME.
FOR THE PRICE OF A SINGLE KISS, I WILL TELL YOU HOW AND WHO IS ACCOUNTABLE FOR HIRING ME.
HOW LONG HAS IT BEEN?

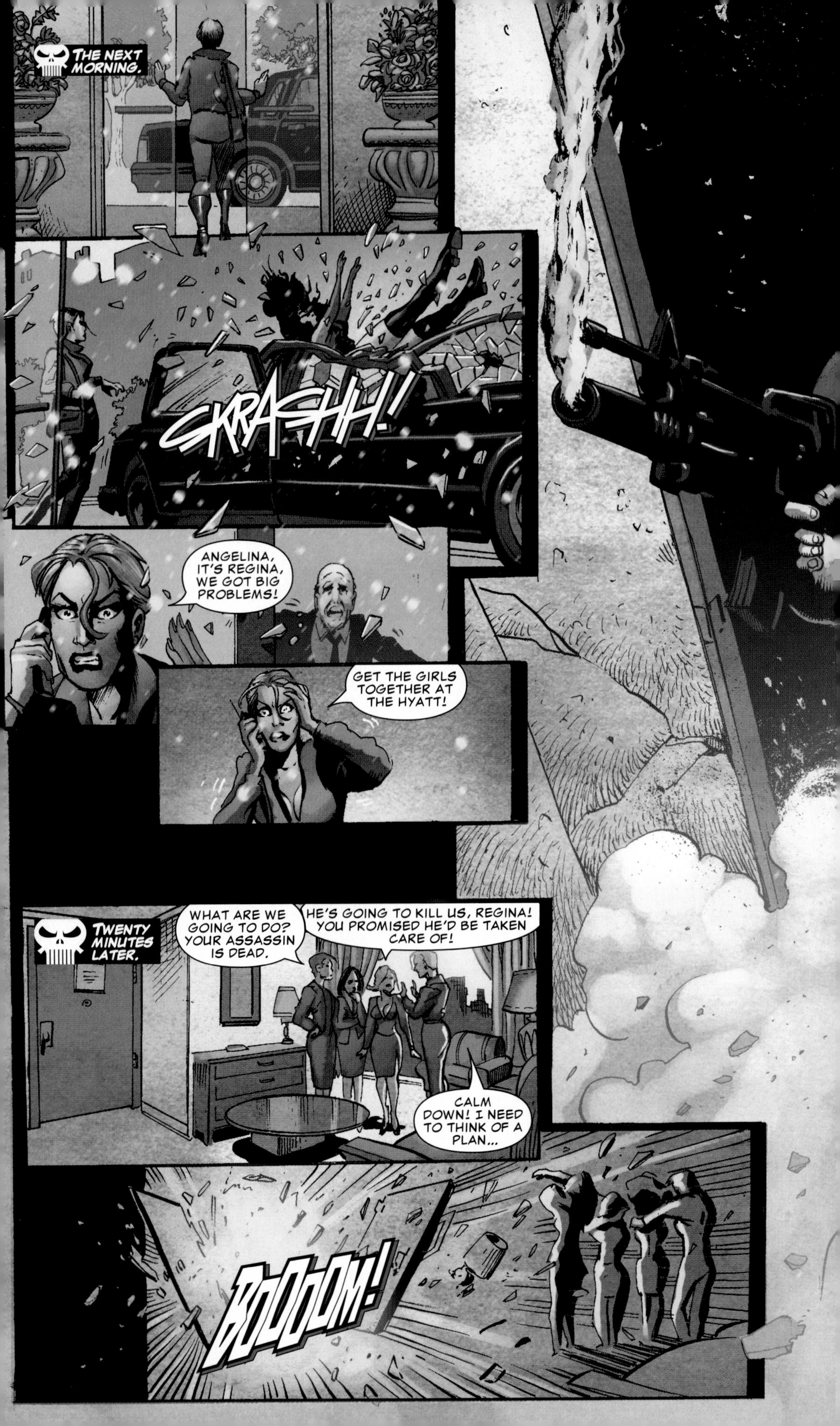
THE NEXT MORNING.
SKRASHH!
ANGELINA, IT'S REGINA, WE GOT BIG PROBLEMS!
GET THE GIRLS TOGETHER AT THE HYATT!
TWENTY MINUTES LATER.
WHAT ARE WE GOING TO DO? YOUR ASSASSIN IS DEAD.
HE'S GOING TO KILL US, REGINA! YOU PROMISED HE'D BE TAKEN CARE OF!
CALM DOWN! I NEED TO THINK OF A PLAN...
BOOOOM!

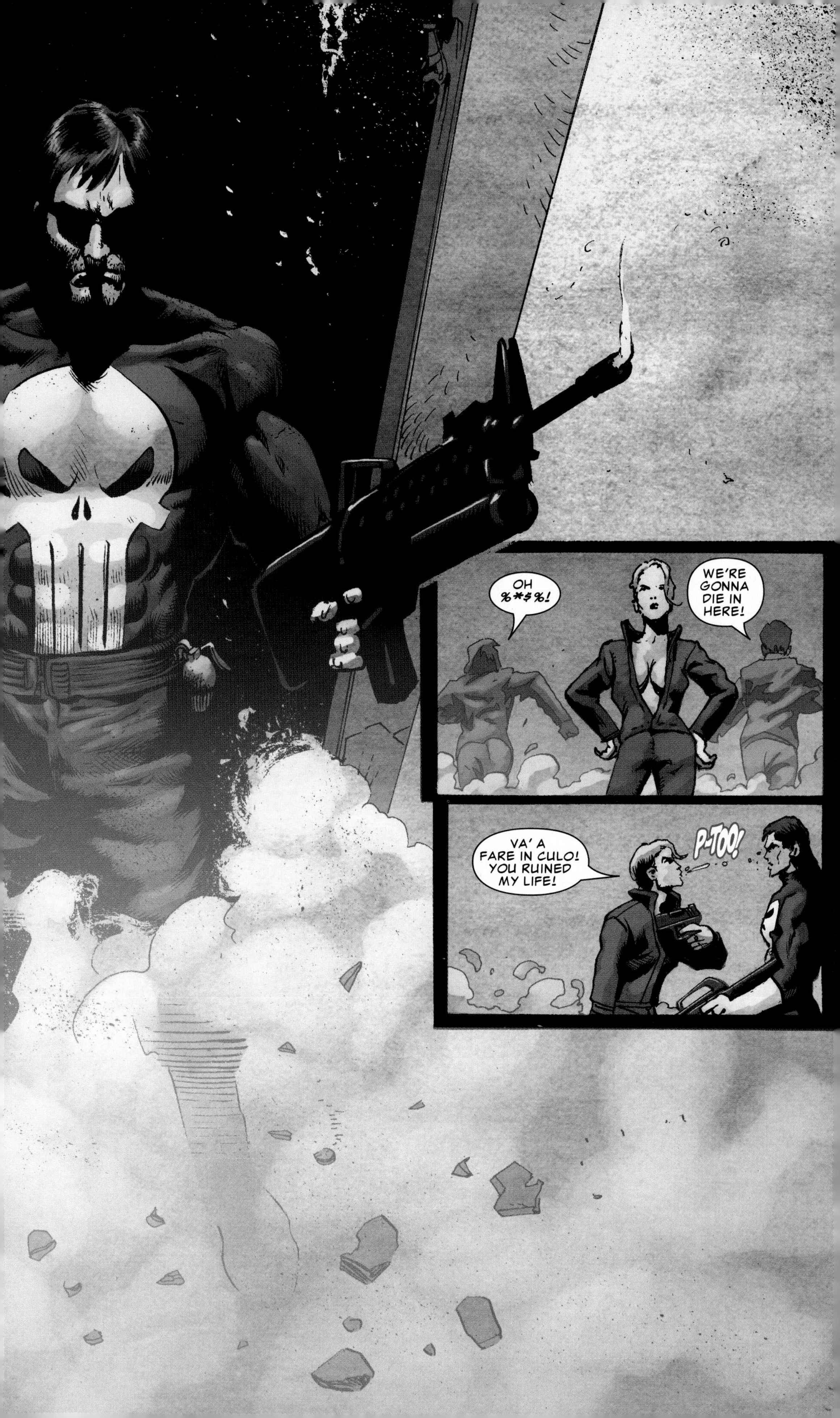
OH %*$%!
WE'RE GONNA DIE IN HERE!
VA' A FARE IN CULO! YOU RUINED MY LIFE!
P-TOO!

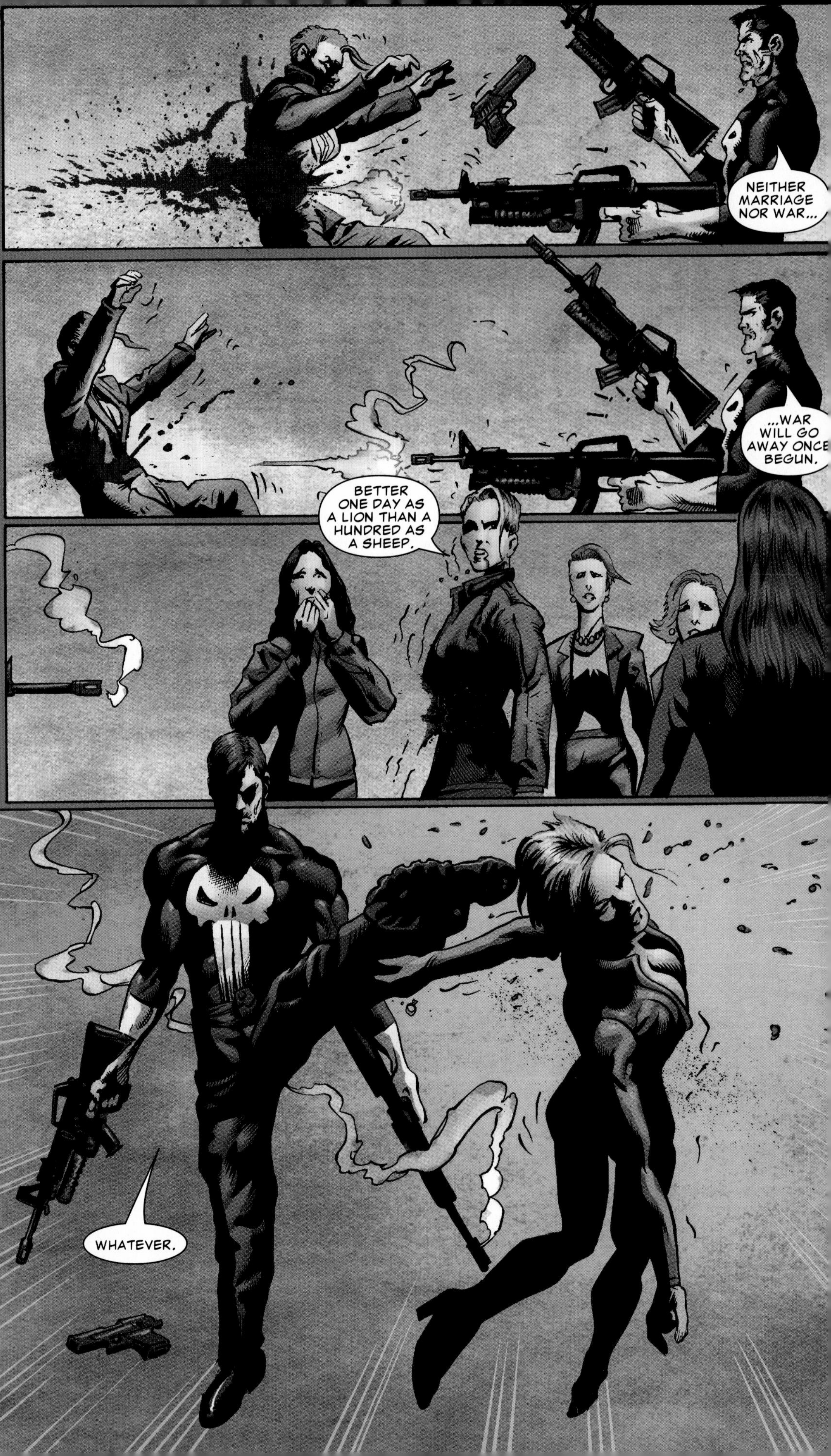
NEITHER MARRIAGE NOR WAR...
...WAR WILL GO AWAY ONCE BEGUN.
BETTER ONE DAY AS A LION THAN A HUNDRED AS A SHEEP.
WHATEVER.

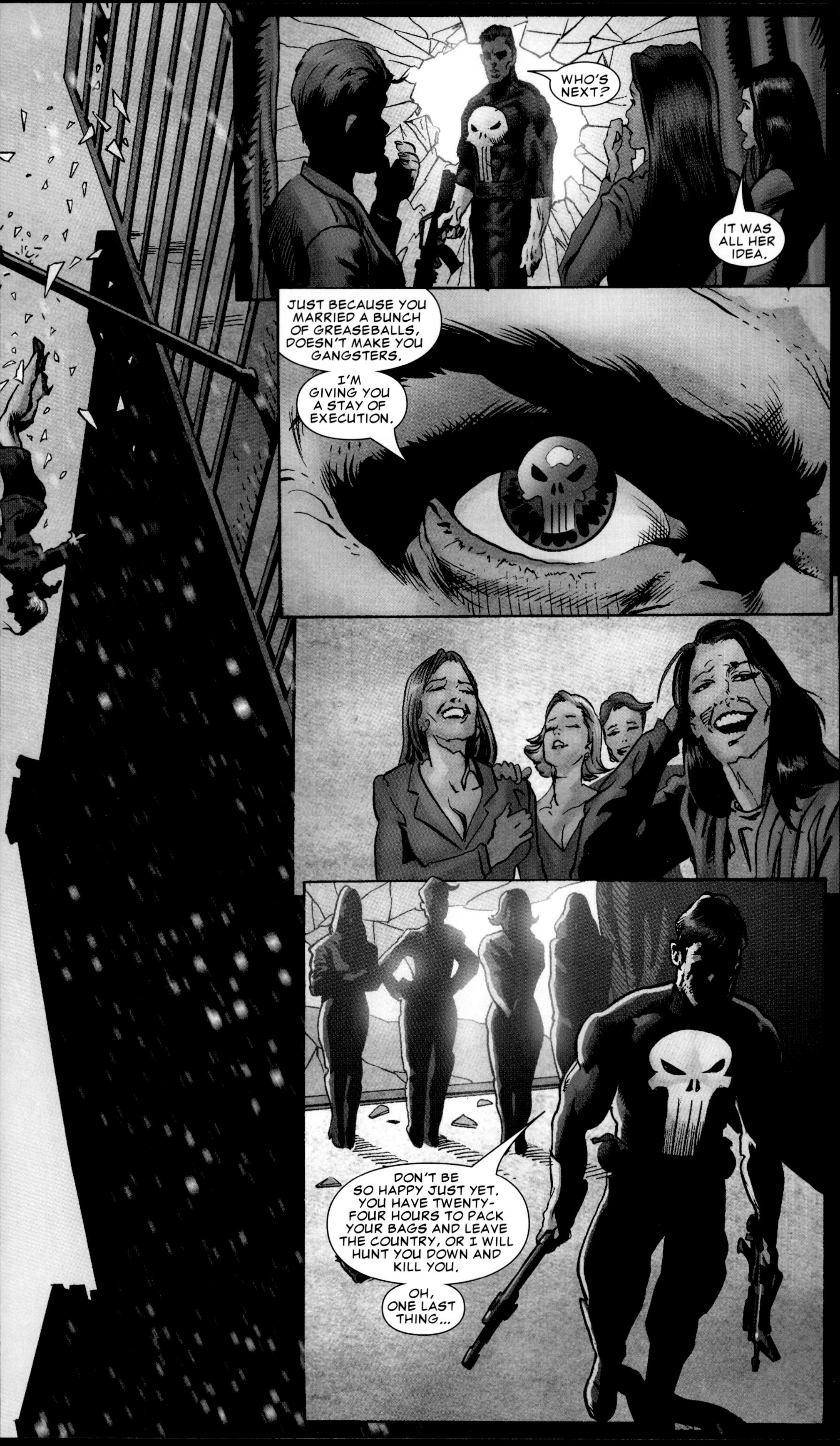

WHO'S NEXT?
IT WAS ALL HER IDEA.
JUST BECAUSE YOU MARRIED A BUNCH OF GREASEBALLS, DOESN'T MAKE YOU GANGSTERS.
I'M GIVING YOU A STAY OF EXECUTION.
DON'T BE SO HAPPY JUST YET. YOU HAVE TWENTY-FOUR HOURS TO PACK YOUR BAGS AND LEAVE THE COUNTRY, OR I WILL HUNT YOU DOWN AND KILL YOU.
OH, ONE LAST THING...

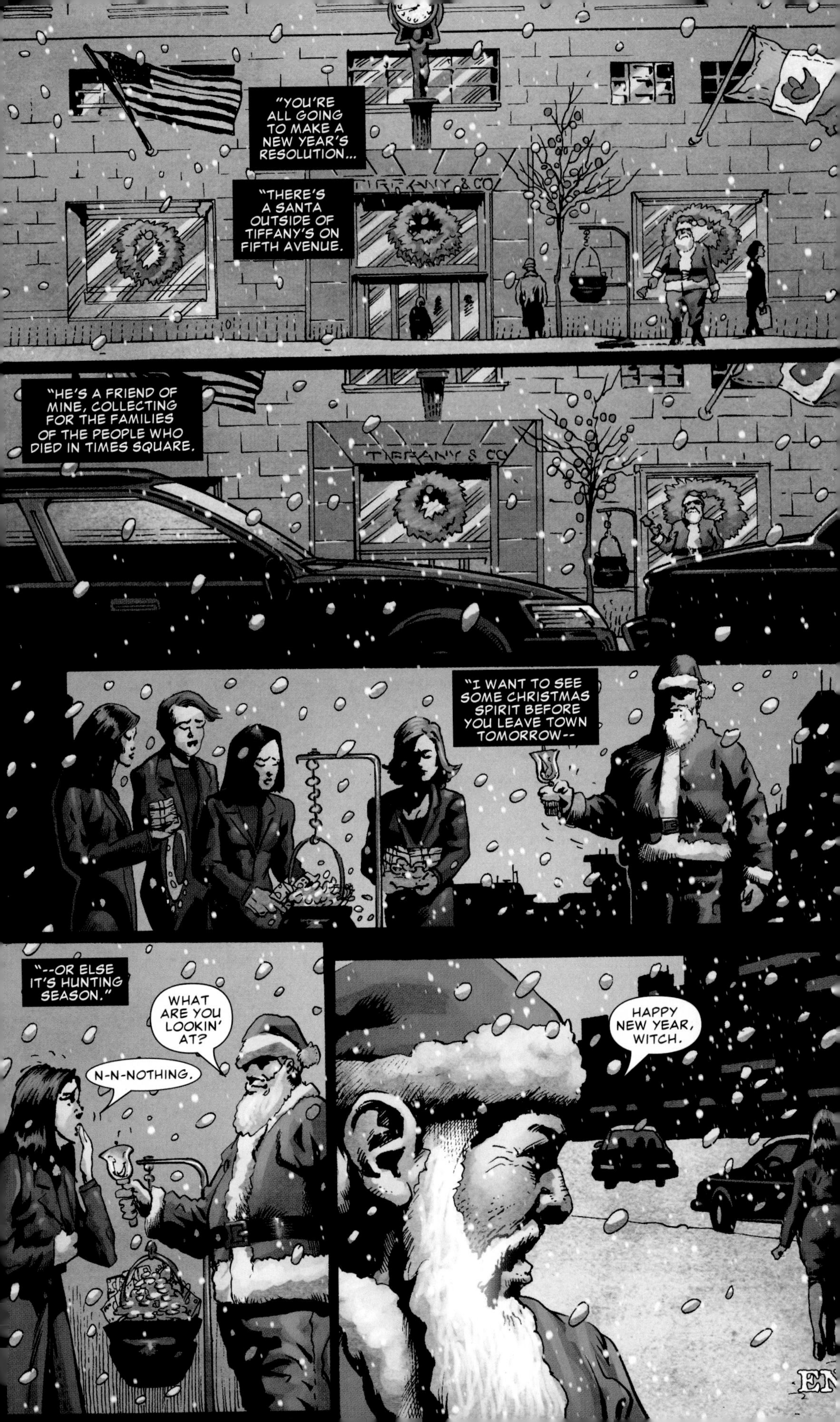

"YOU'RE ALL GOING TO MAKE A NEW YEAR'S RESOLUTION...
"THERE'S A SANTA OUTSIDE OF TIFFANY'S ON FIFTH AVENUE.
TIFFANY & CO
"HE'S A FRIEND OF MINE, COLLECTING FOR THE FAMILIES OF THE PEOPLE WHO DIED IN TIMES SQUARE.
TIFFANY & CO
"I WANT TO SEE SOME CHRISTMAS SPIRIT BEFORE YOU LEAVE TOWN TOMORROW--
"--OR ELSE IT'S HUNTING SEASON."
WHAT ARE YOU LOOKIN' AT?
N-N-NOTHING.
HAPPY NEW YEAR, WITCH.

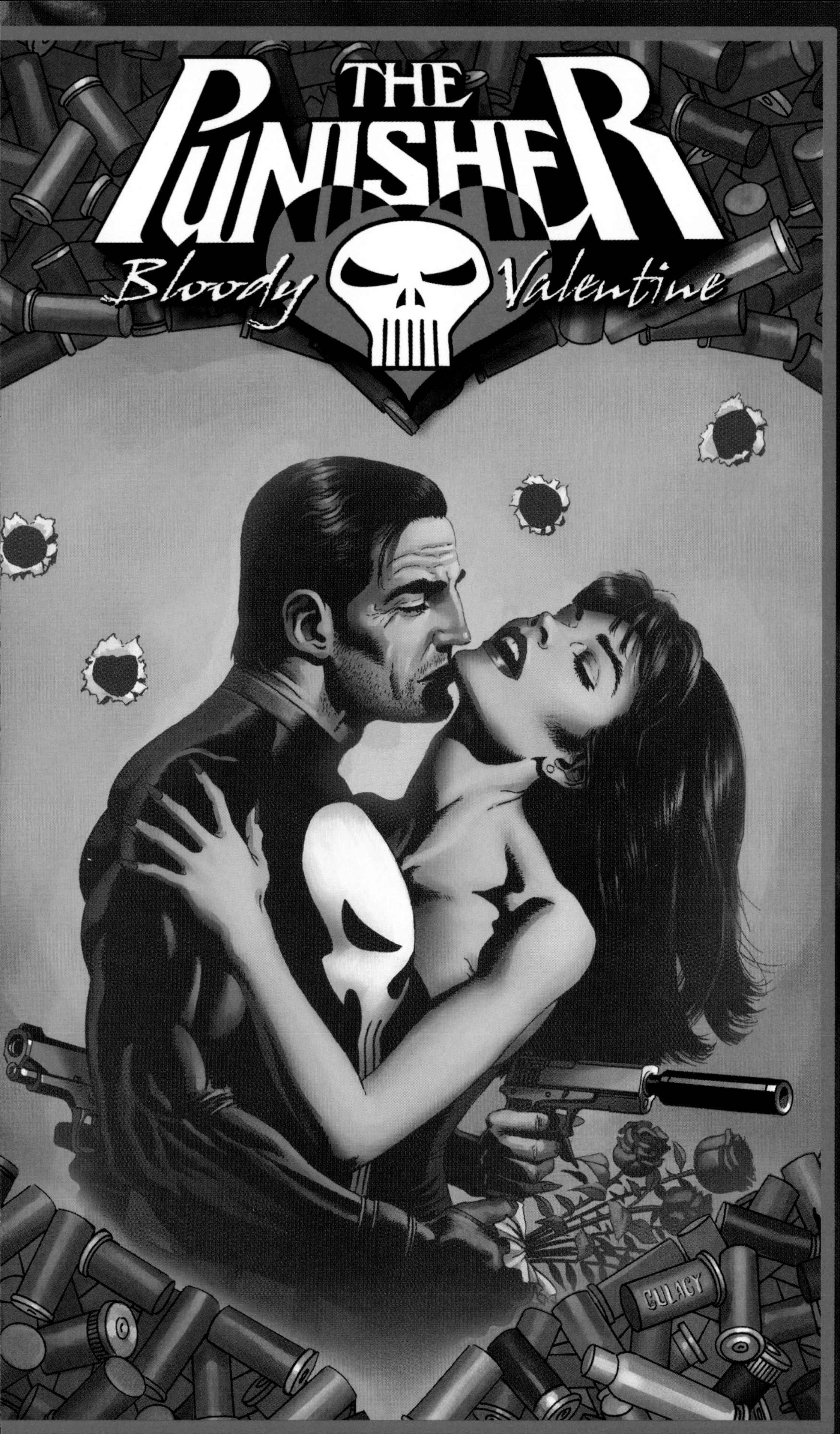
THE PUNISHER
Bloody Valentine
GULACY

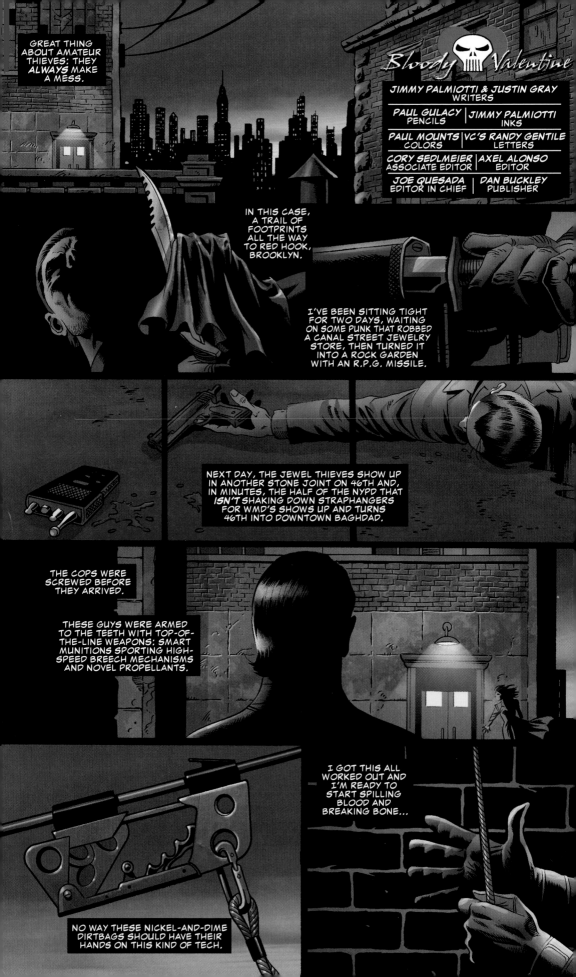

GREAT THING ABOUT AMATEUR THIEVES: THEY ALWAYS MAKE A MESS.

Bloody Valentine

JIMMY PALMIOTTI & JUSTIN GRAY
WRITERS

PAUL GULACY
PENCILS

JIMMY PALMIOTTI
INKS

PAUL MOUNTS
COLORS

VC'S RANDY GENTILE
LETTERS

CORY SEDLMEIER
ASSOCIATE EDITOR

AXEL ALONSO
EDITOR

JOE QUESADA
EDITOR IN CHIEF

DAN BUCKLEY
PUBLISHER

IN THIS CASE, A TRAIL OF FOOTPRINTS ALL THE WAY TO RED HOOK, BROOKLYN.

I'VE BEEN SITTING TIGHT FOR TWO DAYS, WAITING ON SOME PUNK THAT ROBBED A CANAL STREET JEWELRY STORE, THEN TURNED IT INTO A ROCK GARDEN WITH AN R.P.G. MISSILE.

NEXT DAY, THE JEWEL THIEVES SHOW UP IN ANOTHER STONE JOINT ON 46TH AND, IN MINUTES, THE HALF OF THE NYPD THAT *ISN'T* SHAKING DOWN STRAPHANGERS FOR WMD'S SHOWS UP AND TURNS 46TH INTO DOWNTOWN BAGHDAD.

THE COPS WERE SCREWED BEFORE THEY ARRIVED.

THESE GUYS WERE ARMED TO THE TEETH WITH TOP-OF-THE-LINE WEAPONS: SMART MUNITIONS SPORTING HIGH-SPEED BREECH MECHANISMS AND NOVEL PROPELLANTS.

I GOT THIS ALL WORKED OUT AND I'M READY TO START SPILLING BLOOD AND BREAKING BONE...

NO WAY THESE NICKEL-AND-DIME DIRTBAGS SHOULD HAVE THEIR HANDS ON THIS KIND OF TECH.

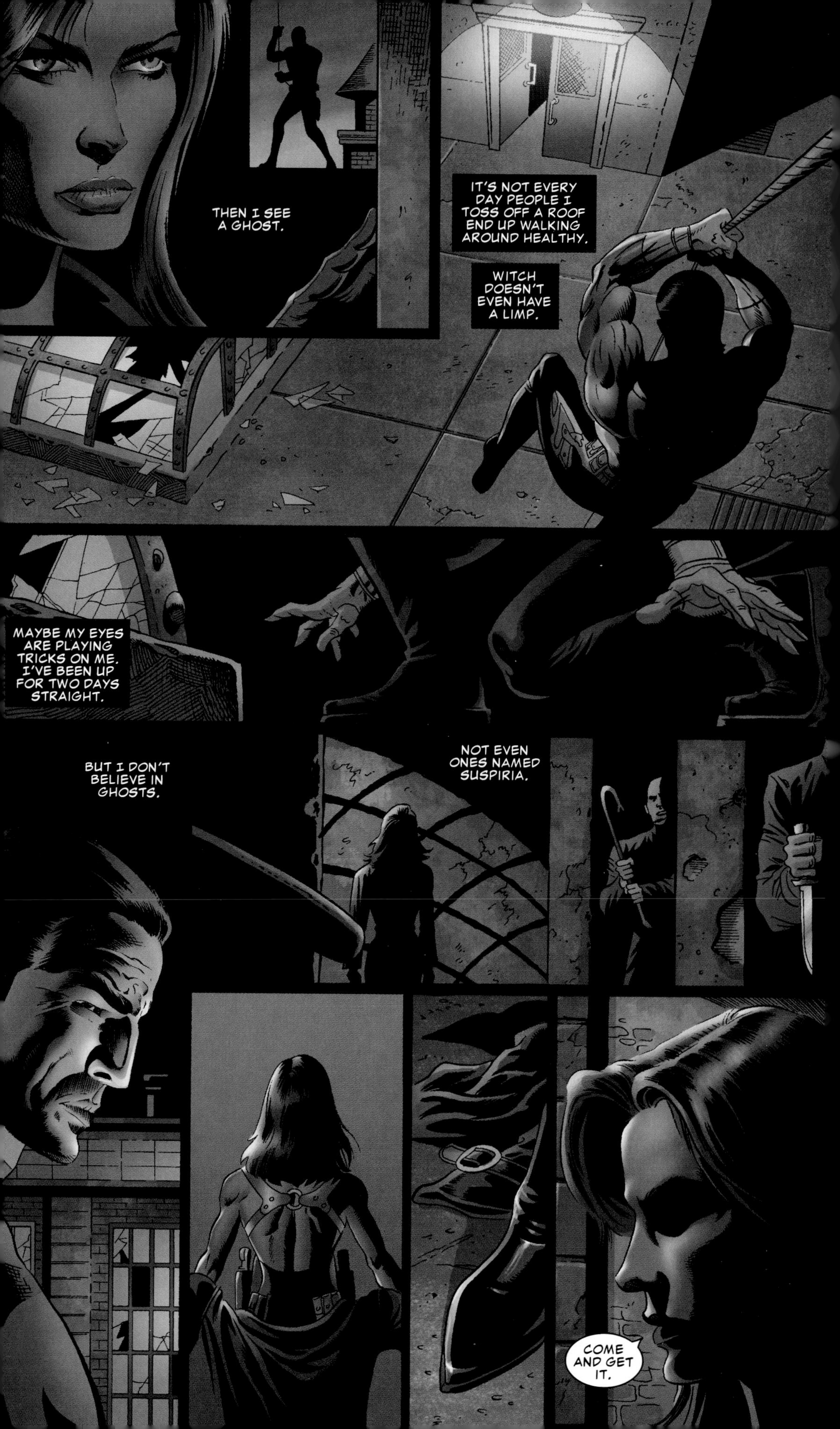
THEN I SEE A GHOST.
IT'S NOT EVERY DAY PEOPLE I TOSS OFF A ROOF END UP WALKING AROUND HEALTHY.
WITCH DOESN'T EVEN HAVE A LIMP.
MAYBE MY EYES ARE PLAYING TRICKS ON ME. I'VE BEEN UP FOR TWO DAYS STRAIGHT.
BUT I DON'T BELIEVE IN GHOSTS.
NOT EVEN ONES NAMED SUSPIRIA.
COME AND GET IT.

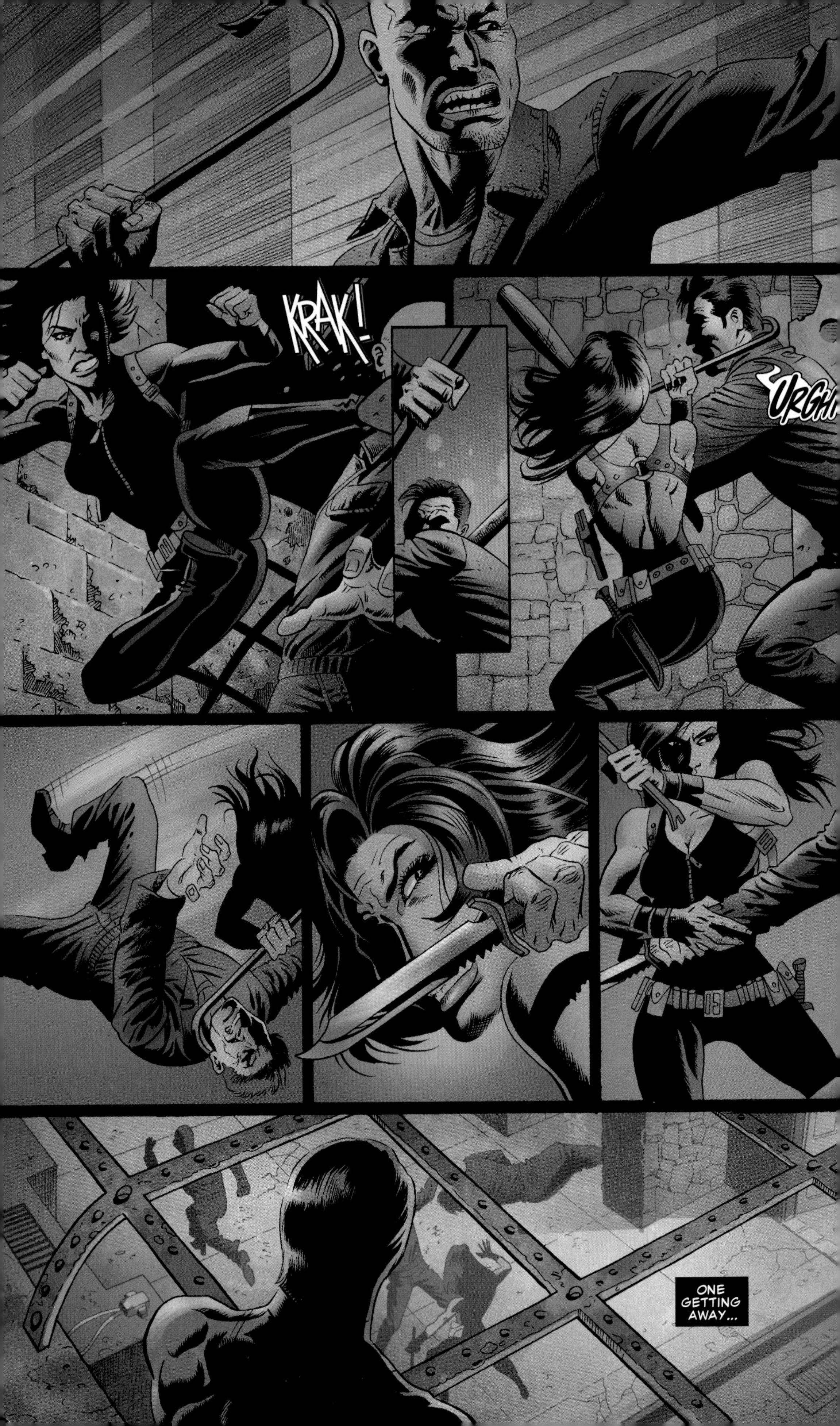

KRAK!
URGH
ONE GETTING AWAY...

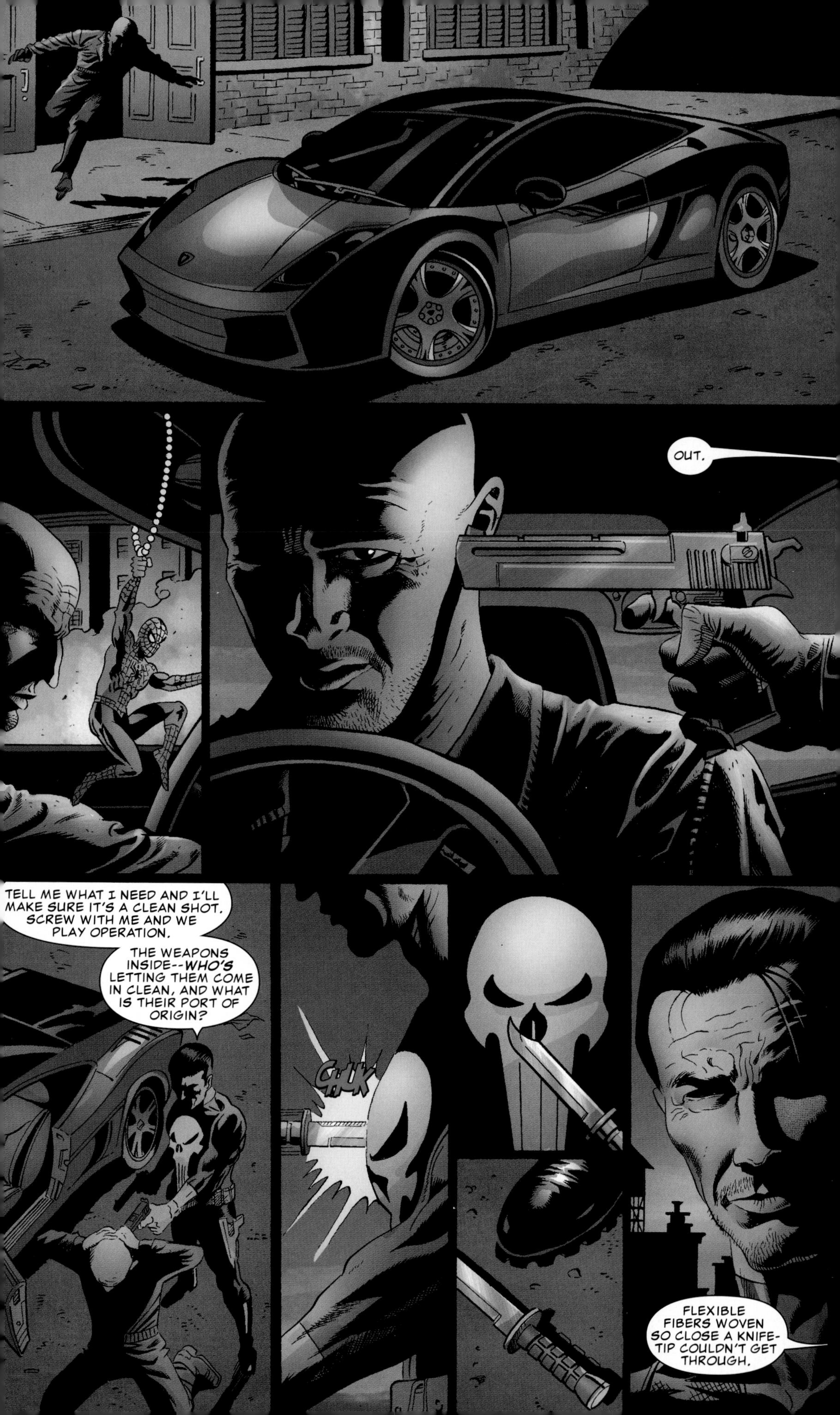
OUT.
TELL ME WHAT I NEED AND I'LL MAKE SURE IT'S A CLEAN SHOT. SCREW WITH ME AND WE PLAY OPERATION.
THE WEAPONS INSIDE--WHO'S LETTING THEM COME IN CLEAN, AND WHAT IS THEIR PORT OF ORIGIN?
CHUK
FLEXIBLE FIBERS WOVEN SO CLOSE A KNIFE-TIP COULDN'T GET THROUGH.

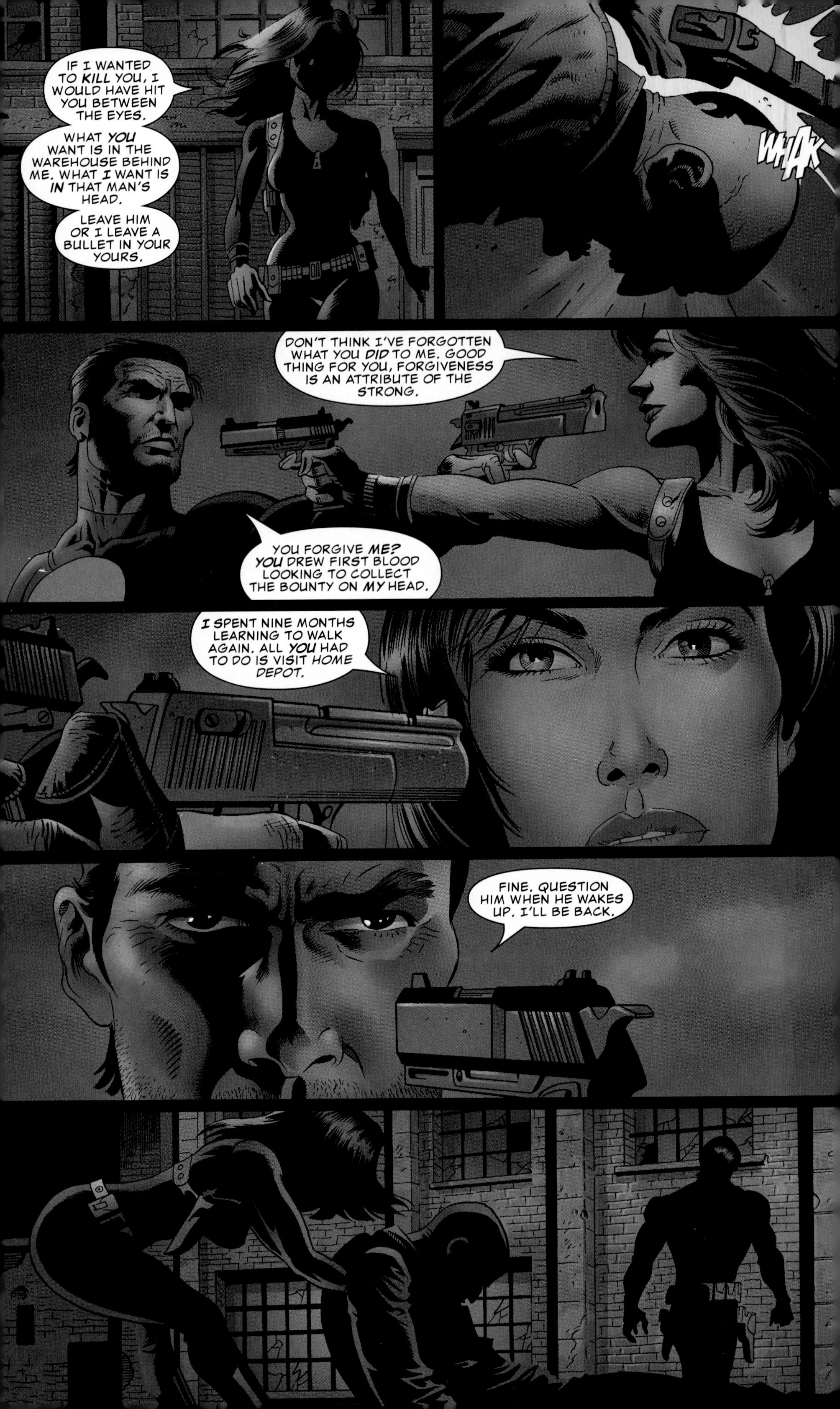

IF I WANTED TO *KILL* YOU, I WOULD HAVE HIT YOU BETWEEN THE EYES.
WHAT *YOU* WANT IS IN THE WAREHOUSE BEHIND ME. WHAT *I* WANT IS *IN* THAT MAN'S HEAD.
LEAVE HIM OR I LEAVE A BULLET IN YOUR YOURS.
WHAK
DON'T THINK I'VE FORGOTTEN WHAT YOU *DID* TO ME. GOOD THING FOR YOU, FORGIVENESS IS AN ATTRIBUTE OF THE STRONG.
YOU FORGIVE *ME? YOU* DREW FIRST BLOOD LOOKING TO COLLECT THE BOUNTY ON *MY* HEAD.
I SPENT NINE MONTHS LEARNING TO WALK AGAIN. ALL *YOU* HAD TO DO IS VISIT HOME DEPOT.
FINE. QUESTION HIM WHEN HE WAKES UP. I'LL BE BACK.

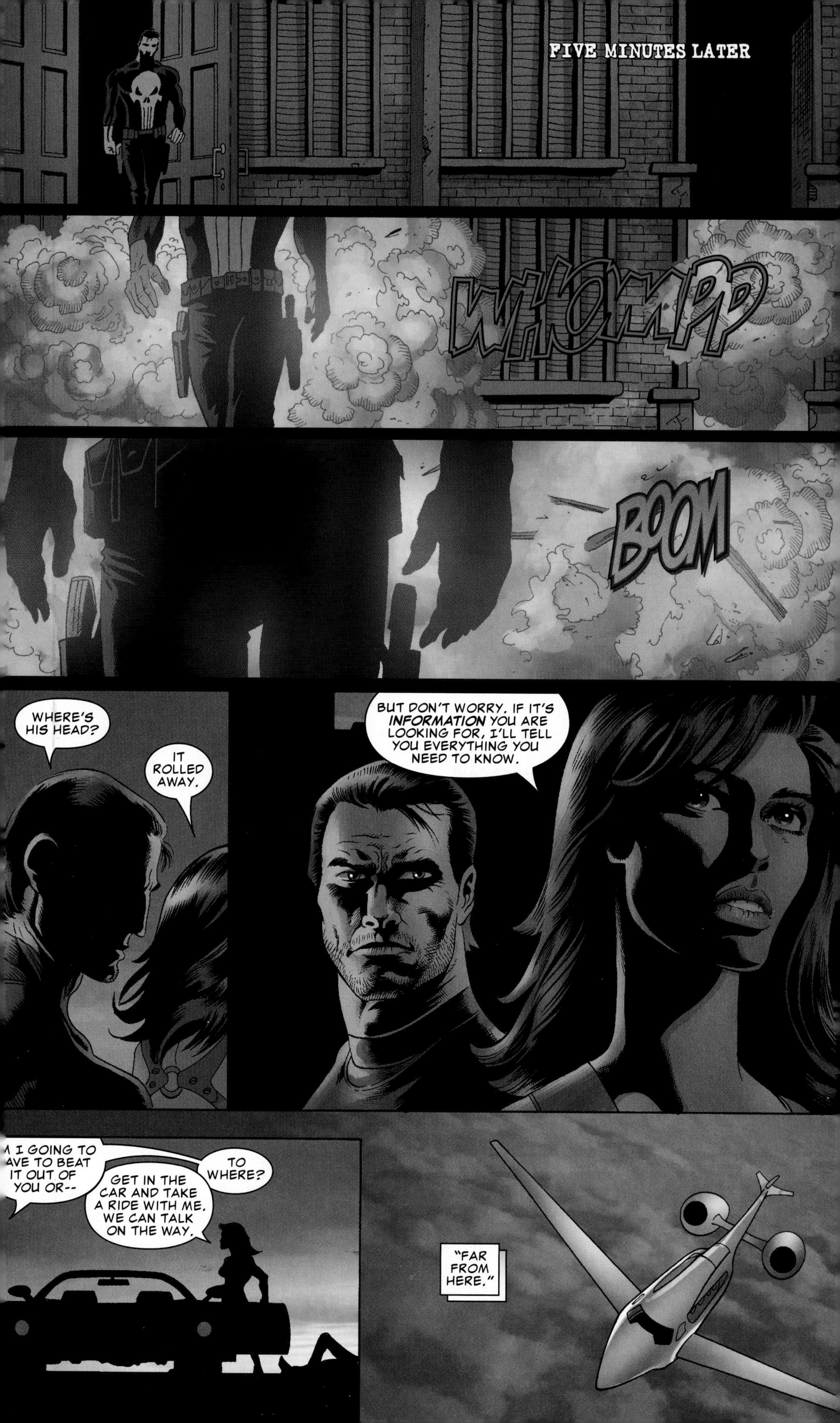
FIVE MINUTES LATER
WHOMPP
BOOM
WHERE'S HIS HEAD?
IT ROLLED AWAY.
BUT DON'T WORRY. IF IT'S *INFORMATION* YOU ARE LOOKING FOR, I'LL TELL YOU EVERYTHING YOU NEED TO KNOW.
I GOING TO AVE TO BEAT IT OUT OF YOU OR--
GET IN THE CAR AND TAKE A RIDE WITH ME. WE CAN TALK ON THE WAY.
TO WHERE?
"FAR FROM HERE."

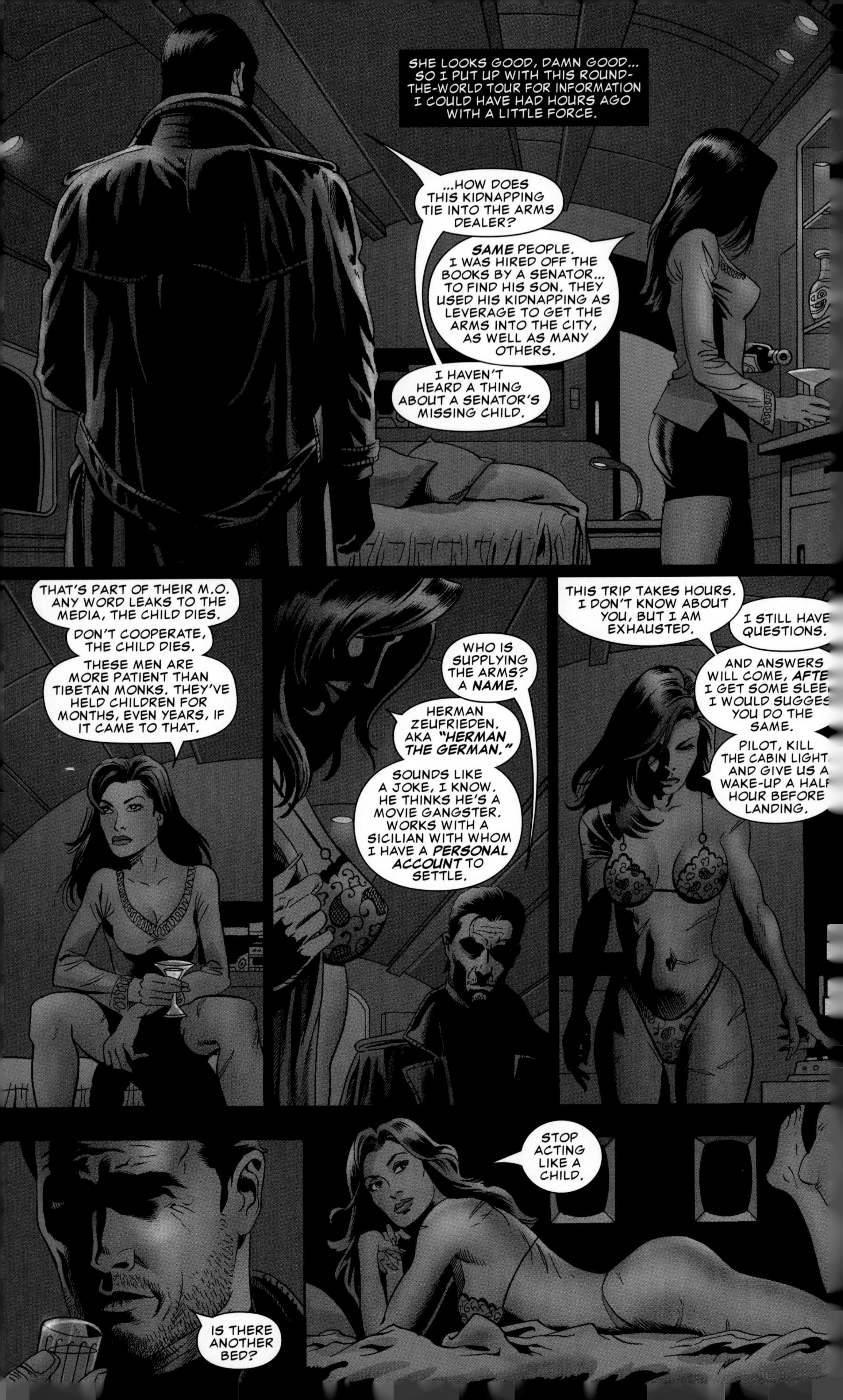
SHE LOOKS GOOD, DAMN GOOD... SO I PUT UP WITH THIS ROUND-THE-WORLD TOUR FOR INFORMATION I COULD HAVE HAD HOURS AGO WITH A LITTLE FORCE.
...HOW DOES THIS KIDNAPPING TIE INTO THE ARMS DEALER?
SAME PEOPLE. I WAS HIRED OFF THE BOOKS BY A SENATOR... TO FIND HIS SON. THEY USED HIS KIDNAPPING AS LEVERAGE TO GET THE ARMS INTO THE CITY, AS WELL AS MANY OTHERS.
I HAVEN'T HEARD A THING ABOUT A SENATOR'S MISSING CHILD.
THAT'S PART OF THEIR M.O. ANY WORD LEAKS TO THE MEDIA, THE CHILD DIES.
DON'T COOPERATE, THE CHILD DIES.
THESE MEN ARE MORE PATIENT THAN TIBETAN MONKS. THEY'VE HELD CHILDREN FOR MONTHS, EVEN YEARS, IF IT CAME TO THAT.
WHO IS SUPPLYING THE ARMS? A NAME.
HERMAN ZEUFRIEDEN. AKA "HERMAN THE GERMAN."
SOUNDS LIKE A JOKE, I KNOW. HE THINKS HE'S A MOVIE GANGSTER. WORKS WITH A SICILIAN WITH WHOM I HAVE A PERSONAL ACCOUNT TO SETTLE.
THIS TRIP TAKES HOURS. I DON'T KNOW ABOUT YOU, BUT I AM EXHAUSTED.
I STILL HAVE QUESTIONS.
AND ANSWERS WILL COME, AFTE I GET SOME SLEE I WOULD SUGGES YOU DO THE SAME.
PILOT, KILL THE CABIN LIGHT AND GIVE US A WAKE-UP A HALF HOUR BEFORE LANDING.
IS THERE ANOTHER BED?
STOP ACTING LIKE A CHILD.

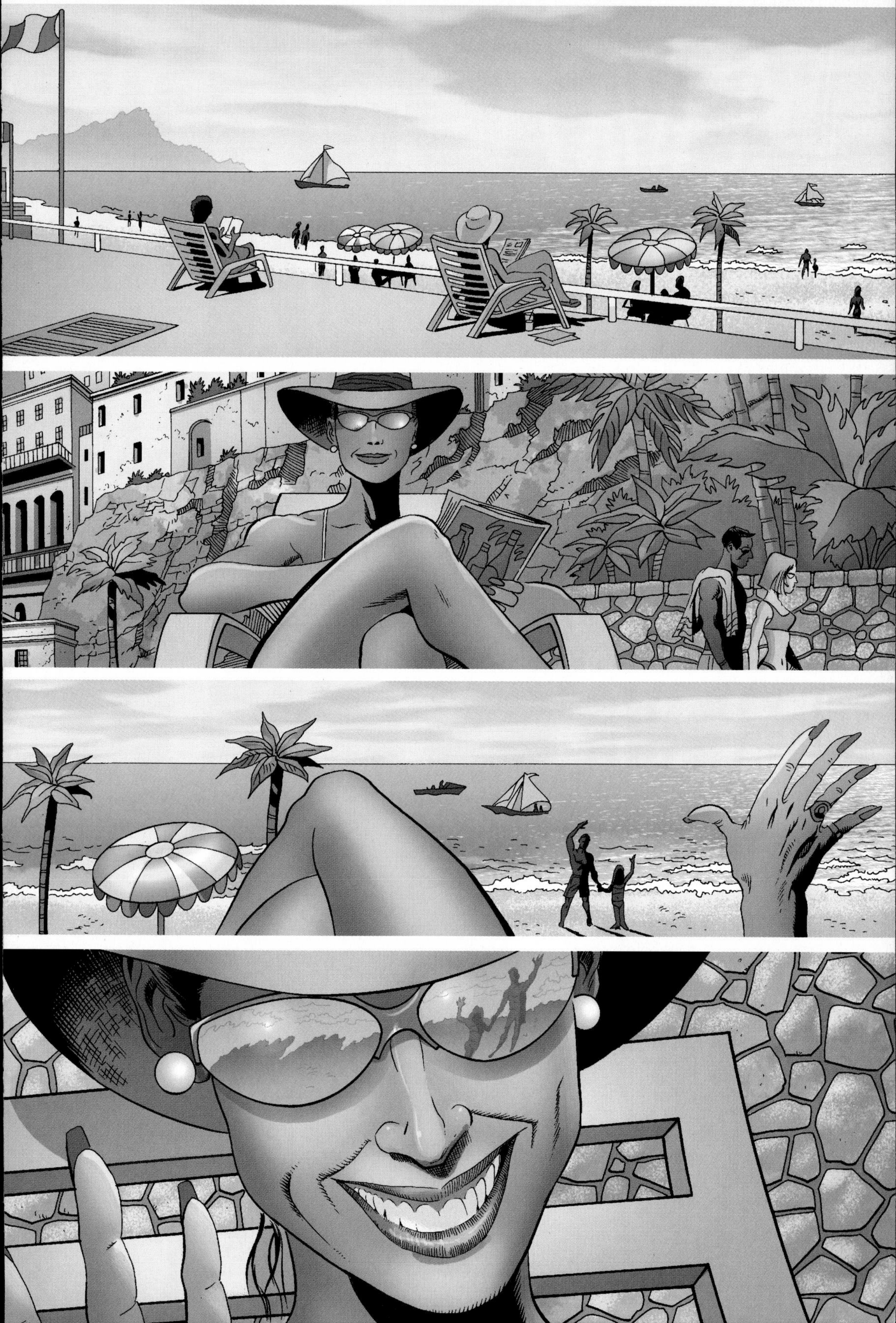

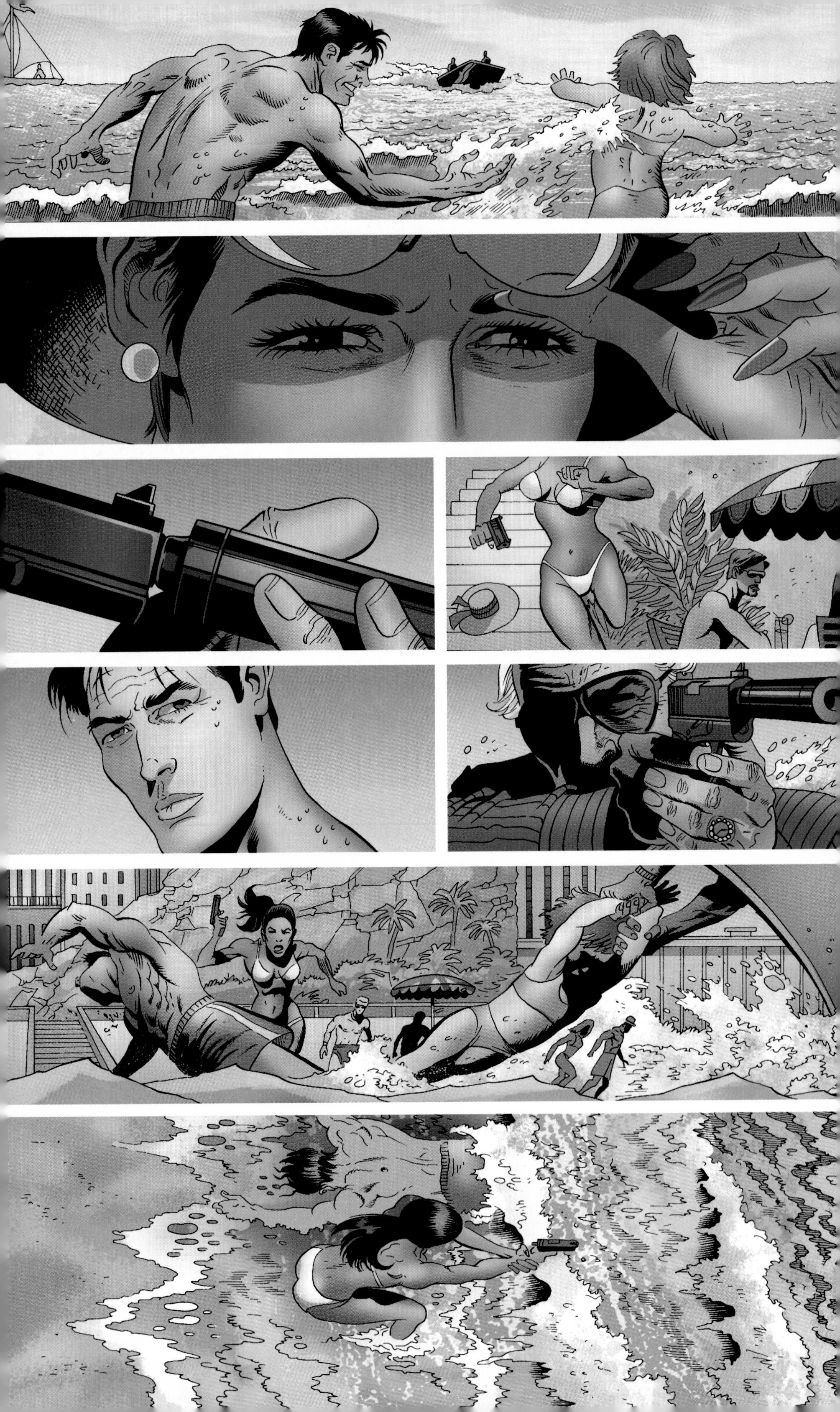

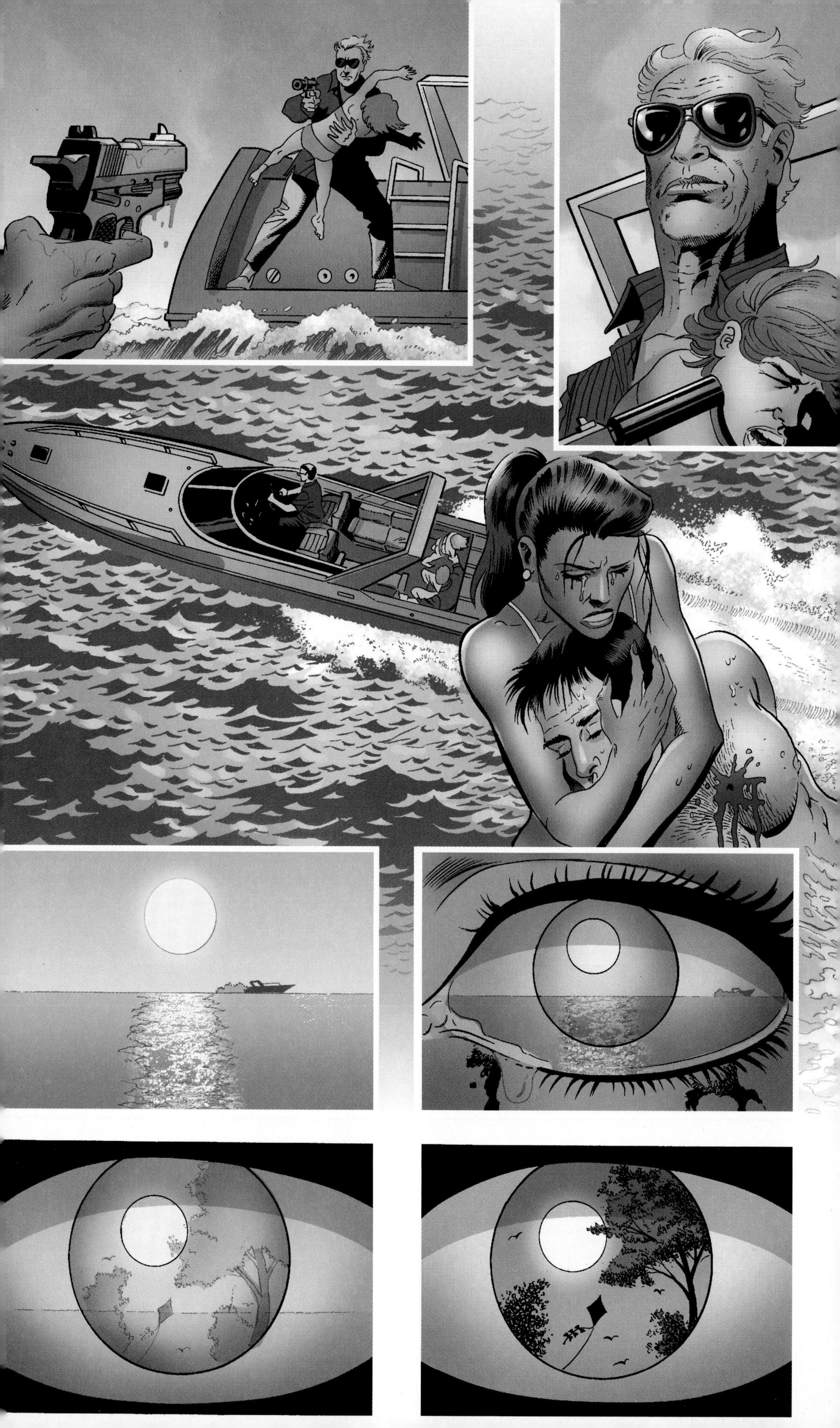

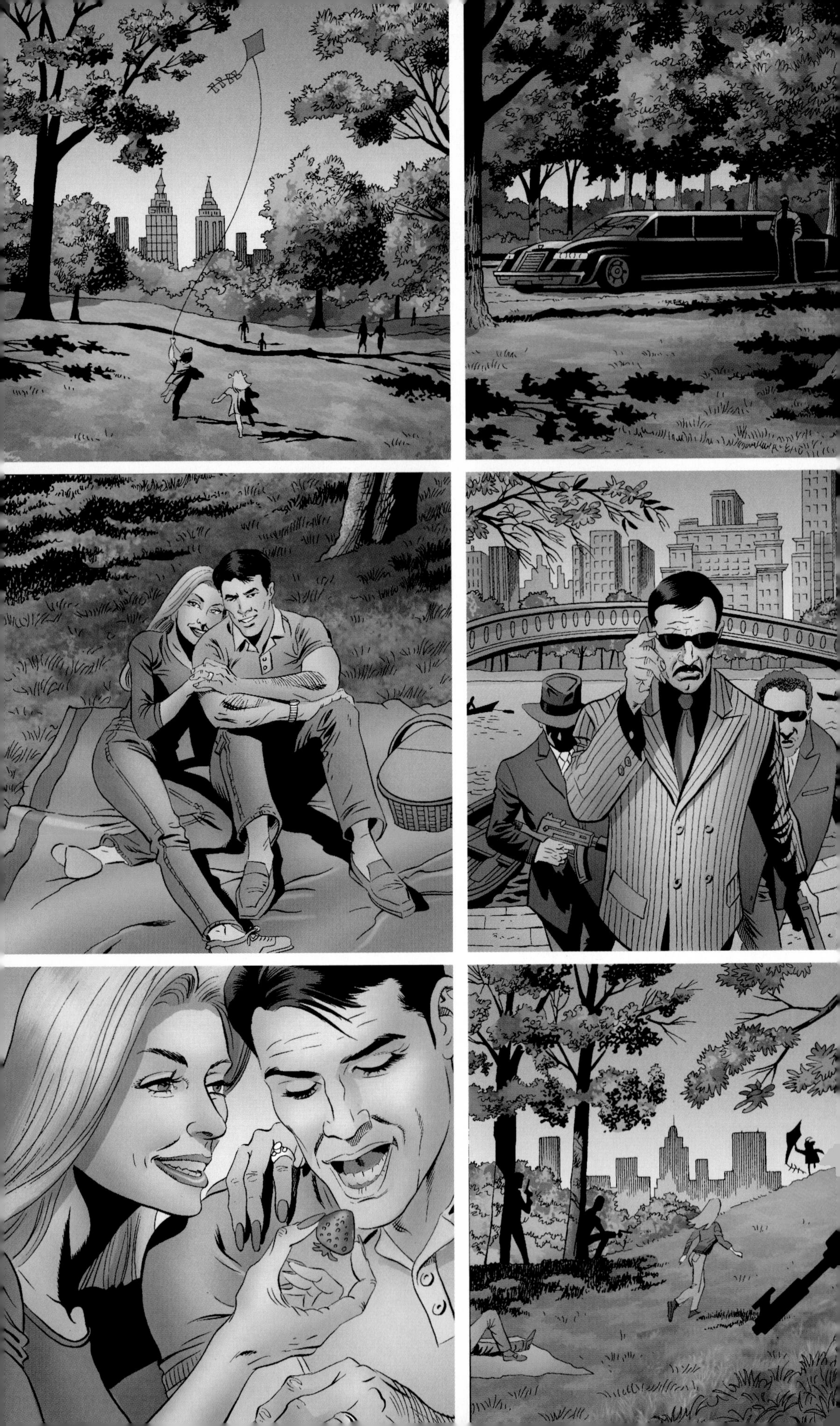

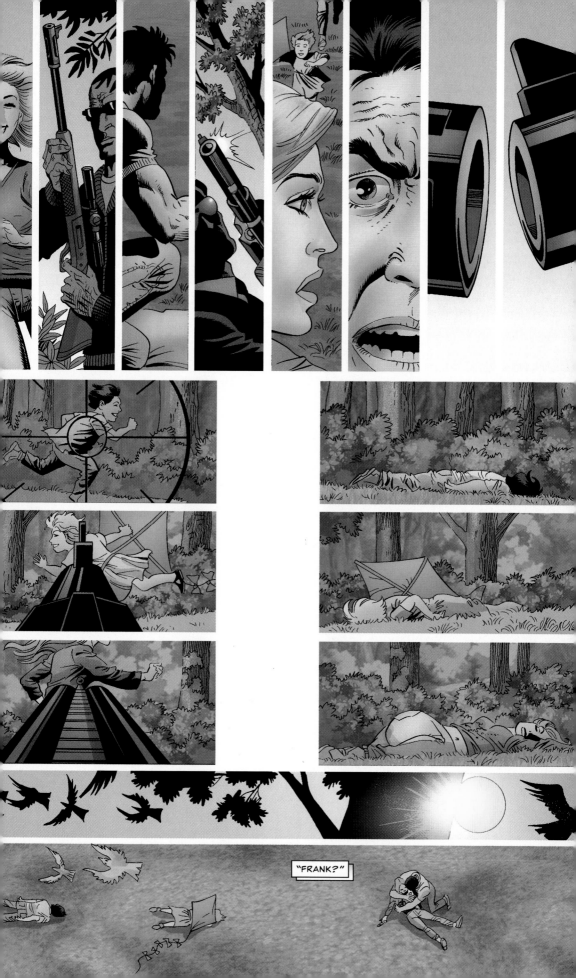

"FRANK?"

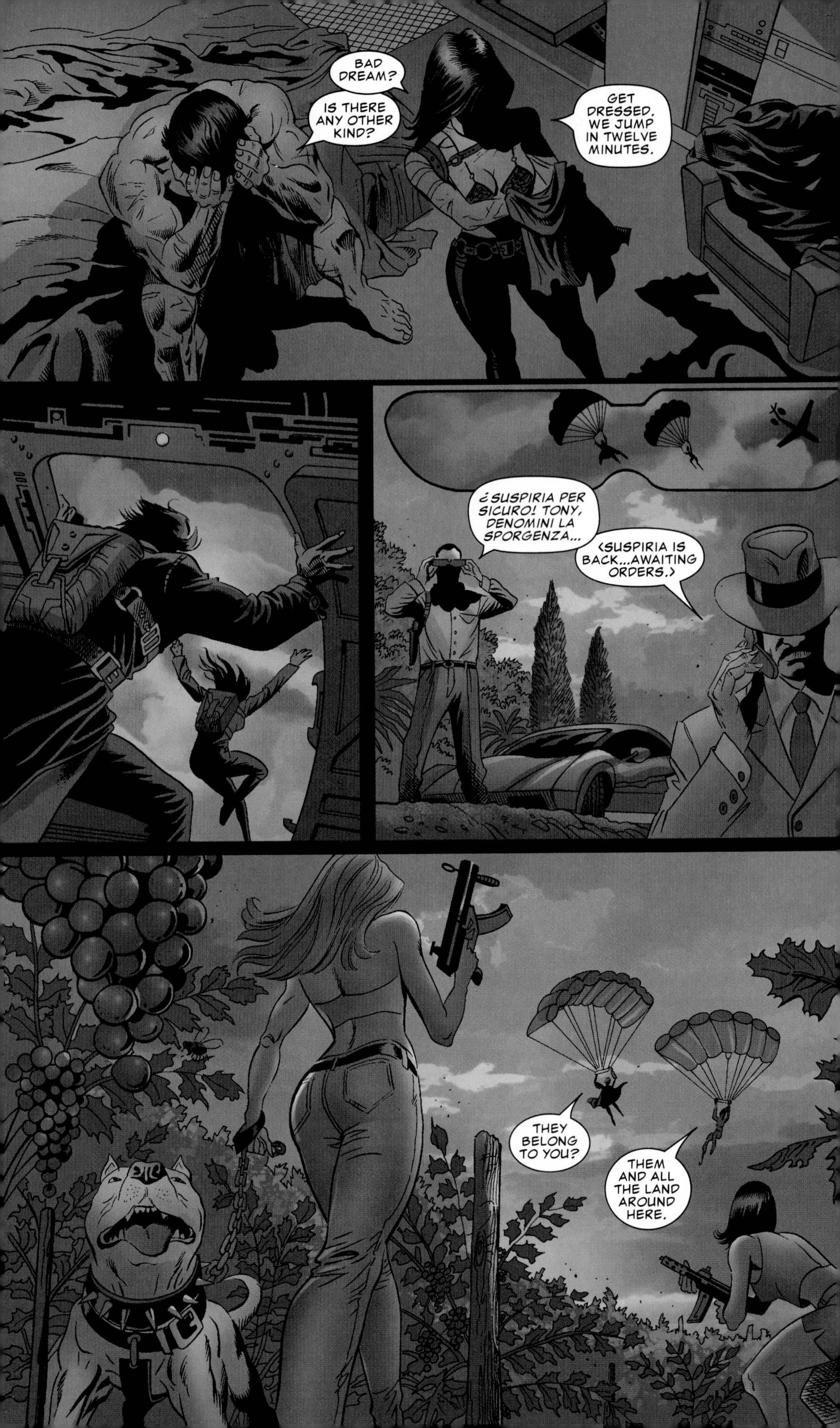
BAD DREAM?
IS THERE ANY OTHER KIND?
GET DRESSED. WE JUMP IN TWELVE MINUTES.
¿SUSPIRIA PER SICURO! TONY, DENOMINI LA SPORGENZA...
‹SUSPIRIA IS BACK...AWAITING ORDERS.›
THEY BELONG TO YOU?
THEM AND ALL THE LAND AROUND HERE.

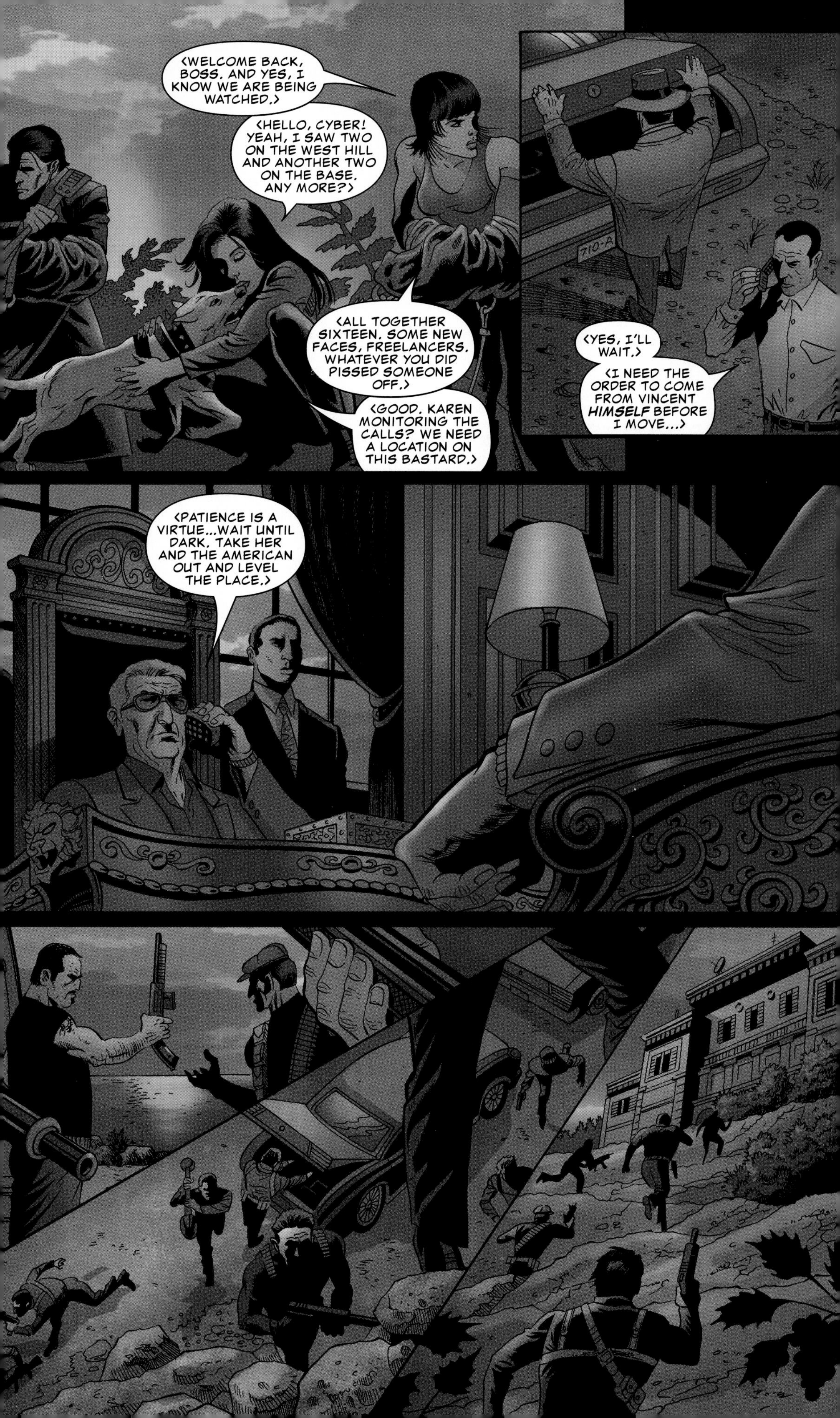
<WELCOME BACK, BOSS. AND YES, I KNOW WE ARE BEING WATCHED.>
<HELLO, CYBER! YEAH, I SAW TWO ON THE WEST HILL AND ANOTHER TWO ON THE BASE. ANY MORE?>
<ALL TOGETHER SIXTEEN. SOME NEW FACES, FREELANCERS. WHATEVER YOU DID PISSED SOMEONE OFF.>
<GOOD. KAREN MONITORING THE CALLS? WE NEED A LOCATION ON THIS BASTARD.>
710-A
<YES, I'LL WAIT.>
<I NEED THE ORDER TO COME FROM VINCENT *HIMSELF* BEFORE I MOVE...>
<PATIENCE IS A VIRTUE...WAIT UNTIL DARK. TAKE HER AND THE AMERICAN OUT AND LEVEL THE PLACE.>

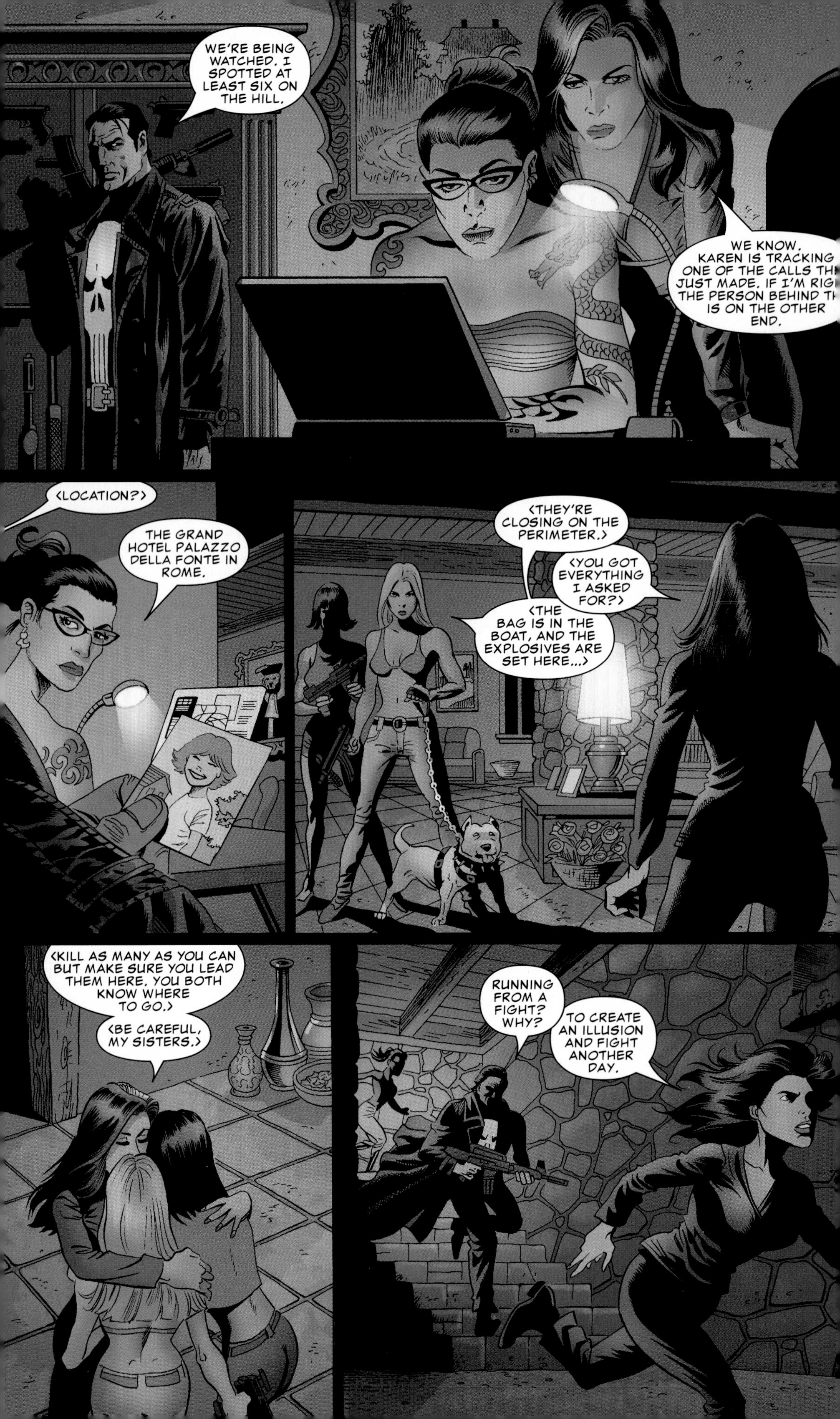
WE'RE BEING WATCHED. I SPOTTED AT LEAST SIX ON THE HILL.
WE KNOW. KAREN IS TRACKING ONE OF THE CALLS TH JUST MADE. IF I'M RIG THE PERSON BEHIND T IS ON THE OTHER END.
<LOCATION?>
THE GRAND HOTEL PALAZZO DELLA FONTE IN ROME.
<THEY'RE CLOSING ON THE PERIMETER.>
<YOU GOT EVERYTHING I ASKED FOR?>
<THE BAG IS IN THE BOAT, AND THE EXPLOSIVES ARE SET HERE...>
<KILL AS MANY AS YOU CAN BUT MAKE SURE YOU LEAD THEM HERE. YOU BOTH KNOW WHERE TO GO.>
<BE CAREFUL, MY SISTERS.>
RUNNING FROM A FIGHT? WHY?
TO CREATE AN ILLUSION AND FIGHT ANOTHER DAY.

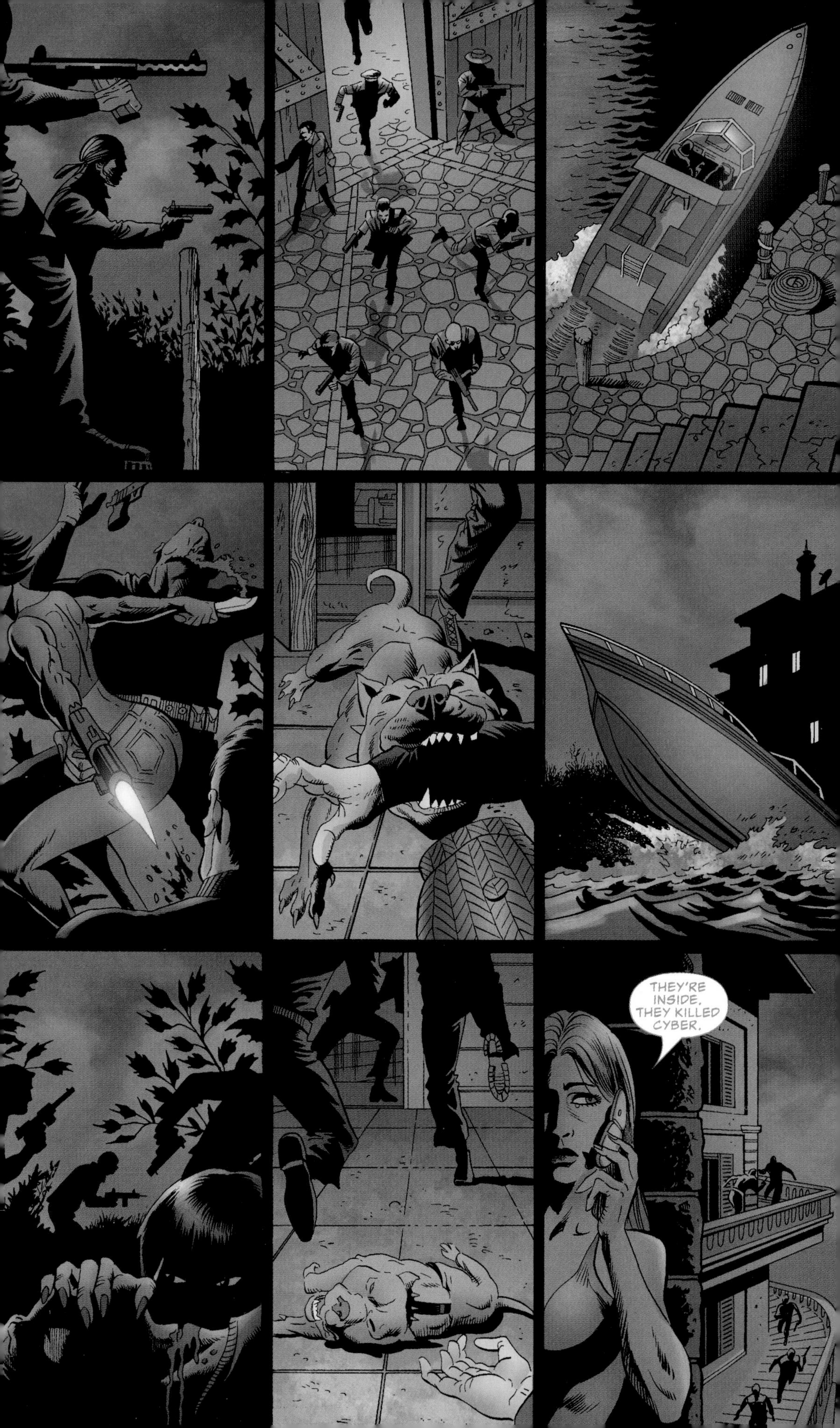
THEY'RE INSIDE. THEY KILLED CYBER.

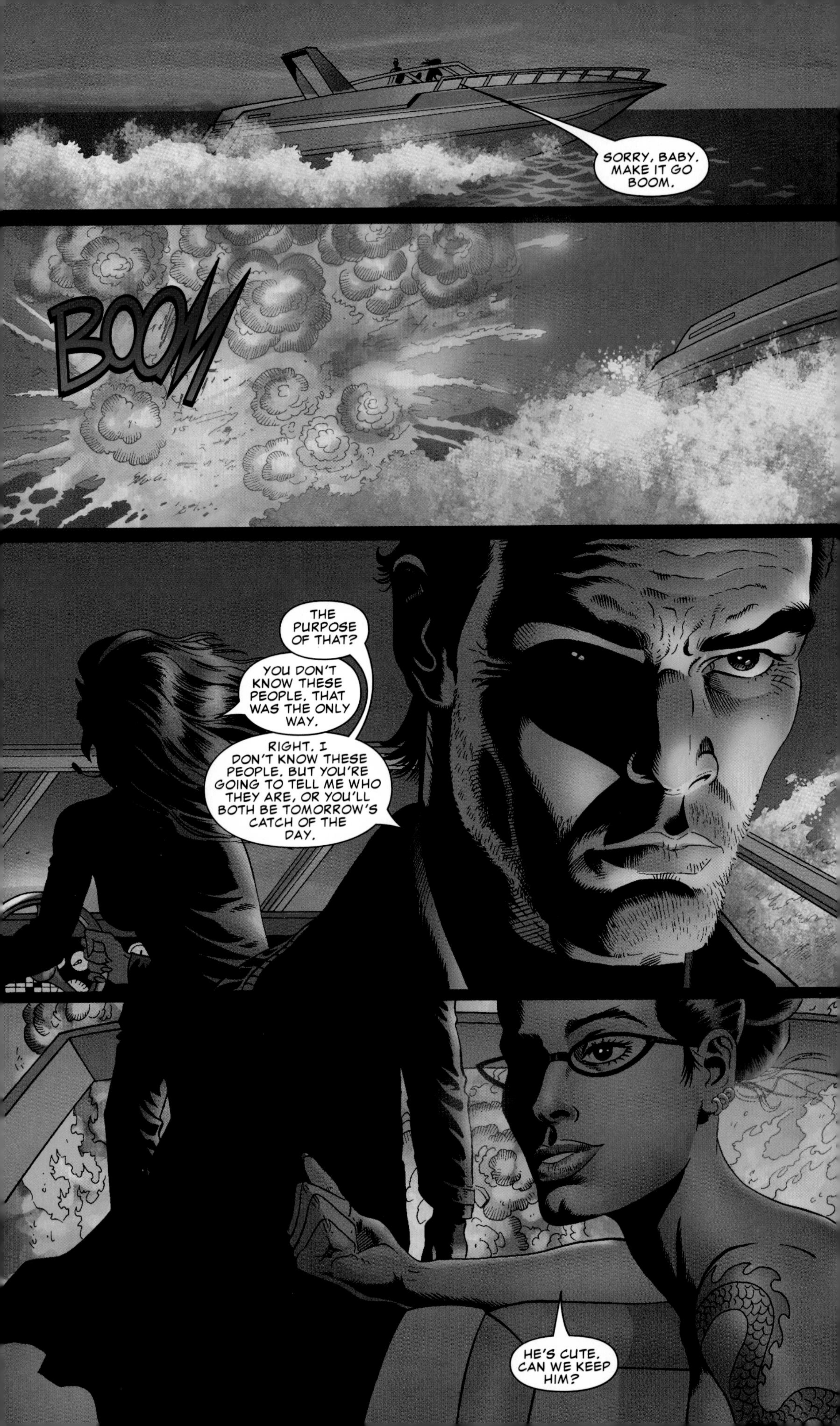
SORRY, BABY. MAKE IT GO BOOM.
BOOM
THE PURPOSE OF THAT?
YOU DON'T KNOW THESE PEOPLE. THAT WAS THE ONLY WAY.
RIGHT. I DON'T KNOW THESE PEOPLE. BUT YOU'RE GOING TO TELL ME WHO THEY ARE, OR YOU'LL BOTH BE TOMORROW'S CATCH OF THE DAY.
HE'S CUTE. CAN WE KEEP HIM?

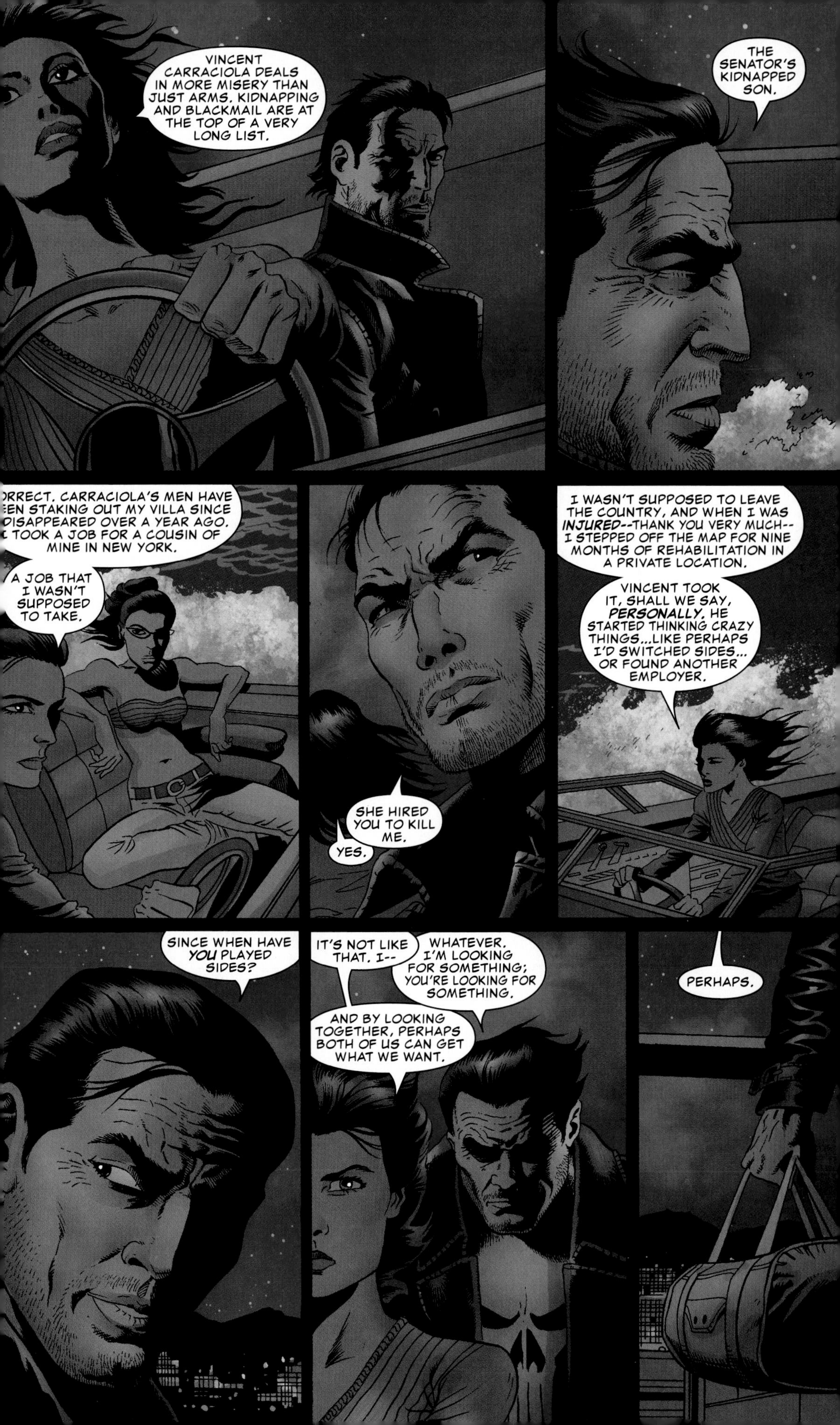
VINCENT CARRACIOLA DEALS IN MORE MISERY THAN JUST ARMS. KIDNAPPING AND BLACKMAIL ARE AT THE TOP OF A VERY LONG LIST.
THE SENATOR'S KIDNAPPED SON.
ORRECT. CARRACIOLA'S MEN HAVE EEN STAKING OUT MY VILLA SINCE DISAPPEARED OVER A YEAR AGO. I TOOK A JOB FOR A COUSIN OF MINE IN NEW YORK.
A JOB THAT I WASN'T SUPPOSED TO TAKE.
SHE HIRED YOU TO KILL ME.
YES.
I WASN'T SUPPOSED TO LEAVE THE COUNTRY, AND WHEN I WAS INJURED--THANK YOU VERY MUCH--I STEPPED OFF THE MAP FOR NINE MONTHS OF REHABILITATION IN A PRIVATE LOCATION.
VINCENT TOOK IT, SHALL WE SAY, PERSONALLY. HE STARTED THINKING CRAZY THINGS...LIKE PERHAPS I'D SWITCHED SIDES... OR FOUND ANOTHER EMPLOYER.
SINCE WHEN HAVE YOU PLAYED SIDES?
IT'S NOT LIKE THAT. I--
WHATEVER. I'M LOOKING FOR SOMETHING; YOU'RE LOOKING FOR SOMETHING.
AND BY LOOKING TOGETHER, PERHAPS BOTH OF US CAN GET WHAT WE WANT.
PERHAPS.

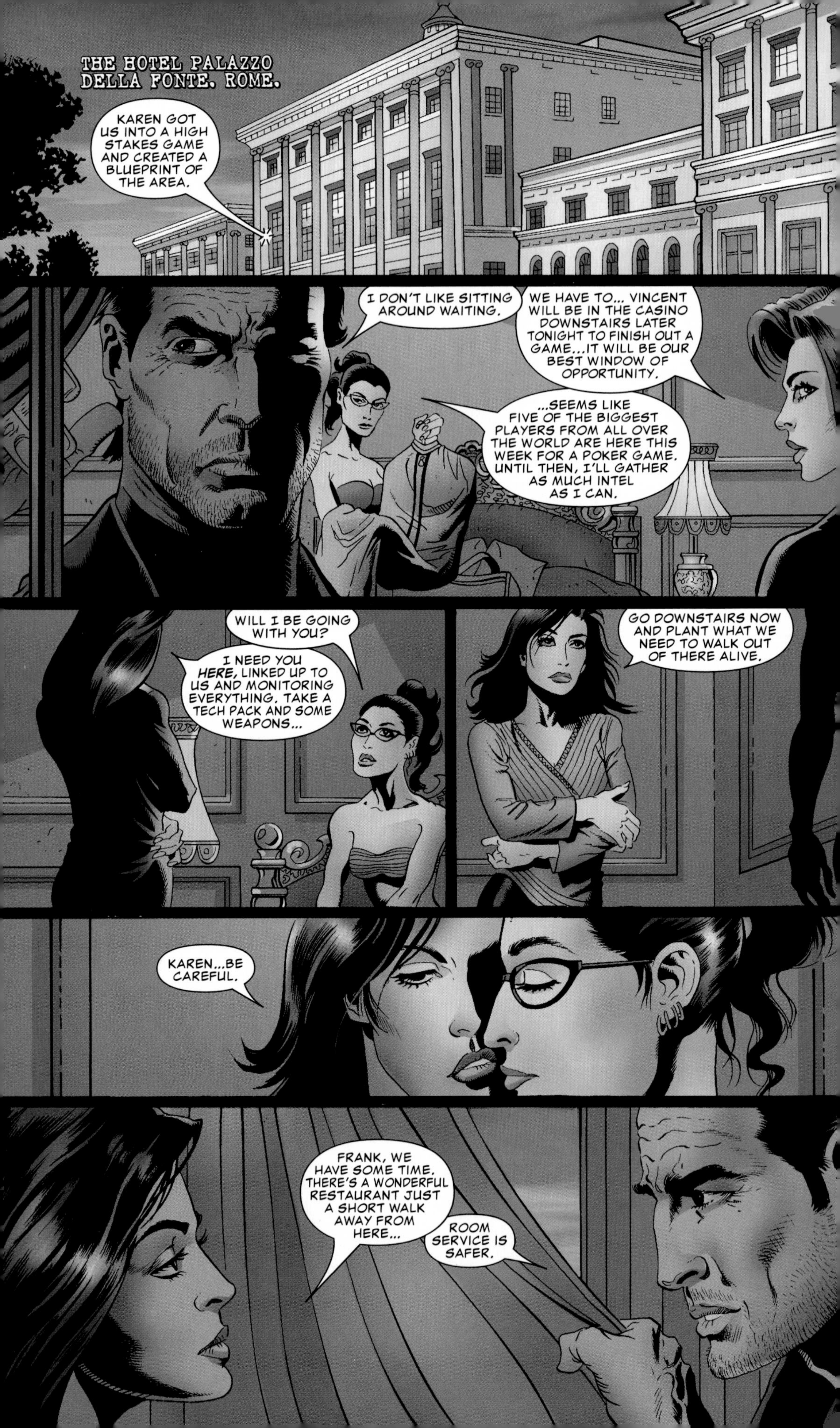
THE HOTEL PALAZZO DELLA FONTE. ROME.
KAREN GOT US INTO A HIGH STAKES GAME AND CREATED A BLUEPRINT OF THE AREA.
I DON'T LIKE SITTING AROUND WAITING.
WE HAVE TO... VINCENT WILL BE IN THE CASINO DOWNSTAIRS LATER TONIGHT TO FINISH OUT A GAME...IT WILL BE OUR BEST WINDOW OF OPPORTUNITY.
...SEEMS LIKE FIVE OF THE BIGGEST PLAYERS FROM ALL OVER THE WORLD ARE HERE THIS WEEK FOR A POKER GAME. UNTIL THEN, I'LL GATHER AS MUCH INTEL AS I CAN.
WILL I BE GOING WITH YOU?
I NEED YOU HERE, LINKED UP TO US AND MONITORING EVERYTHING. TAKE A TECH PACK AND SOME WEAPONS...
GO DOWNSTAIRS NOW AND PLANT WHAT WE NEED TO WALK OUT OF THERE ALIVE.
KAREN...BE CAREFUL.
FRANK, WE HAVE SOME TIME. THERE'S A WONDERFUL RESTAURANT JUST A SHORT WALK AWAY FROM HERE...
ROOM SERVICE IS SAFER.

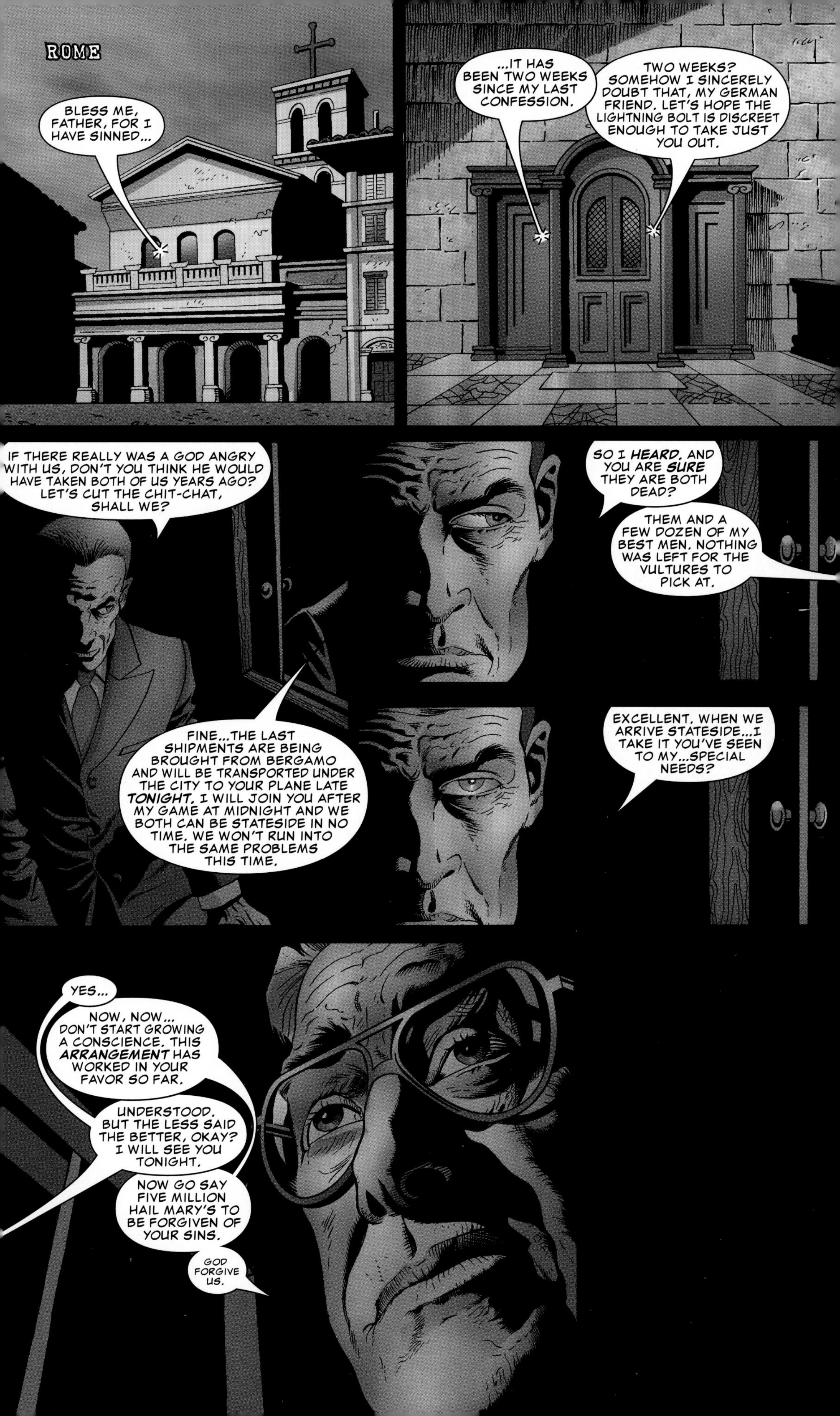
ROME
BLESS ME, FATHER, FOR I HAVE SINNED...
...IT HAS BEEN TWO WEEKS SINCE MY LAST CONFESSION.
TWO WEEKS? SOMEHOW I SINCERELY DOUBT THAT, MY GERMAN FRIEND. LET'S HOPE THE LIGHTNING BOLT IS DISCREET ENOUGH TO TAKE JUST YOU OUT.
IF THERE REALLY WAS A GOD ANGRY WITH US, DON'T YOU THINK HE WOULD HAVE TAKEN BOTH OF US YEARS AGO? LET'S CUT THE CHIT-CHAT, SHALL WE?
SO I HEARD. AND YOU ARE SURE THEY ARE BOTH DEAD?
THEM AND A FEW DOZEN OF MY BEST MEN. NOTHING WAS LEFT FOR THE VULTURES TO PICK AT.
FINE...THE LAST SHIPMENTS ARE BEING BROUGHT FROM BERGAMO AND WILL BE TRANSPORTED UNDER THE CITY TO YOUR PLANE LATE TONIGHT. I WILL JOIN YOU AFTER MY GAME AT MIDNIGHT AND WE BOTH CAN BE STATESIDE IN NO TIME. WE WON'T RUN INTO THE SAME PROBLEMS THIS TIME.
EXCELLENT. WHEN WE ARRIVE STATESIDE...I TAKE IT YOU'VE SEEN TO MY...SPECIAL NEEDS?
YES...
NOW, NOW... DON'T START GROWING A CONSCIENCE. THIS ARRANGEMENT HAS WORKED IN YOUR FAVOR SO FAR.
UNDERSTOOD. BUT THE LESS SAID THE BETTER, OKAY? I WILL SEE YOU TONIGHT.
NOW GO SAY FIVE MILLION HAIL MARY'S TO BE FORGIVEN OF YOUR SINS.
GOD FORGIVE US.

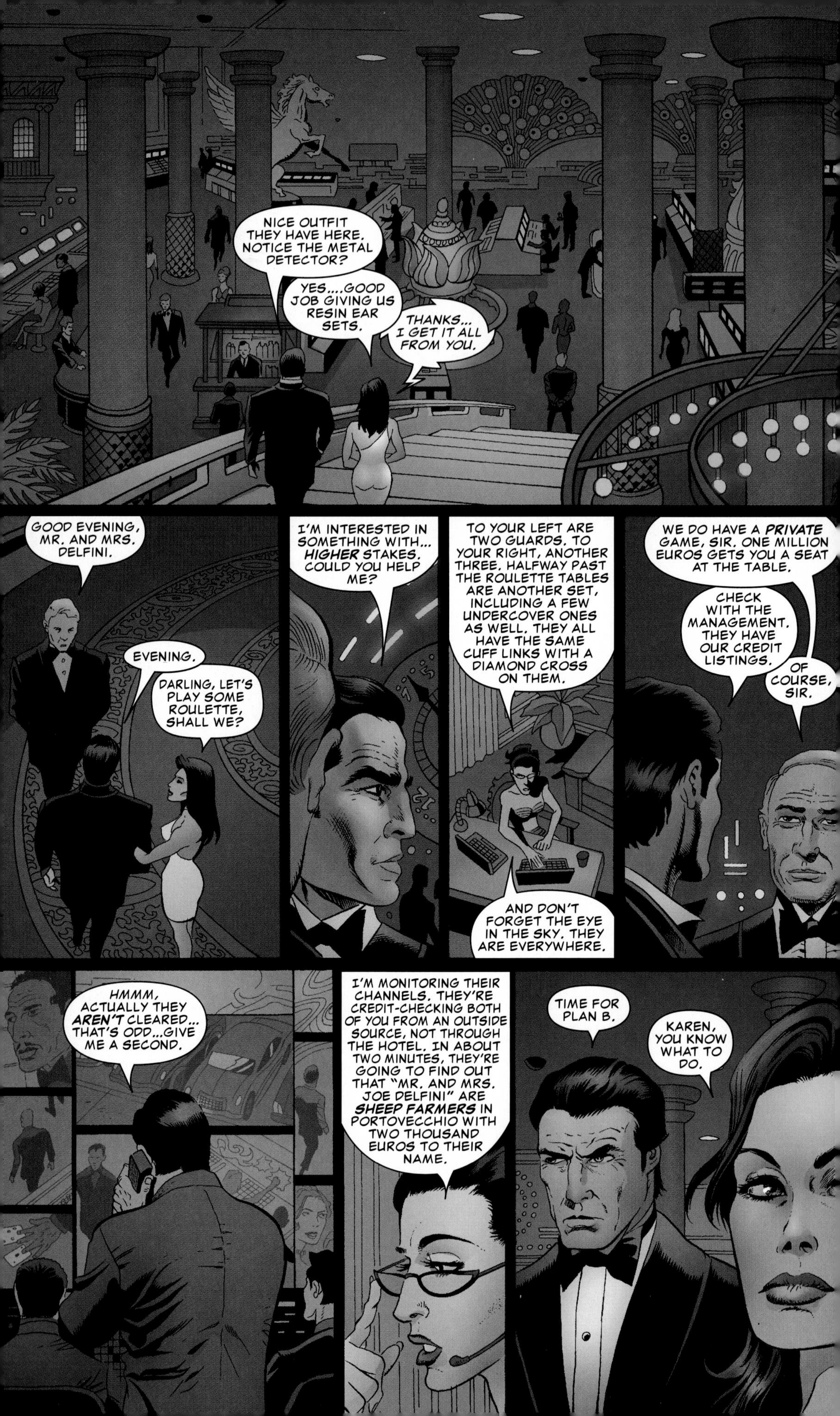
NICE OUTFIT THEY HAVE HERE. NOTICE THE METAL DETECTOR?
YES....GOOD JOB GIVING US RESIN EAR SETS.
THANKS... I GET IT ALL FROM YOU.
GOOD EVENING, MR. AND MRS. DELFINI.
EVENING.
DARLING, LET'S PLAY SOME ROULETTE, SHALL WE?
I'M INTERESTED IN SOMETHING WITH... HIGHER STAKES. COULD YOU HELP ME?
TO YOUR LEFT ARE TWO GUARDS. TO YOUR RIGHT, ANOTHER THREE. HALFWAY PAST THE ROULETTE TABLES ARE ANOTHER SET, INCLUDING A FEW UNDERCOVER ONES AS WELL. THEY ALL HAVE THE SAME CUFF LINKS WITH A DIAMOND CROSS ON THEM.
AND DON'T FORGET THE EYE IN THE SKY. THEY ARE EVERYWHERE.
WE DO HAVE A PRIVATE GAME, SIR. ONE MILLION EUROS GETS YOU A SEAT AT THE TABLE.
CHECK WITH THE MANAGEMENT. THEY HAVE OUR CREDIT LISTINGS.
OF COURSE, SIR.
HMMM, ACTUALLY THEY AREN'T CLEARED... THAT'S ODD...GIVE ME A SECOND.
I'M MONITORING THEIR CHANNELS. THEY'RE CREDIT-CHECKING BOTH OF YOU FROM AN OUTSIDE SOURCE, NOT THROUGH THE HOTEL. IN ABOUT TWO MINUTES, THEY'RE GOING TO FIND OUT THAT "MR. AND MRS. JOE DELFINI" ARE SHEEP FARMERS IN PORTOVECCHIO WITH TWO THOUSAND EUROS TO THEIR NAME.
TIME FOR PLAN B.
KAREN, YOU KNOW WHAT TO DO.

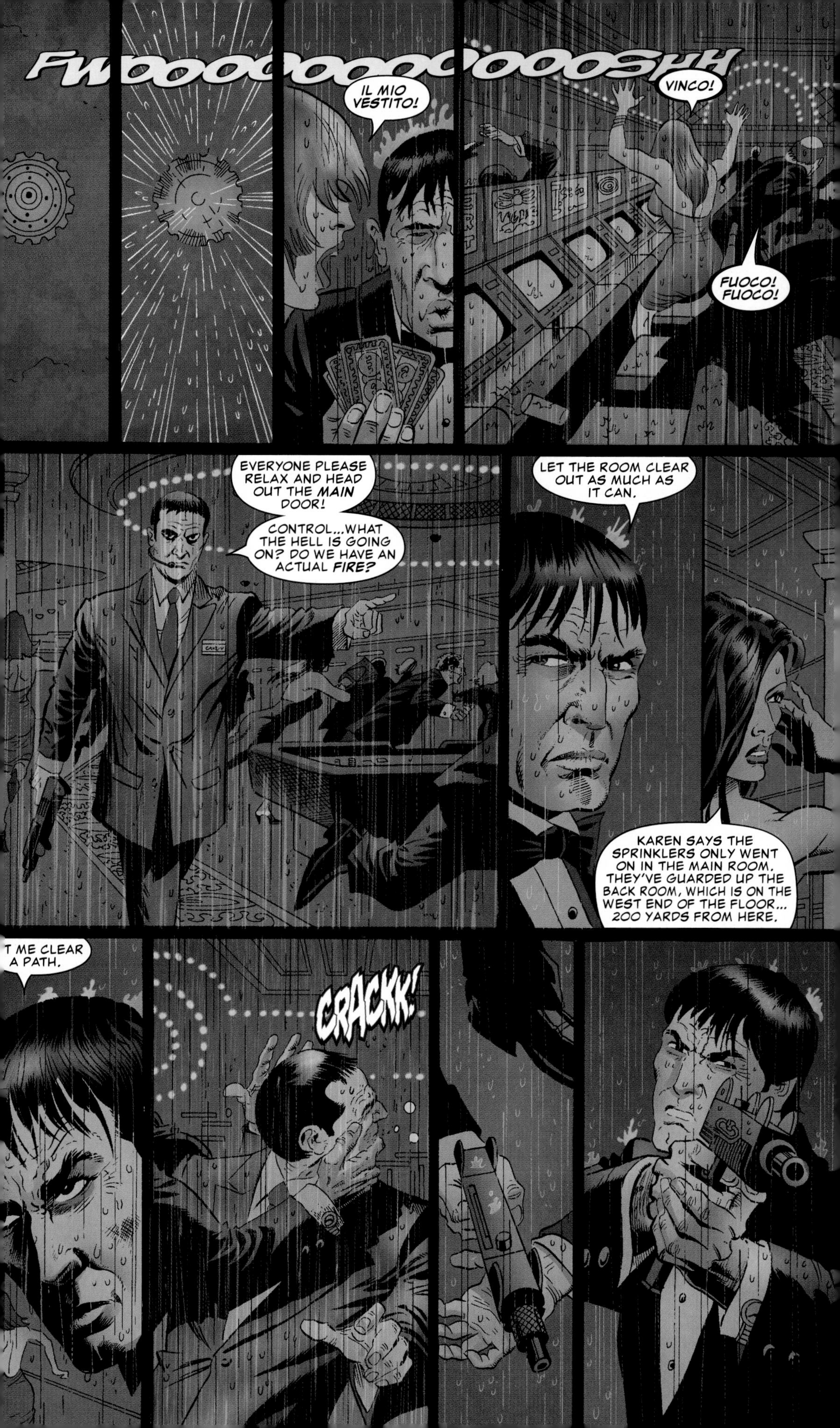
FWOOOOOOOOOOOSHH
IL MIO VESTITO!
VINCO!
FUOCO! FUOCO!
EVERYONE PLEASE RELAX AND HEAD OUT THE MAIN DOOR!
CONTROL...WHAT THE HELL IS GOING ON? DO WE HAVE AN ACTUAL FIRE?
LET THE ROOM CLEAR OUT AS MUCH AS IT CAN.
KAREN SAYS THE SPRINKLERS ONLY WENT ON IN THE MAIN ROOM. THEY'VE GUARDED UP THE BACK ROOM, WHICH IS ON THE WEST END OF THE FLOOR... 200 YARDS FROM HERE.
T ME CLEAR A PATH.
CRACKK!

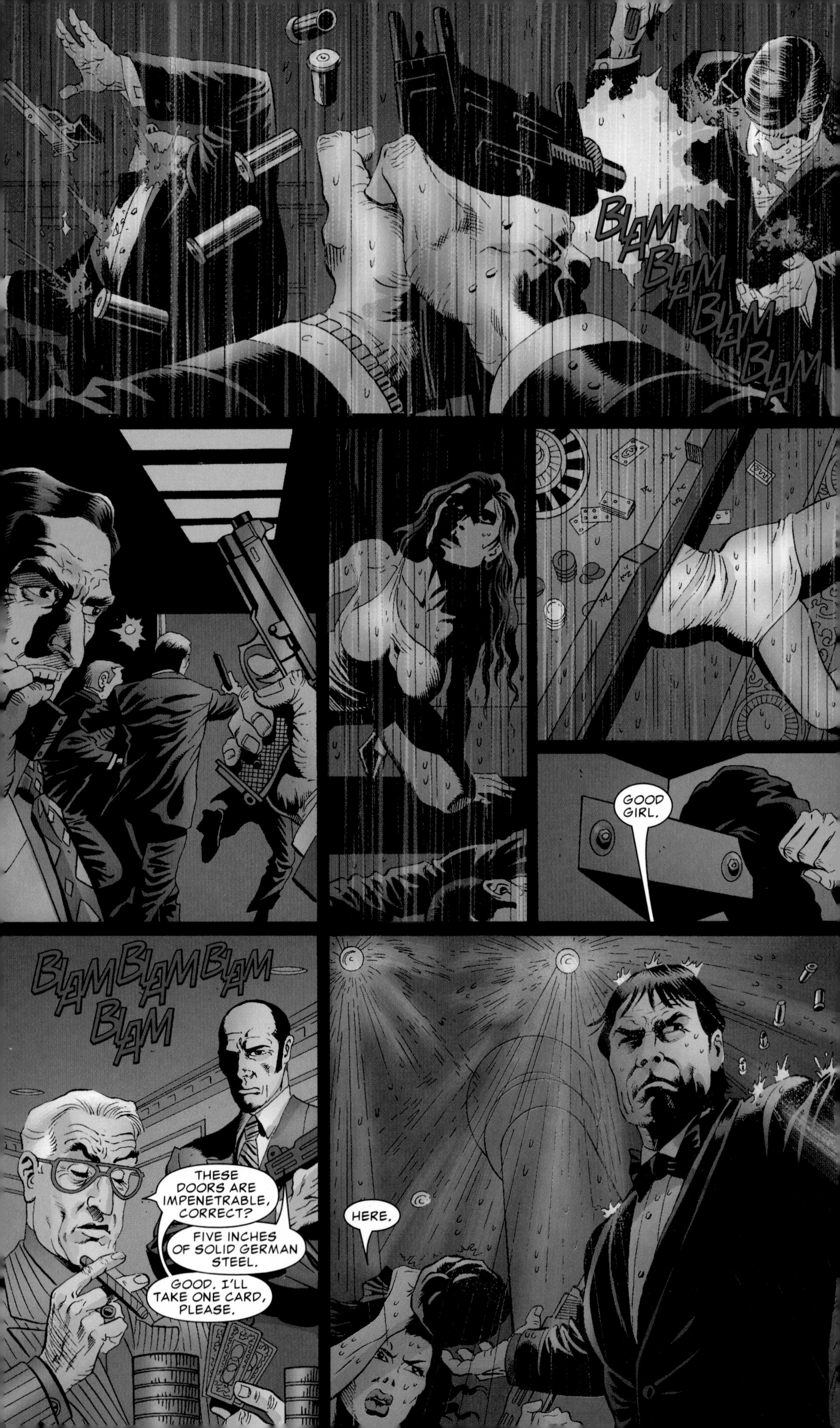
BLAM BLAM BLAM BLAM
GOOD GIRL.
BLAM BLAM BLAM BLAM
THESE DOORS ARE IMPENETRABLE, CORRECT?
FIVE INCHES OF SOLID GERMAN STEEL.
GOOD. I'LL TAKE ONE CARD, PLEASE.
HERE.

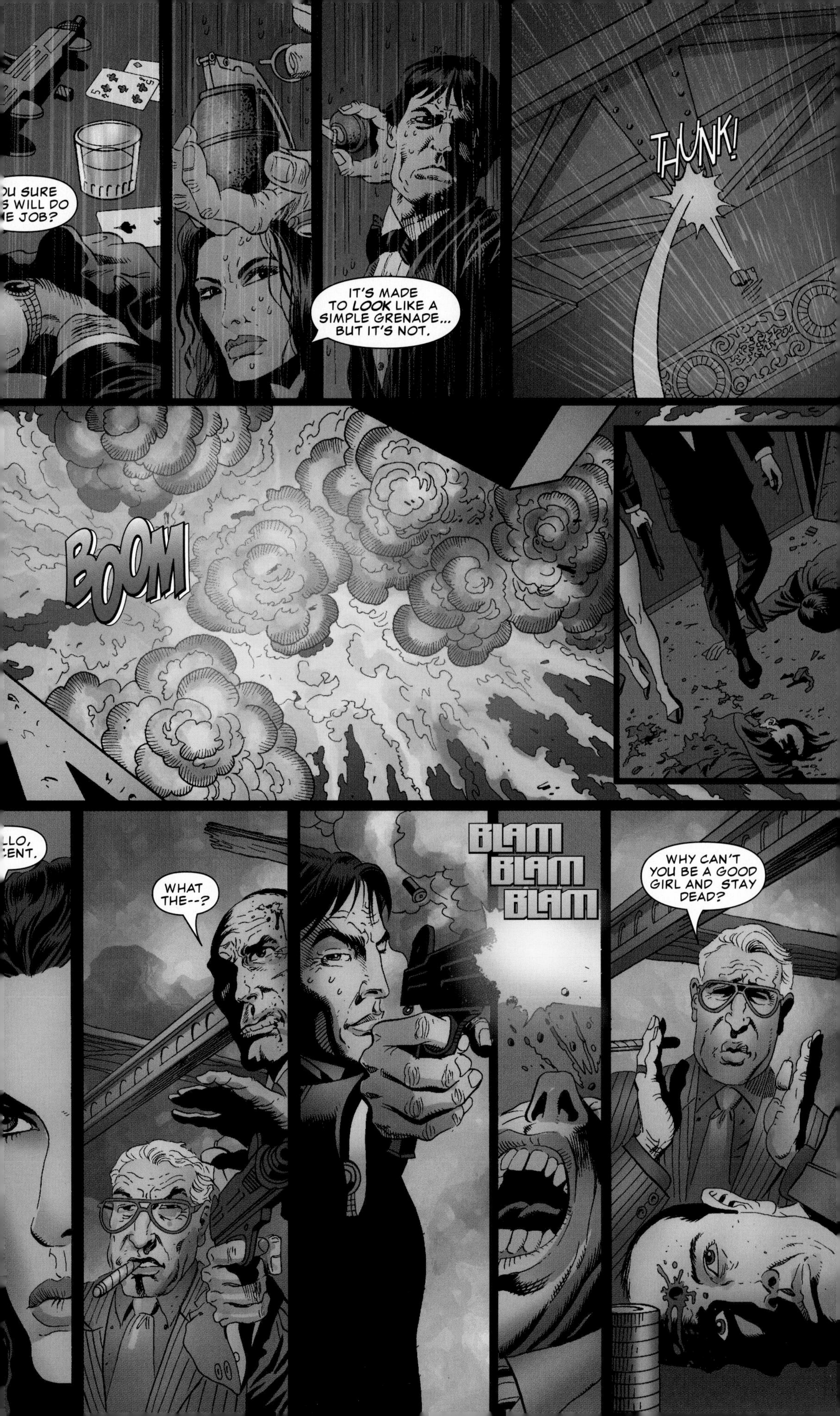

OU SURE
S WILL DO
E JOB?
IT'S MADE
TO LOOK LIKE A
SIMPLE GRENADE...
BUT IT'S NOT.
THUNK!
BOOM
LLO,
CENT.
WHAT
THE--?
BLAM
BLAM
BLAM
WHY CAN'T
YOU BE A GOOD
GIRL AND STAY
DEAD?

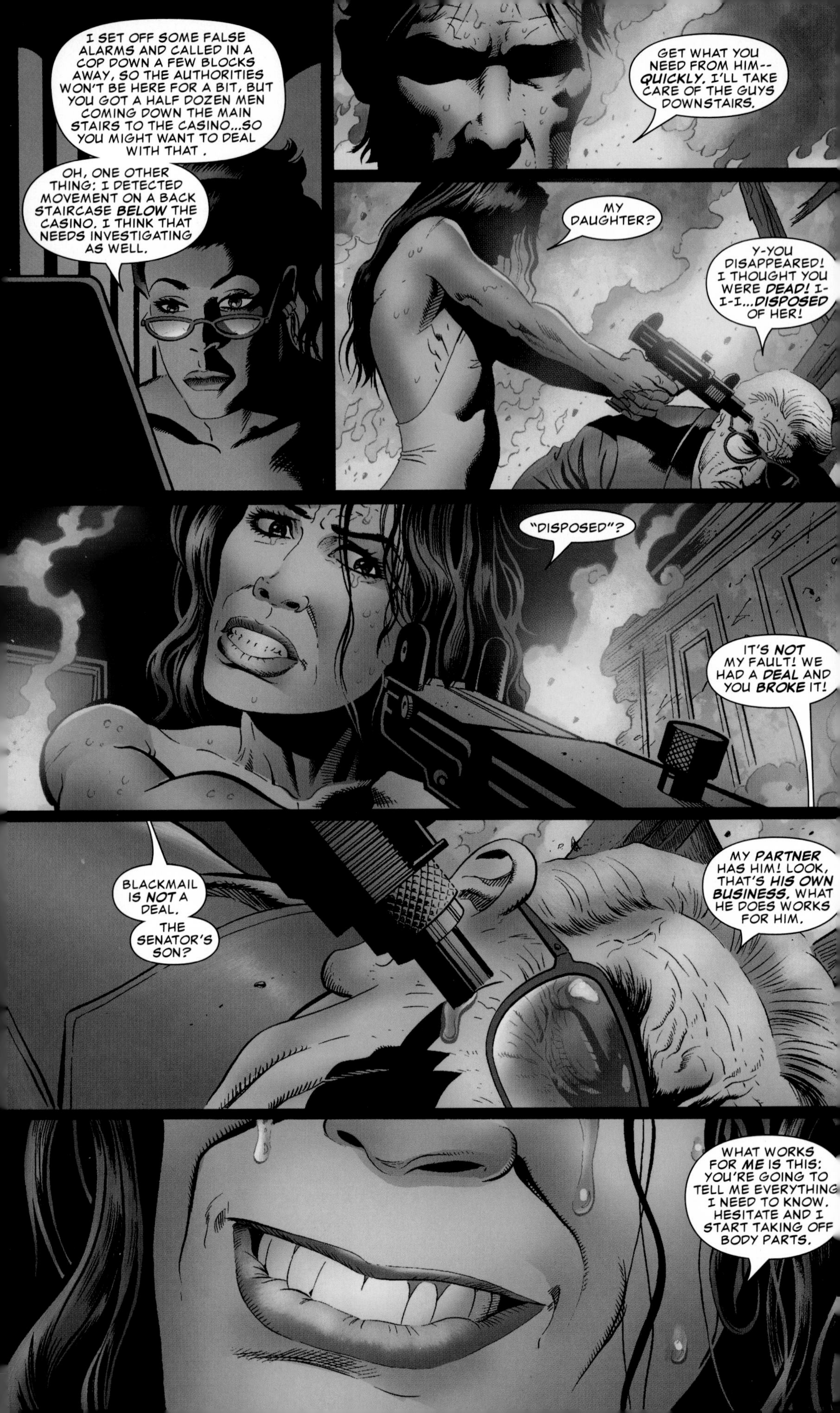

I SET OFF SOME FALSE ALARMS AND CALLED IN A COP DOWN A FEW BLOCKS AWAY, SO THE AUTHORITIES WON'T BE HERE FOR A BIT, BUT YOU GOT A HALF DOZEN MEN COMING DOWN THE MAIN STAIRS TO THE CASINO...SO YOU MIGHT WANT TO DEAL WITH THAT.
OH, ONE OTHER THING: I DETECTED MOVEMENT ON A BACK STAIRCASE **BELOW** THE CASINO. I THINK THAT NEEDS INVESTIGATING AS WELL.
GET WHAT YOU NEED FROM HIM-- **QUICKLY.** I'LL TAKE CARE OF THE GUYS DOWNSTAIRS.
MY DAUGHTER?
Y-YOU DISAPPEARED! I THOUGHT YOU WERE **DEAD!** I-I-I...**DISPOSED** OF HER!
"DISPOSED"?
IT'S **NOT** MY FAULT! WE HAD A **DEAL** AND YOU **BROKE** IT!
BLACKMAIL IS **NOT** A DEAL.
THE SENATOR'S SON?
MY **PARTNER** HAS HIM! LOOK, THAT'S **HIS OWN BUSINESS.** WHAT HE DOES WORKS FOR HIM.
WHAT WORKS FOR **ME** IS THIS: YOU'RE GOING TO TELL ME EVERYTHING I NEED TO KNOW. HESITATE AND I START TAKING OFF BODY PARTS.

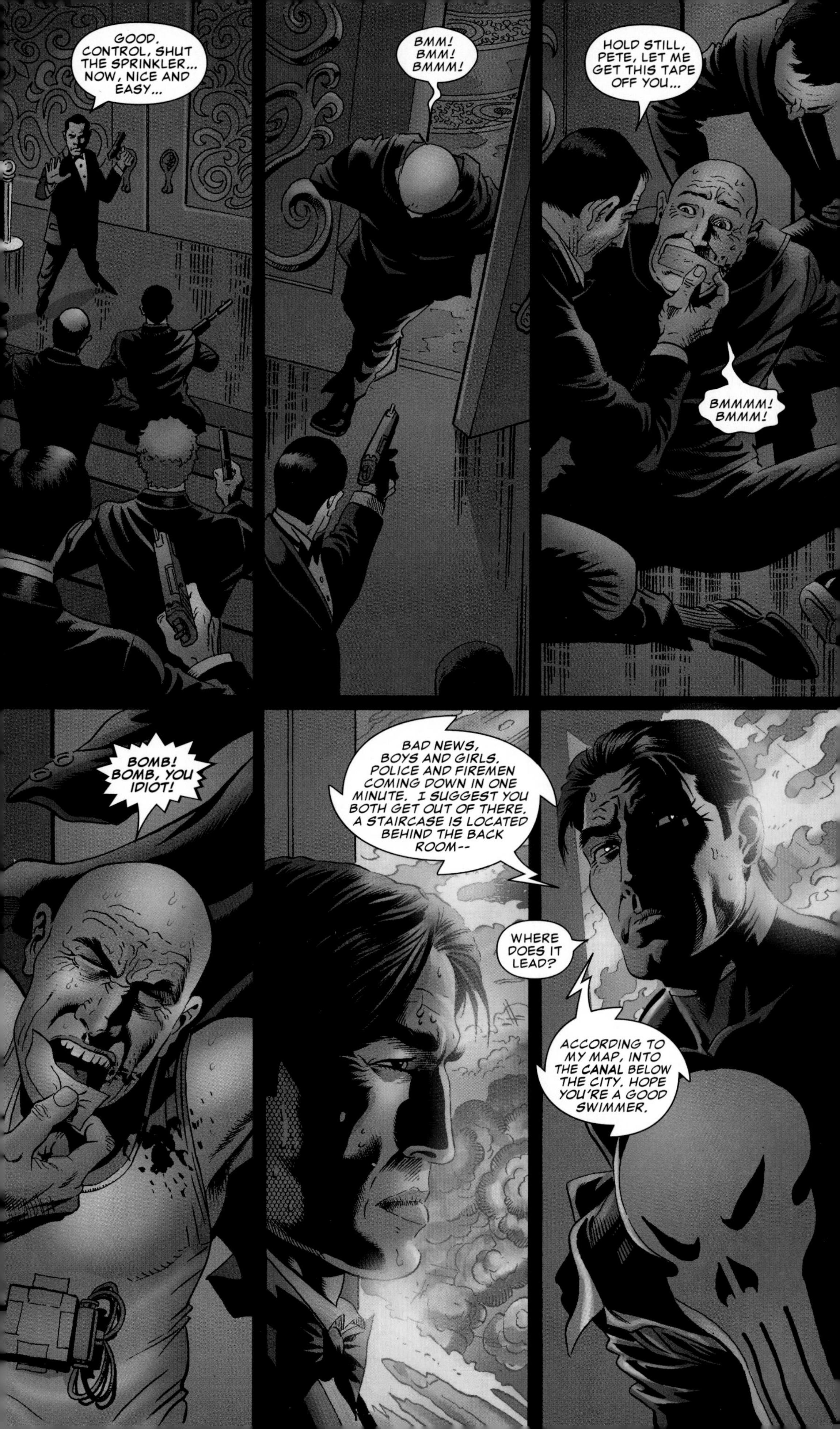

GOOD. CONTROL, SHUT THE SPRINKLER... NOW, NICE AND EASY...
BMM! BMM! BMMM!
HOLD STILL, PETE, LET ME GET THIS TAPE OFF YOU...
BMMMM! BMMM!
BOMB! BOMB, YOU IDIOT!
BAD NEWS, BOYS AND GIRLS. POLICE AND FIREMEN COMING DOWN IN ONE MINUTE. I SUGGEST YOU BOTH GET OUT OF THERE. A STAIRCASE IS LOCATED BEHIND THE BACK ROOM--
WHERE DOES IT LEAD?
ACCORDING TO MY MAP, INTO THE CANAL BELOW THE CITY. HOPE YOU'RE A GOOD SWIMMER.

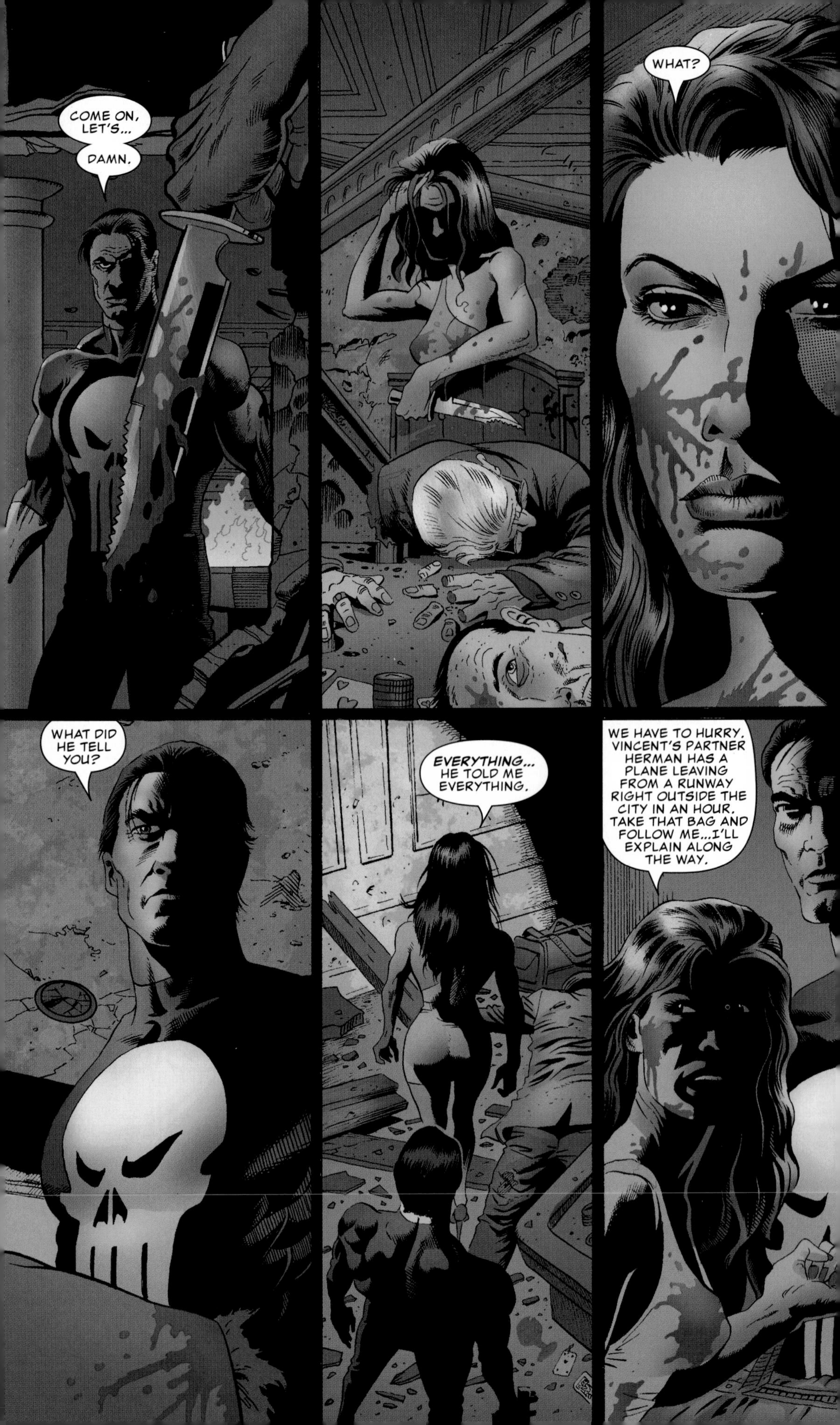
COME ON, LET'S...
DAMN.
WHAT?
WHAT DID HE TELL YOU?
EVERYTHING... HE TOLD ME EVERYTHING.
WE HAVE TO HURRY. VINCENT'S PARTNER HERMAN HAS A PLANE LEAVING FROM A RUNWAY RIGHT OUTSIDE THE CITY IN AN HOUR. TAKE THAT BAG AND FOLLOW ME...I'LL EXPLAIN ALONG THE WAY.

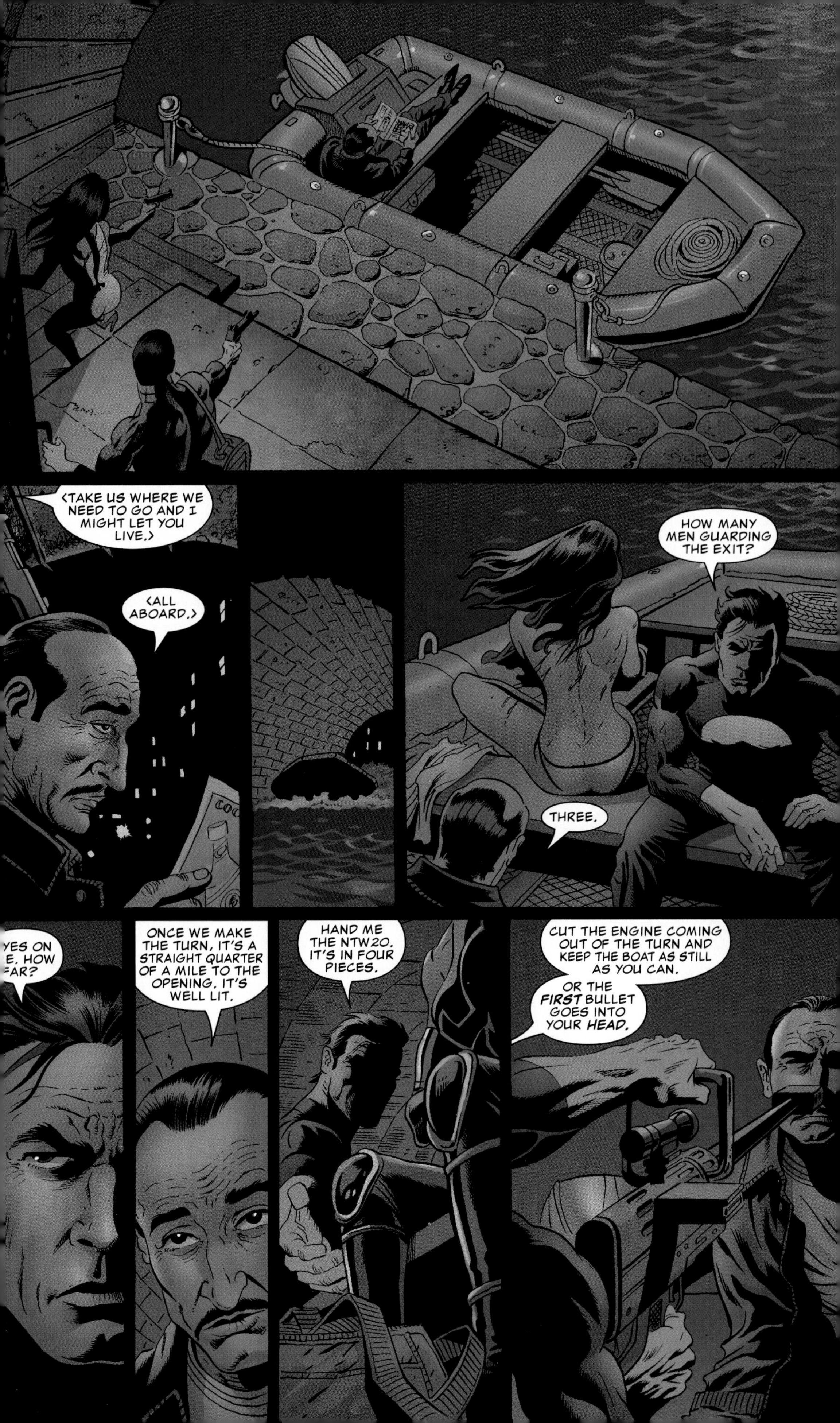

<TAKE US WHERE WE NEED TO GO AND I MIGHT LET YOU LIVE.>
<ALL ABOARD.>
HOW MANY MEN GUARDING THE EXIT?
THREE.
YES ON E. HOW FAR?
ONCE WE MAKE THE TURN, IT'S A STRAIGHT QUARTER OF A MILE TO THE OPENING. IT'S WELL LIT.
HAND ME THE NTW20. IT'S IN FOUR PIECES.
CUT THE ENGINE COMING OUT OF THE TURN AND KEEP THE BOAT AS STILL AS YOU CAN.
OR THE *FIRST* BULLET GOES INTO YOUR *HEAD*.

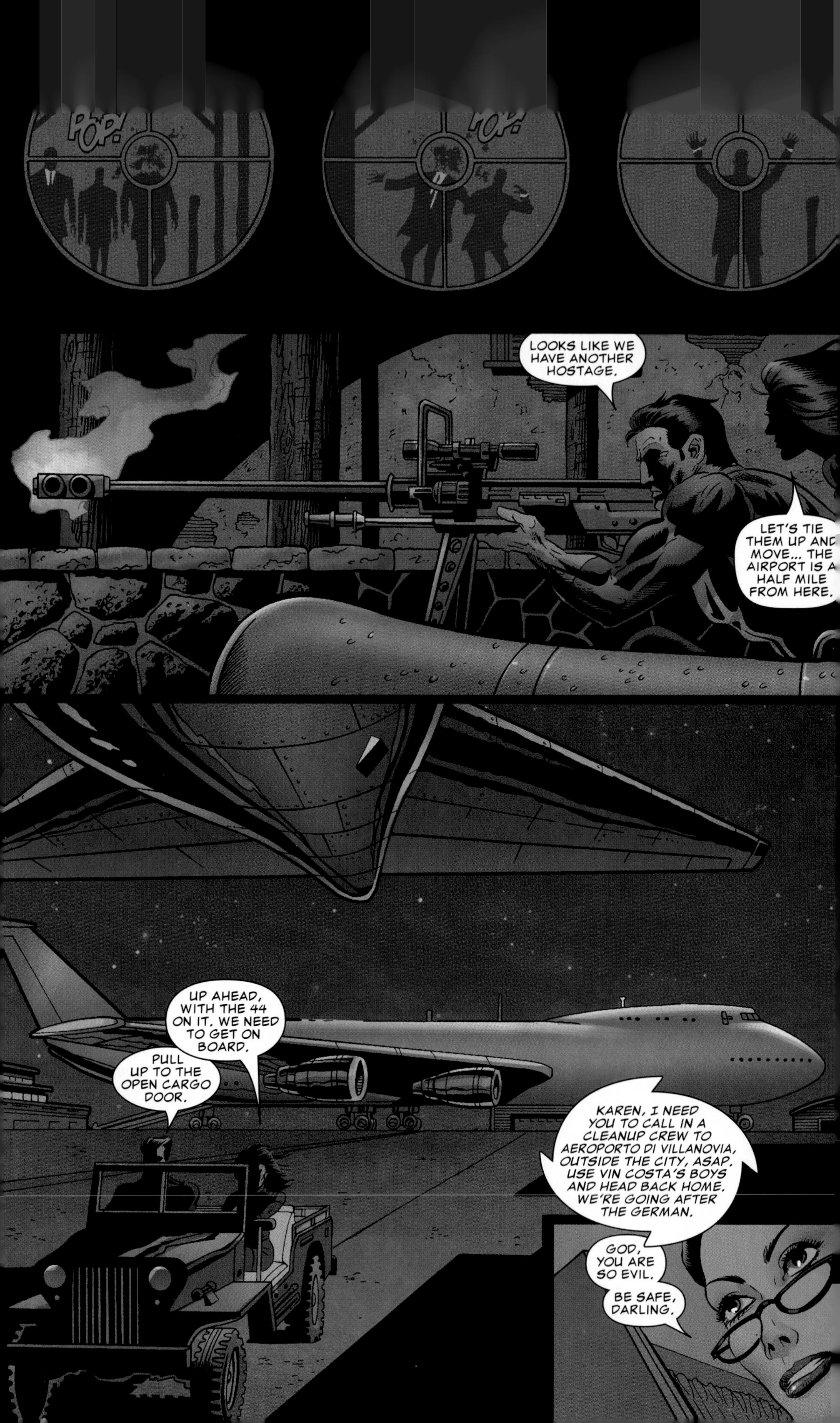
POP!
POP!
LOOKS LIKE WE HAVE ANOTHER HOSTAGE.
LET'S TIE THEM UP AND MOVE... THE AIRPORT IS A HALF MILE FROM HERE.
UP AHEAD, WITH THE 44 ON IT. WE NEED TO GET ON BOARD.
PULL UP TO THE OPEN CARGO DOOR.
KAREN, I NEED YOU TO CALL IN A CLEANUP CREW TO AEROPORTO DI VILLANOVIA, OUTSIDE THE CITY, ASAP. USE VIN COSTA'S BOYS AND HEAD BACK HOME. WE'RE GOING AFTER THE GERMAN.
GOD, YOU ARE SO EVIL.
BE SAFE, DARLING.

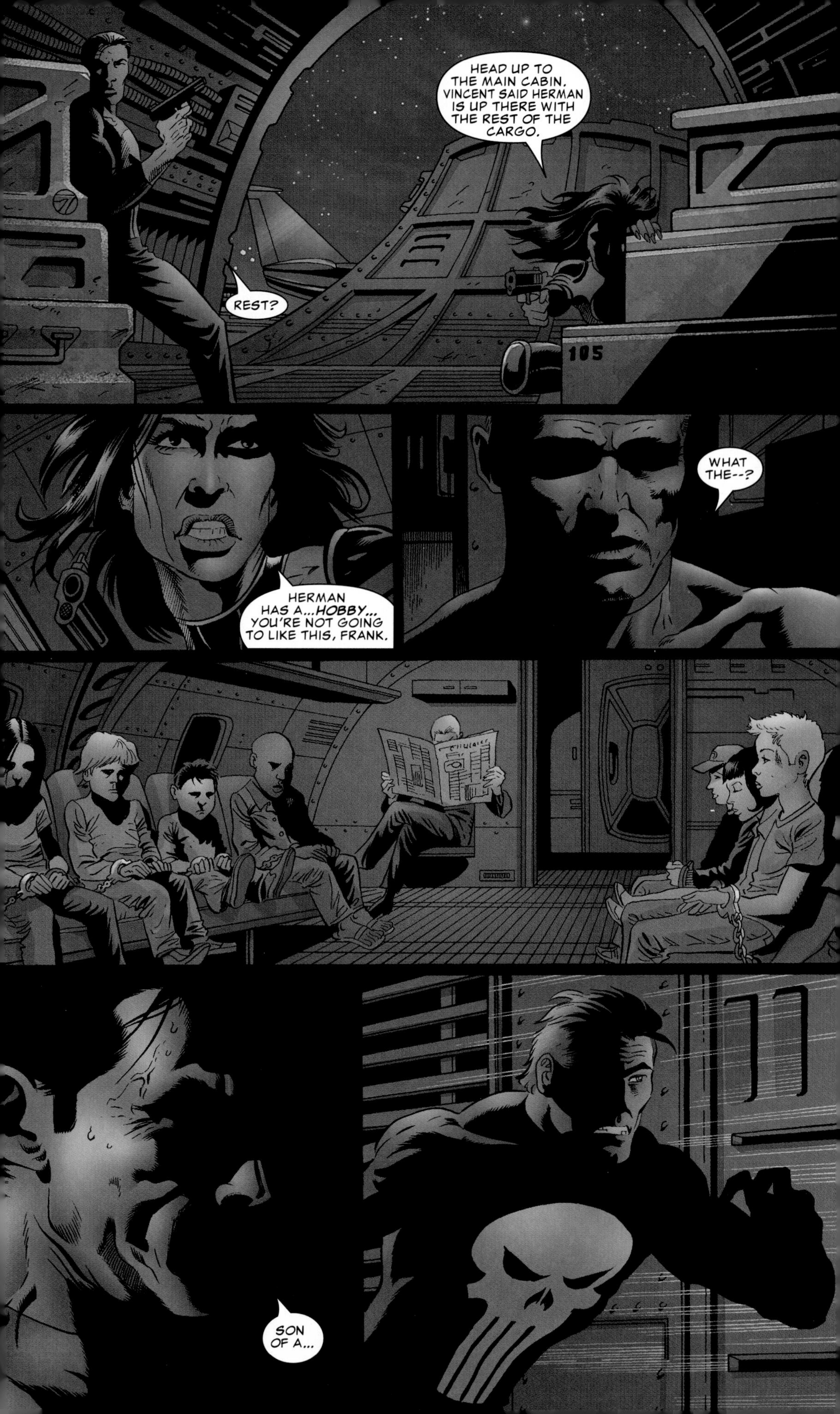

HEAD UP TO THE MAIN CABIN. VINCENT SAID HERMAN IS UP THERE WITH THE REST OF THE CARGO.
REST?
105
HERMAN HAS A...HOBBY... YOU'RE NOT GOING TO LIKE THIS, FRANK.
WHAT THE--?
105
SON OF A...

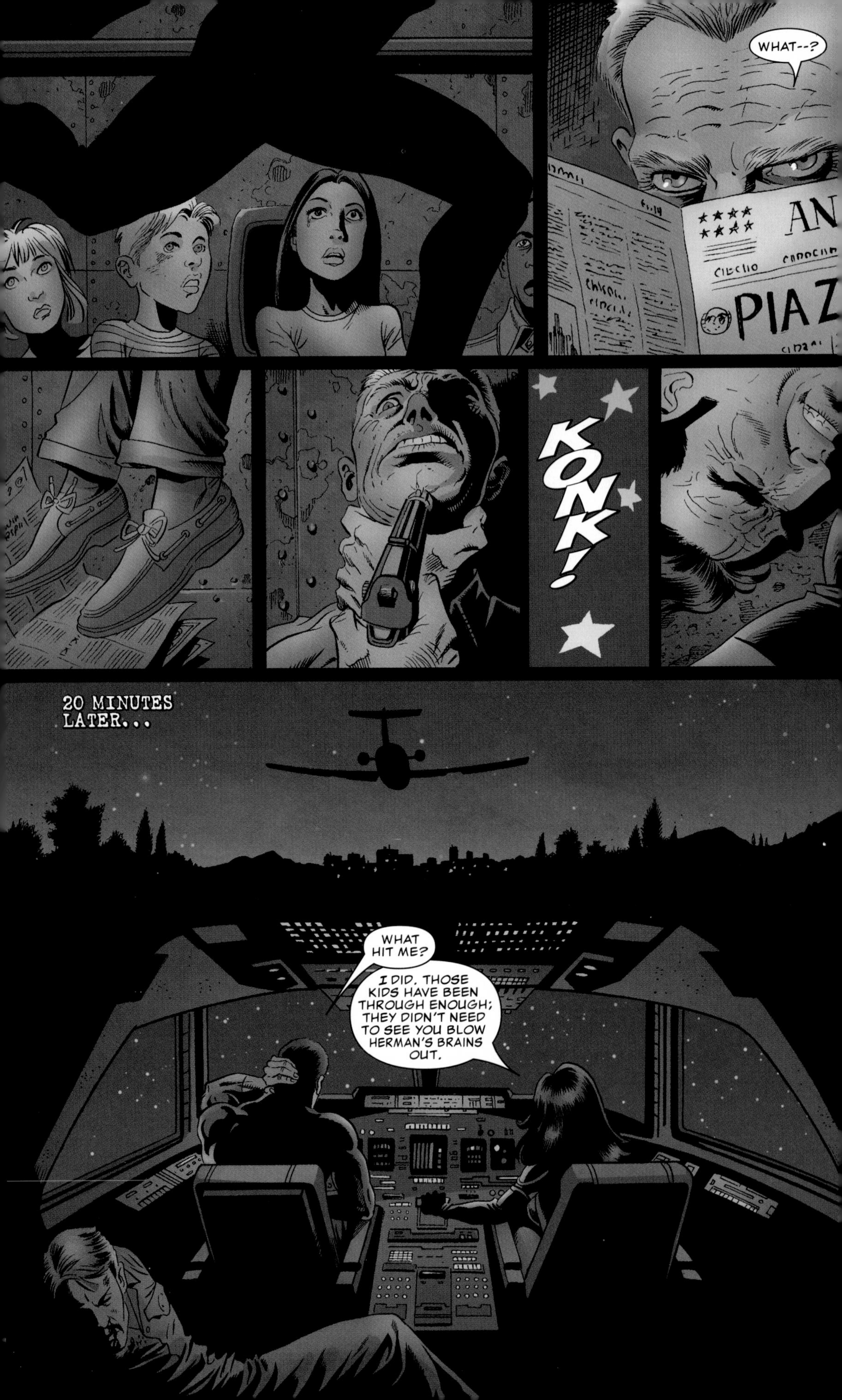
WHAT--?
KONK!
20 MINUTES LATER...
WHAT HIT ME?
I DID. THOSE KIDS HAVE BEEN THROUGH ENOUGH; THEY DIDN'T NEED TO SEE YOU BLOW HERMAN'S BRAINS OUT.

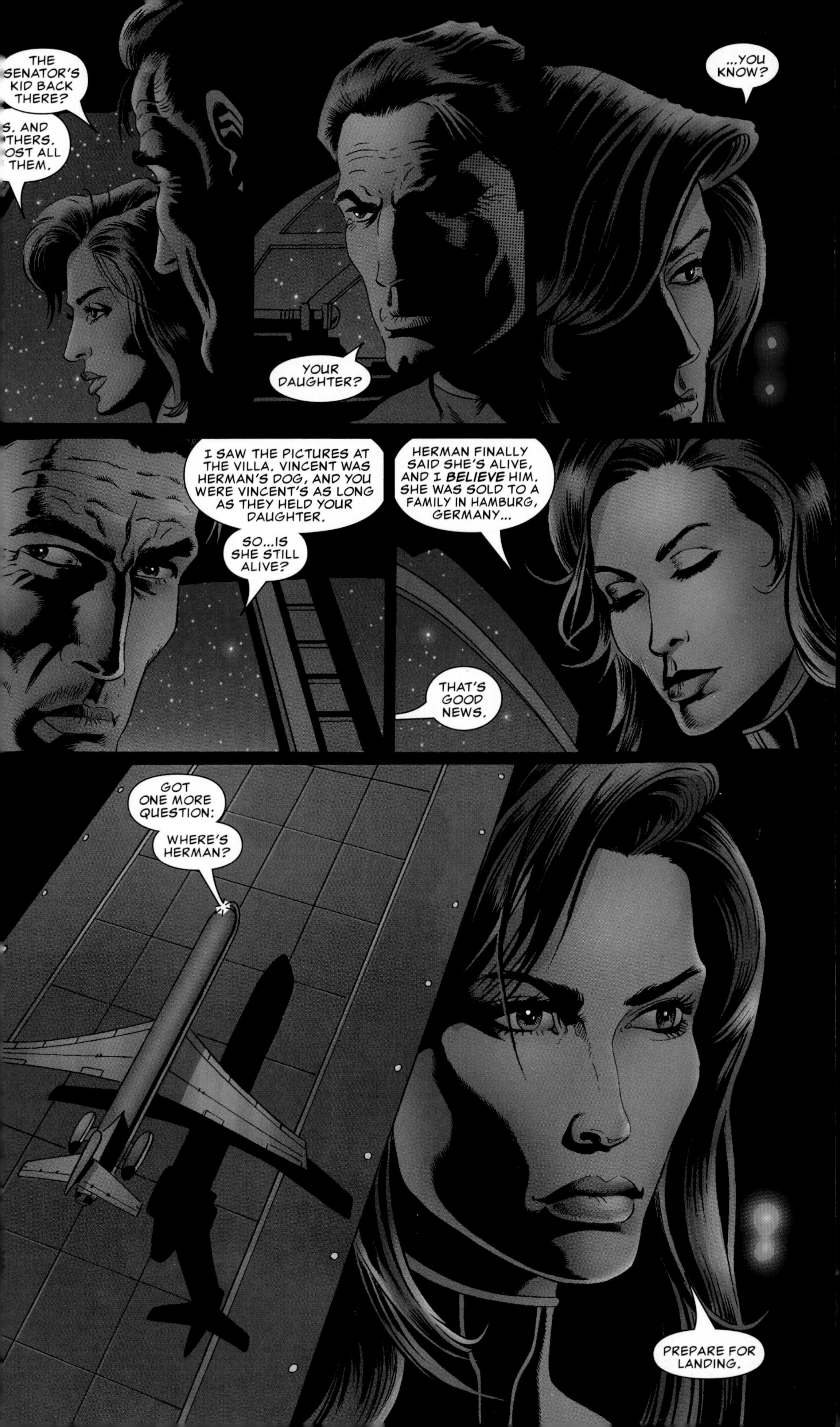
THE SENATOR'S KID BACK THERE?
S. AND
THERS.
OST ALL
THEM.
YOUR DAUGHTER?
...YOU KNOW?
I SAW THE PICTURES AT THE VILLA. VINCENT WAS HERMAN'S DOG, AND YOU WERE VINCENT'S AS LONG AS THEY HELD YOUR DAUGHTER.
SO...IS SHE STILL ALIVE?
HERMAN FINALLY SAID SHE'S ALIVE, AND I BELIEVE HIM. SHE WAS SOLD TO A FAMILY IN HAMBURG, GERMANY...
THAT'S GOOD NEWS.
GOT ONE MORE QUESTION:
WHERE'S HERMAN?
PREPARE FOR LANDING.

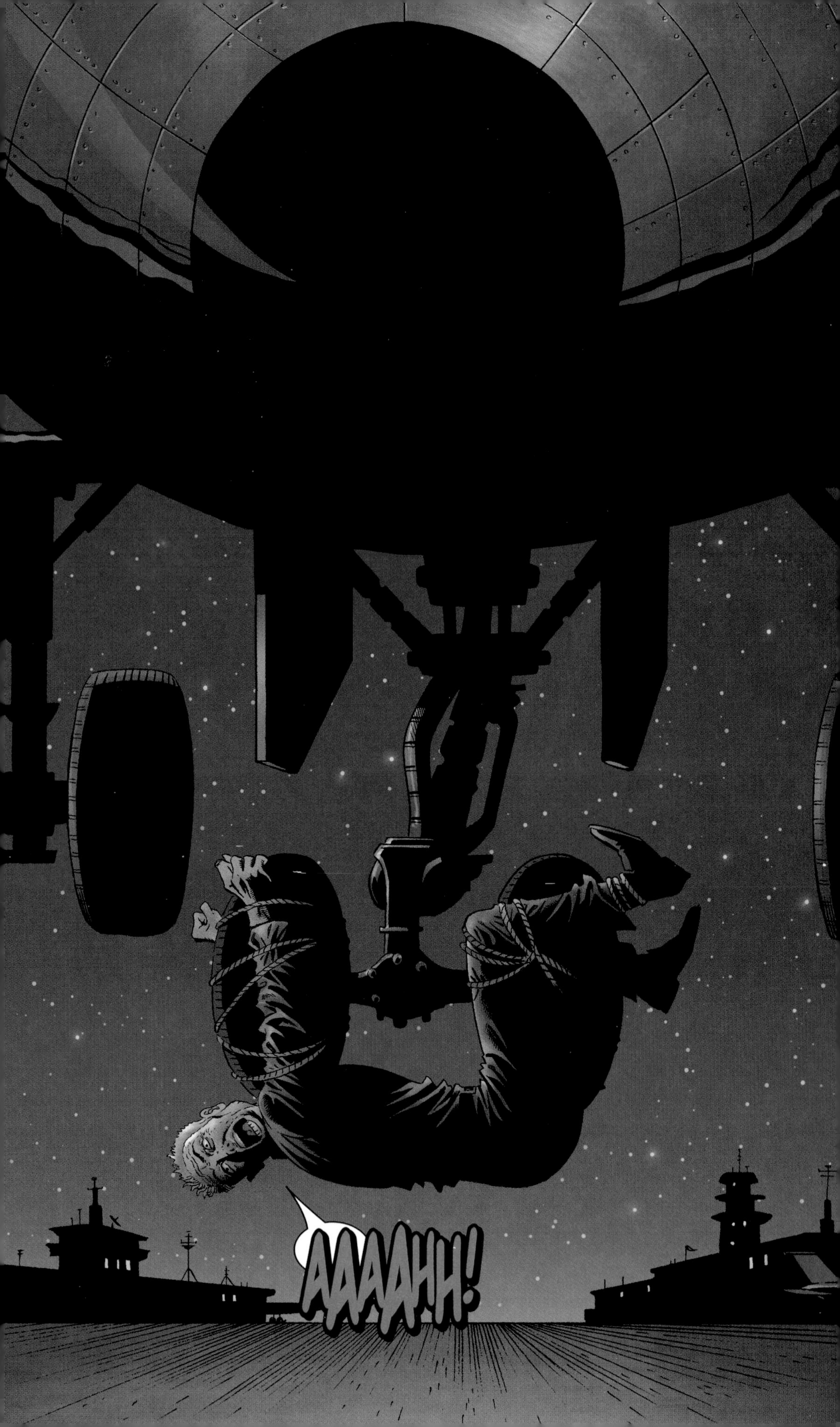
AAAAHH!

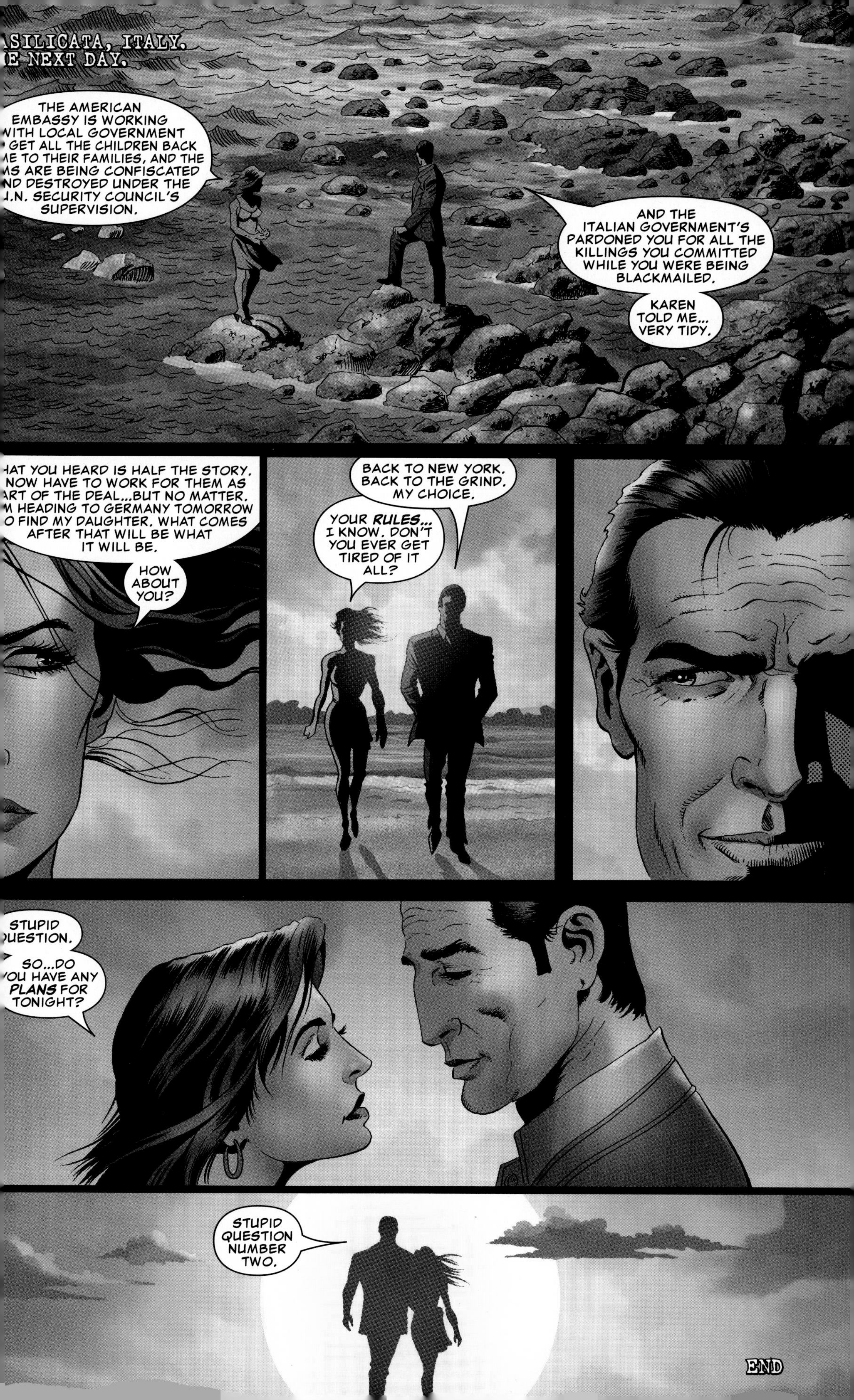
ASILICATA, ITALY.
E NEXT DAY.
THE AMERICAN EMBASSY IS WORKING WITH LOCAL GOVERNMENT GET ALL THE CHILDREN BACK ME TO THEIR FAMILIES, AND THE MS ARE BEING CONFISCATED ND DESTROYED UNDER THE .N. SECURITY COUNCIL'S SUPERVISION.
AND THE ITALIAN GOVERNMENT'S PARDONED YOU FOR ALL THE KILLINGS YOU COMMITTED WHILE YOU WERE BEING BLACKMAILED.
KAREN TOLD ME... VERY TIDY.
HAT YOU HEARD IS HALF THE STORY. NOW HAVE TO WORK FOR THEM AS ART OF THE DEAL...BUT NO MATTER. M HEADING TO GERMANY TOMORROW O FIND MY DAUGHTER. WHAT COMES AFTER THAT WILL BE WHAT IT WILL BE.
HOW ABOUT YOU?
BACK TO NEW YORK. BACK TO THE GRIND. MY CHOICE.
YOUR RULES... I KNOW. DON'T YOU EVER GET TIRED OF IT ALL?
STUPID UESTION.
SO...DO OU HAVE ANY PLANS FOR TONIGHT?
STUPID QUESTION NUMBER TWO.
END

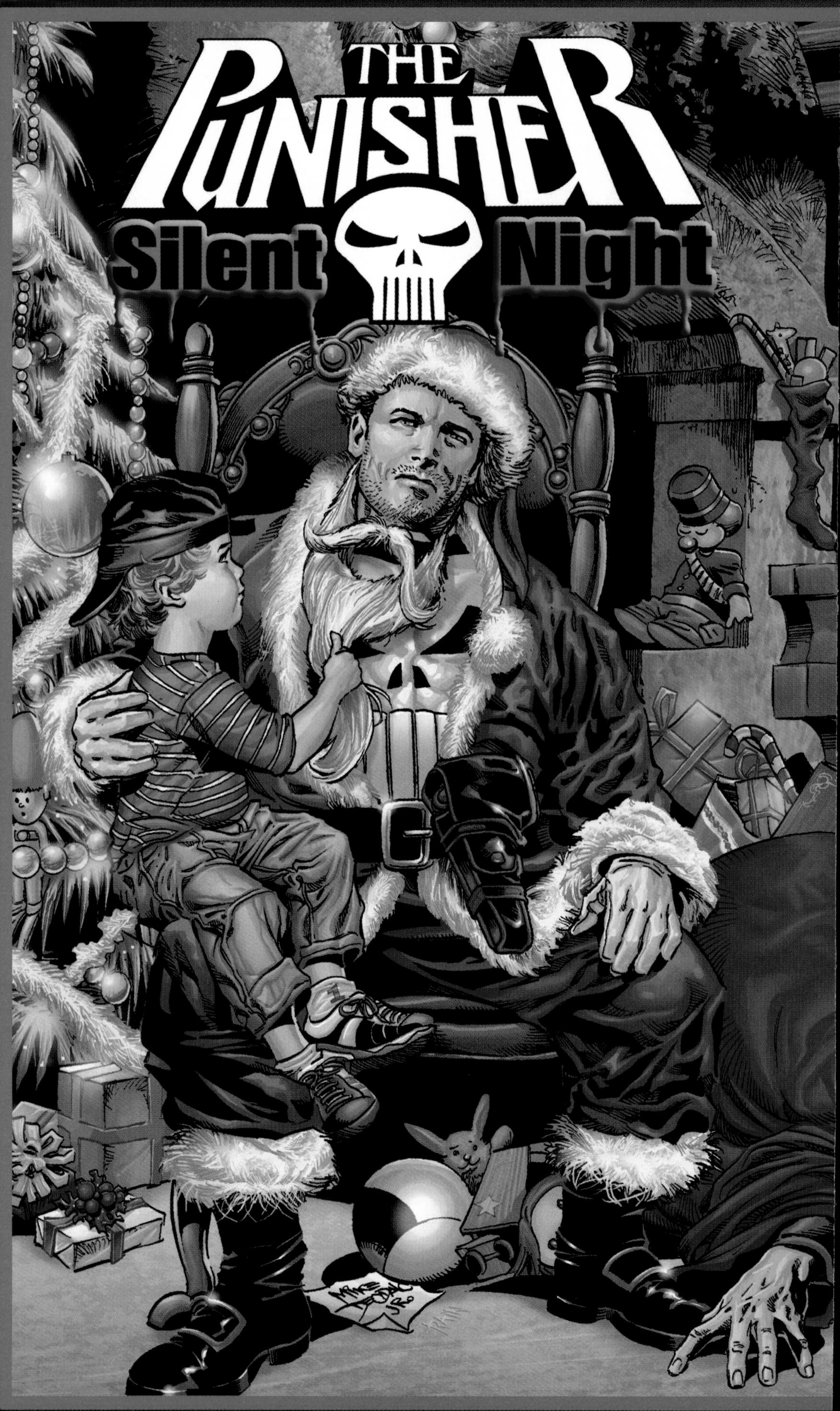
THE PUNISHER
Silent Night

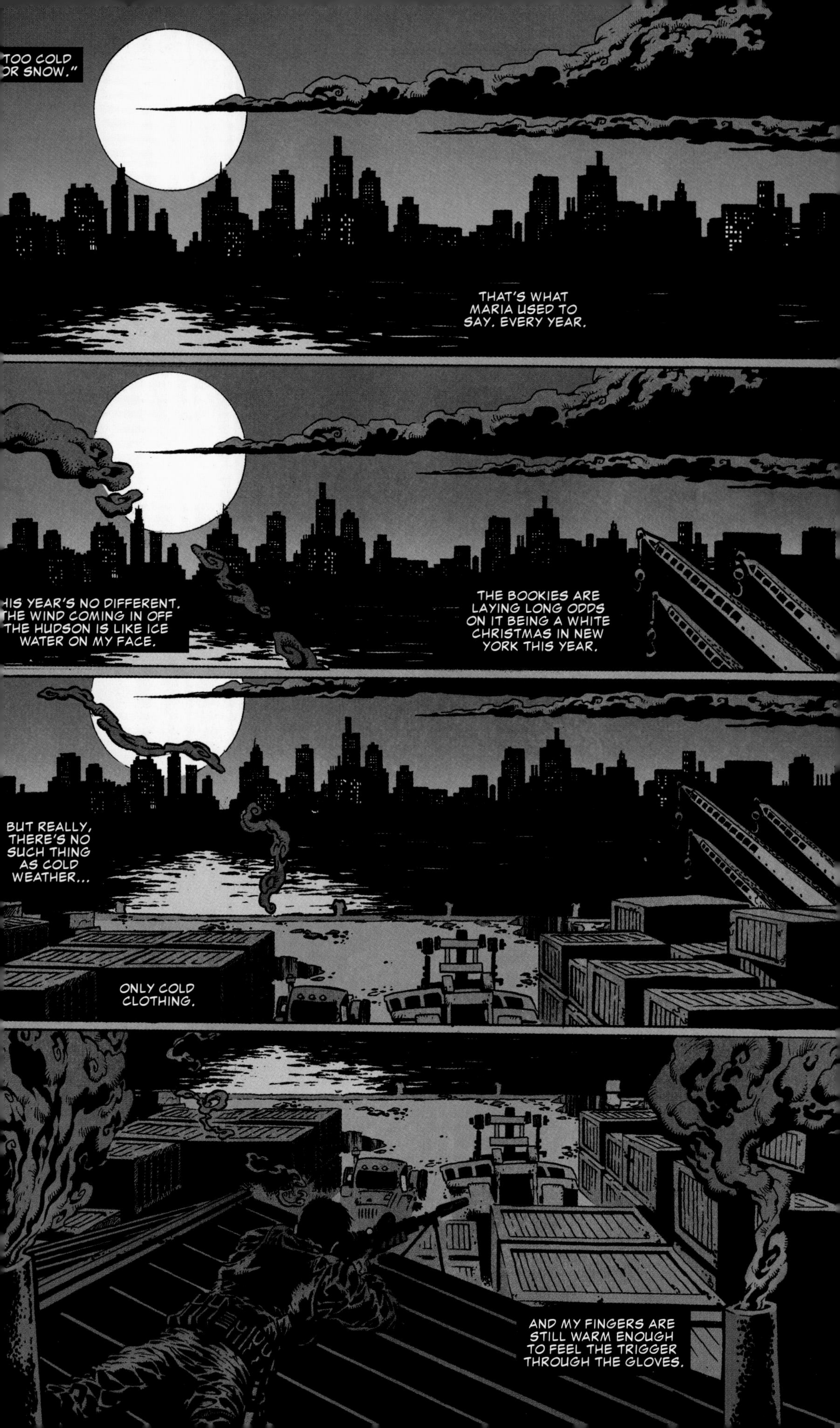
TOO COLD
OR SNOW."
THAT'S WHAT MARIA USED TO SAY. EVERY YEAR.
HIS YEAR'S NO DIFFERENT. THE WIND COMING IN OFF THE HUDSON IS LIKE ICE WATER ON MY FACE.
THE BOOKIES ARE LAYING LONG ODDS ON IT BEING A WHITE CHRISTMAS IN NEW YORK THIS YEAR.
BUT REALLY, THERE'S NO SUCH THING AS COLD WEATHER...
ONLY COLD CLOTHING.
AND MY FINGERS ARE STILL WARM ENOUGH TO FEEL THE TRIGGER THROUGH THE GLOVES.

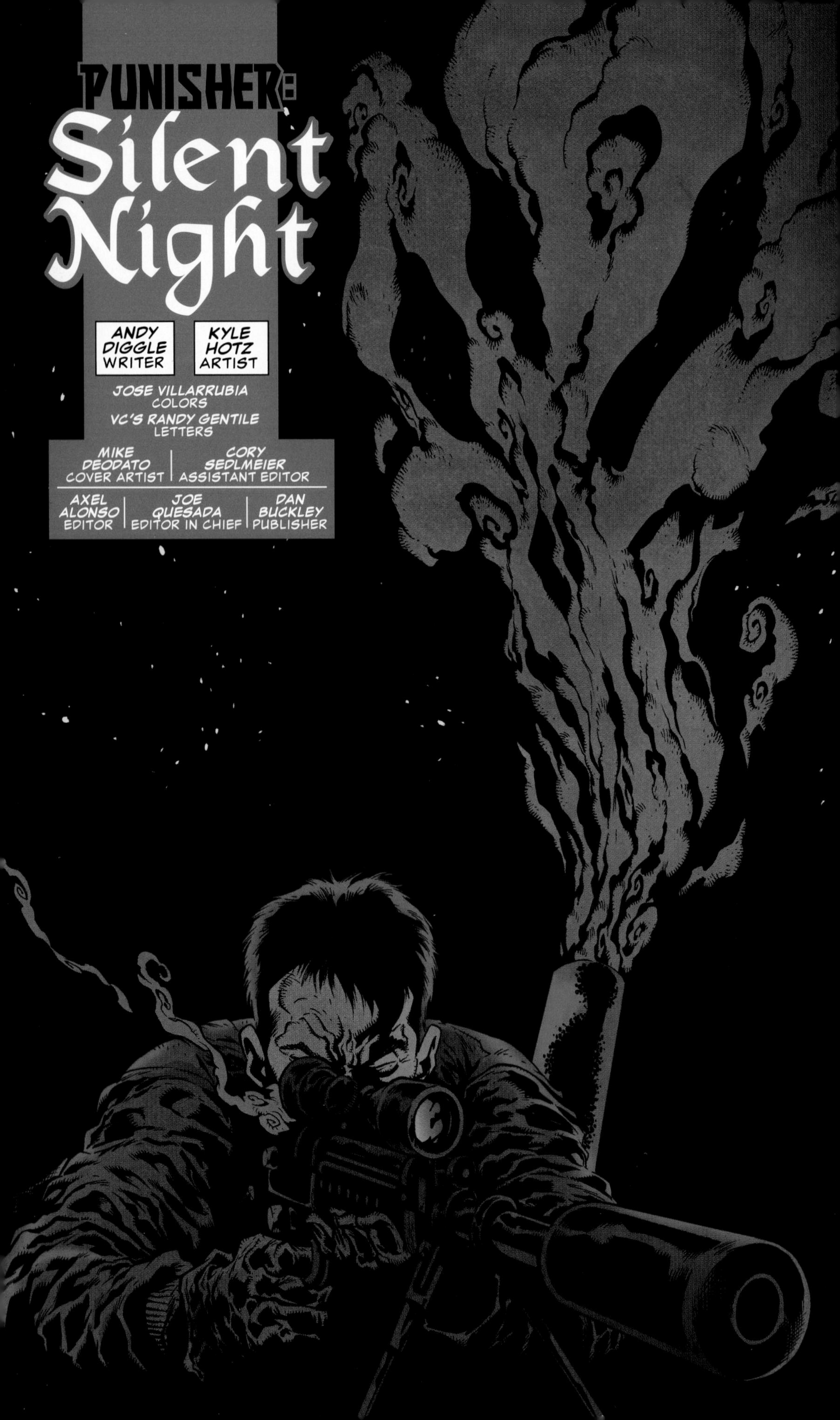

PUNISHER:
Silent Night
ANDY DIGGLE WRITER
KYLE HOTZ ARTIST
JOSE VILLARRUBIA COLORS
VC'S RANDY GENTILE LETTERS
MIKE DEODATO COVER ARTIST
CORY SEDLMEIER ASSISTANT EDITOR
AXEL ALONSO EDITOR
JOE QUESADA EDITOR IN CHIEF
DAN BUCKLEY PUBLISHER

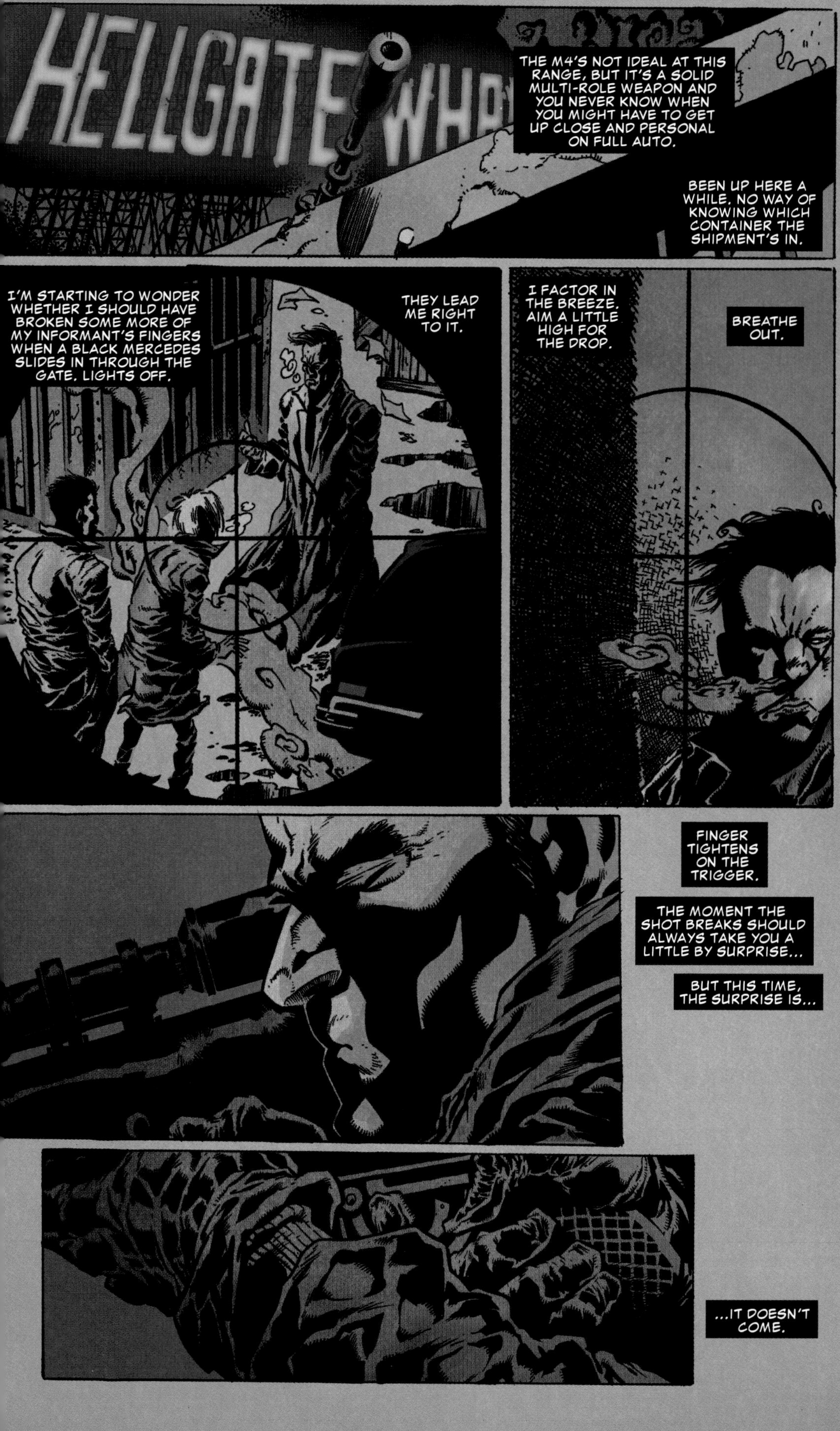

HELLGATE WHA
THE M4'S NOT IDEAL AT THIS RANGE, BUT IT'S A SOLID MULTI-ROLE WEAPON AND YOU NEVER KNOW WHEN YOU MIGHT HAVE TO GET UP CLOSE AND PERSONAL ON FULL AUTO.
BEEN UP HERE A WHILE. NO WAY OF KNOWING WHICH CONTAINER THE SHIPMENT'S IN.
I'M STARTING TO WONDER WHETHER I SHOULD HAVE BROKEN SOME MORE OF MY INFORMANT'S FINGERS WHEN A BLACK MERCEDES SLIDES IN THROUGH THE GATE. LIGHTS OFF.
THEY LEAD ME RIGHT TO IT.
I FACTOR IN THE BREEZE. AIM A LITTLE HIGH FOR THE DROP.
BREATHE OUT.
FINGER TIGHTENS ON THE TRIGGER.
THE MOMENT THE SHOT BREAKS SHOULD ALWAYS TAKE YOU A LITTLE BY SURPRISE...
BUT THIS TIME, THE SURPRISE IS...
...IT DOESN'T COME.

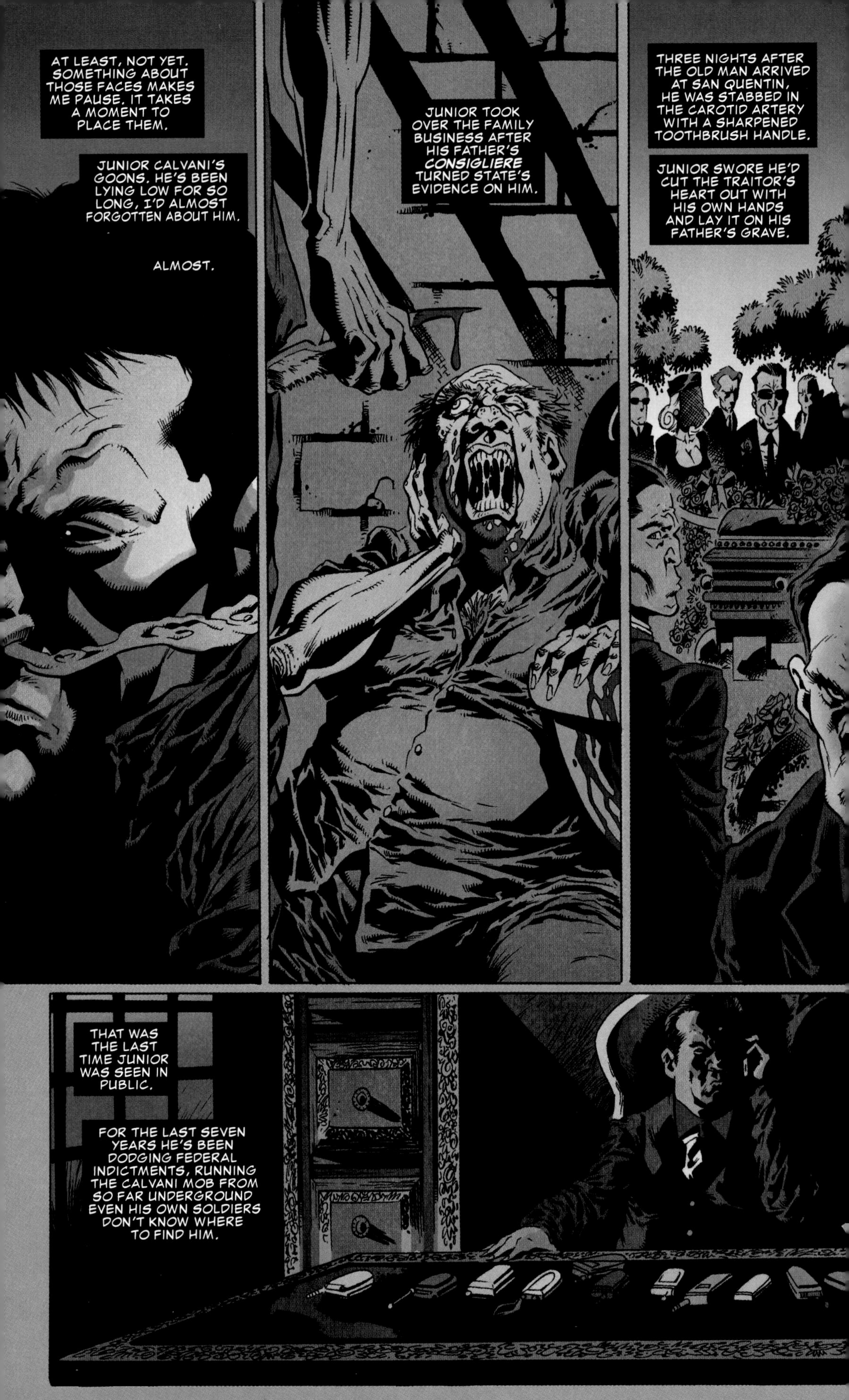
AT LEAST, NOT YET. SOMETHING ABOUT THOSE FACES MAKES ME PAUSE. IT TAKES A MOMENT TO PLACE THEM.
JUNIOR CALVANI'S GOONS. HE'S BEEN LYING LOW FOR SO LONG, I'D ALMOST FORGOTTEN ABOUT HIM.
ALMOST.
JUNIOR TOOK OVER THE FAMILY BUSINESS AFTER HIS FATHER'S *CONSIGLIERE* TURNED STATE'S EVIDENCE ON HIM.
THREE NIGHTS AFTER THE OLD MAN ARRIVED AT SAN QUENTIN, HE WAS STABBED IN THE CAROTID ARTERY WITH A SHARPENED TOOTHBRUSH HANDLE.
JUNIOR SWORE HE'D CUT THE TRAITOR'S HEART OUT WITH HIS OWN HANDS AND LAY IT ON HIS FATHER'S GRAVE.
THAT WAS THE LAST TIME JUNIOR WAS SEEN IN PUBLIC.
FOR THE LAST SEVEN YEARS HE'S BEEN DODGING FEDERAL INDICTMENTS, RUNNING THE CALVANI MOB FROM SO FAR UNDERGROUND EVEN HIS OWN SOLDIERS DON'T KNOW WHERE TO FIND HIM.

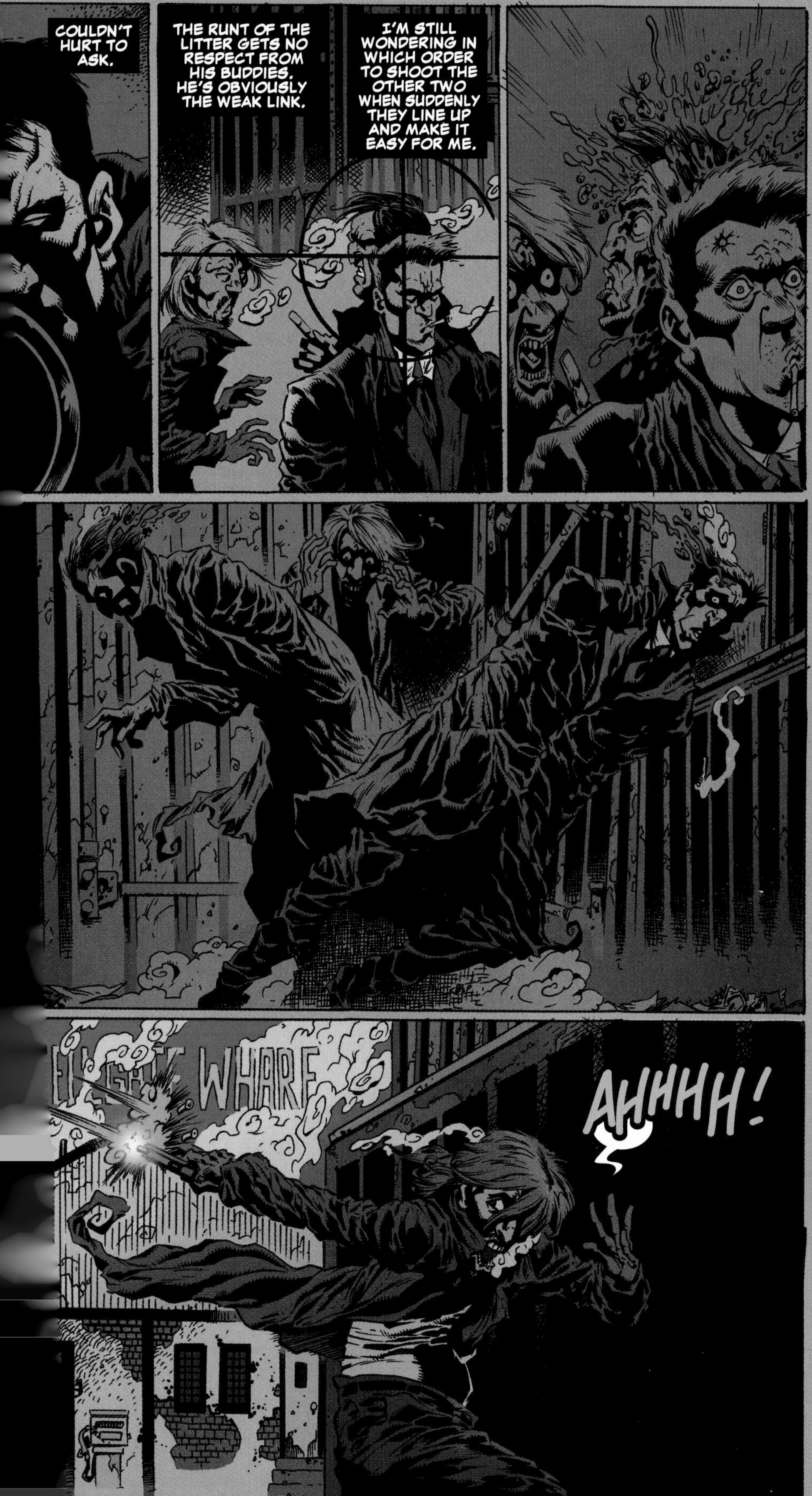
COULDN'T HURT TO ASK.
THE RUNT OF THE LITTER GETS NO RESPECT FROM HIS BUDDIES. HE'S OBVIOUSLY THE WEAK LINK.
I'M STILL WONDERING IN WHICH ORDER TO SHOOT THE OTHER TWO WHEN SUDDENLY THEY LINE UP AND MAKE IT EASY FOR ME.
WHARF
AHHHH!

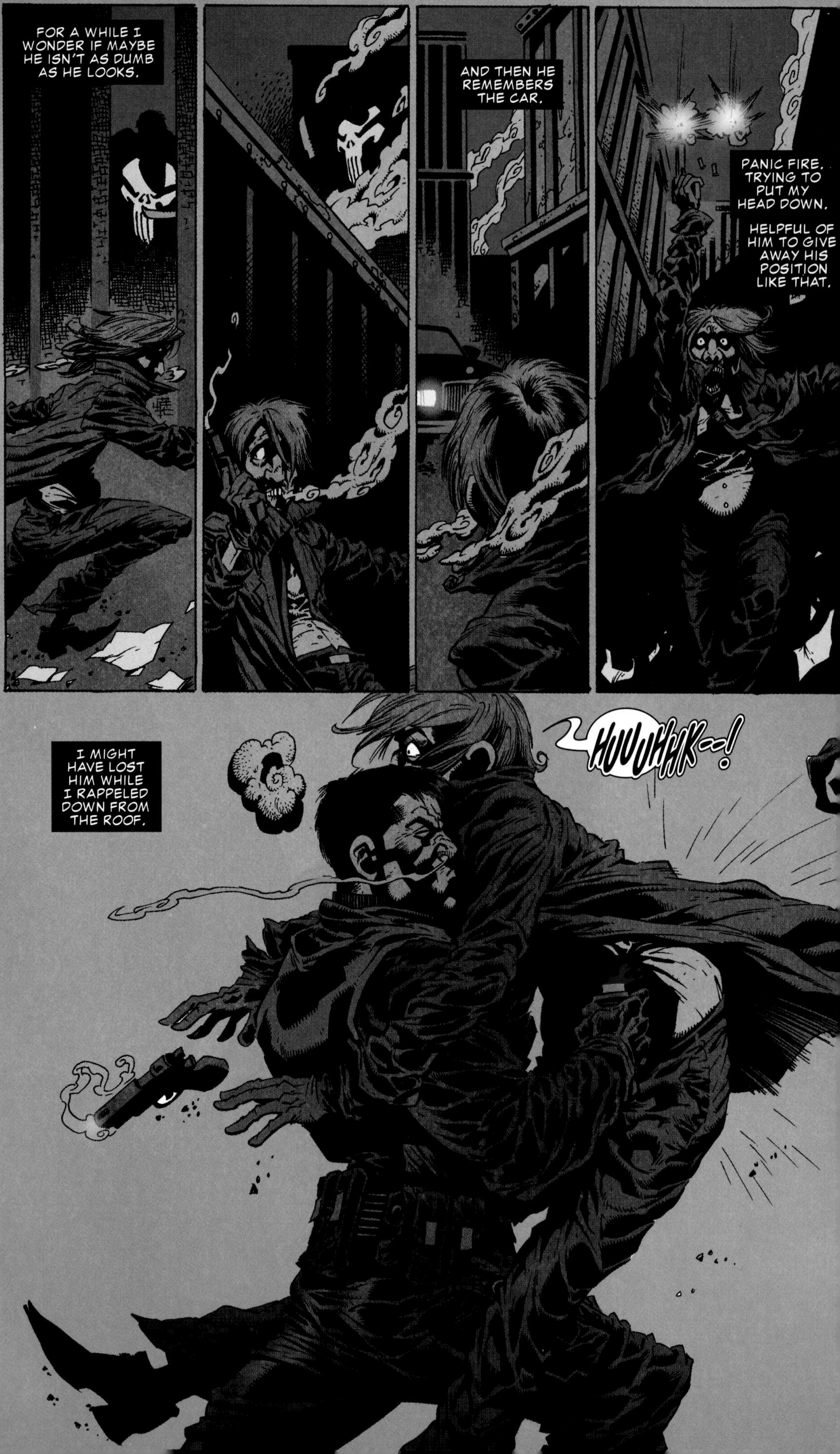

FOR A WHILE I WONDER IF MAYBE HE ISN'T AS DUMB AS HE LOOKS.
AND THEN HE REMEMBERS THE CAR.
PANIC FIRE. TRYING TO PUT MY HEAD DOWN.
HELPFUL OF HIM TO GIVE AWAY HIS POSITION LIKE THAT.
I MIGHT HAVE LOST HIM WHILE I RAPPELED DOWN FROM THE ROOF.
HUUUHHK--!

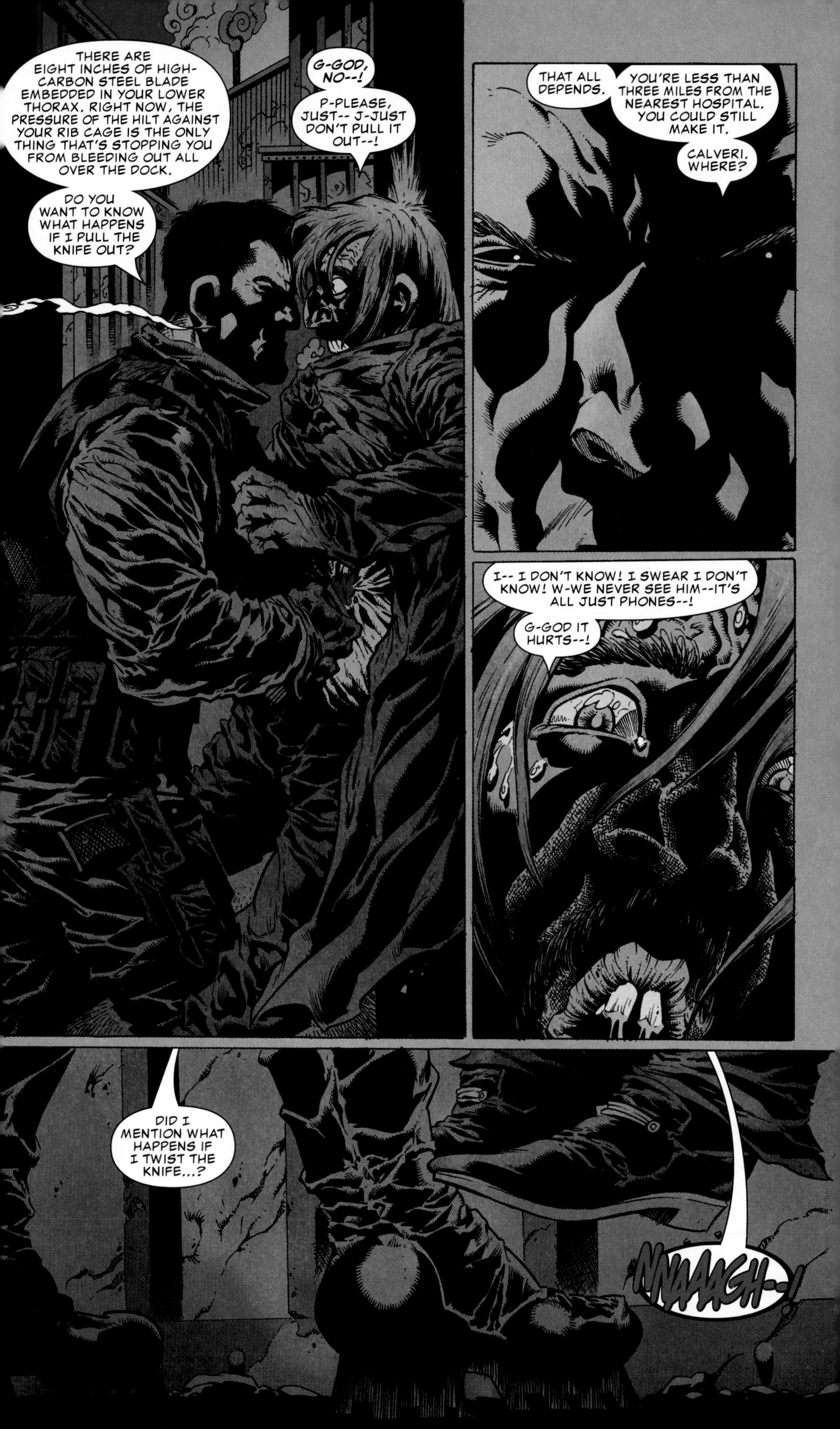
THERE ARE EIGHT INCHES OF HIGH-CARBON STEEL BLADE EMBEDDED IN YOUR LOWER THORAX. RIGHT NOW, THE PRESSURE OF THE HILT AGAINST YOUR RIB CAGE IS THE ONLY THING THAT'S STOPPING YOU FROM BLEEDING OUT ALL OVER THE DOCK.
DO YOU WANT TO KNOW WHAT HAPPENS IF I PULL THE KNIFE OUT?
G-GOD, NO--!
P-PLEASE, JUST-- J-JUST DON'T PULL IT OUT--!
THAT ALL DEPENDS.
YOU'RE LESS THAN THREE MILES FROM THE NEAREST HOSPITAL. YOU COULD STILL MAKE IT.
CALVERI. WHERE?
I-- I DON'T KNOW! I SWEAR I DON'T KNOW! W-WE NEVER SEE HIM--IT'S ALL JUST PHONES--!
G-GOD IT HURTS--!
DID I MENTION WHAT HAPPENS IF I TWIST THE KNIFE...?
NNAAAGH--!

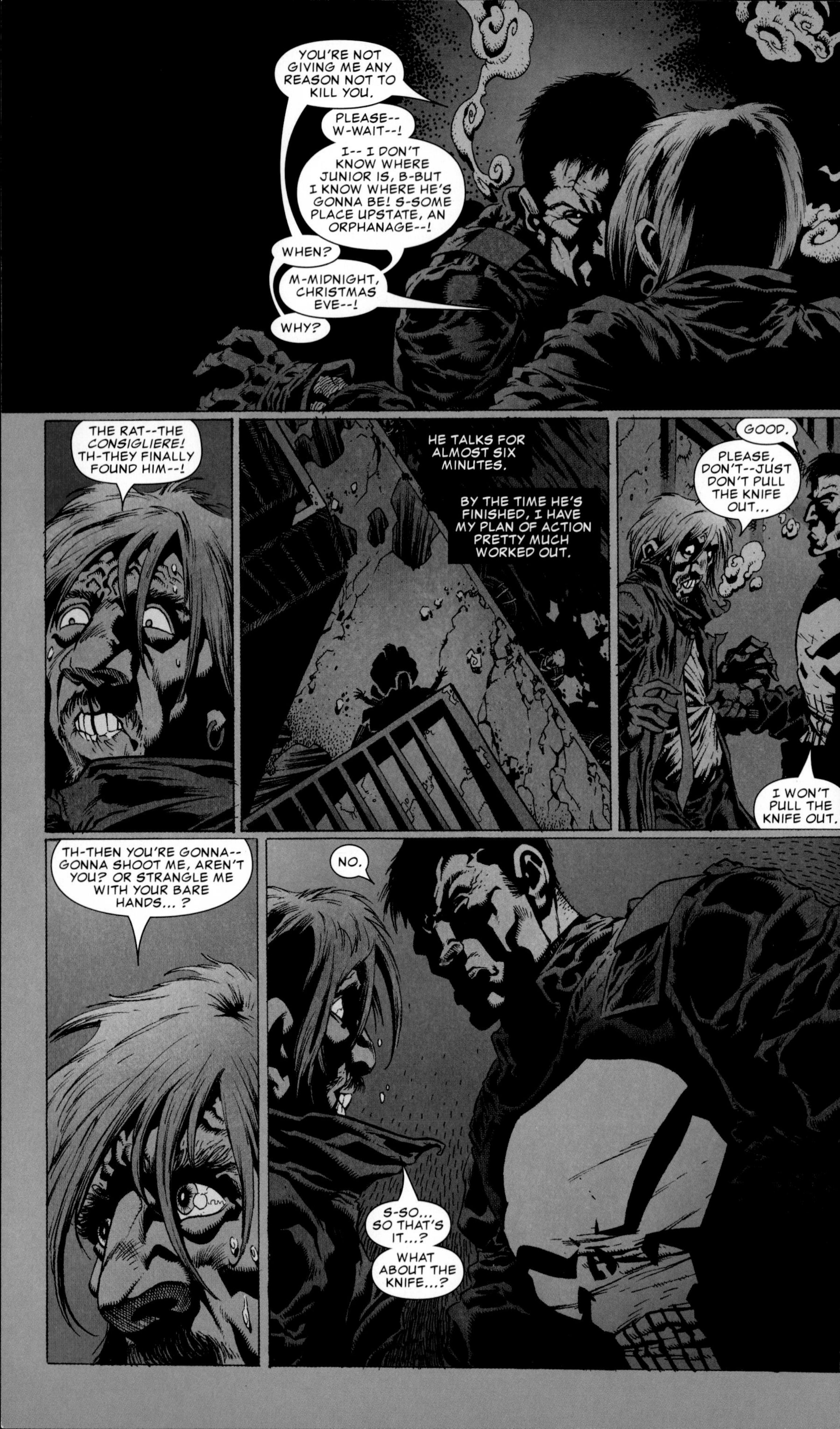
YOU'RE NOT GIVING ME ANY REASON NOT TO KILL YOU.
PLEASE-- W-WAIT--!
I-- I DON'T KNOW WHERE JUNIOR IS, B-BUT I KNOW WHERE HE'S GONNA BE! S-SOME PLACE UPSTATE, AN ORPHANAGE--!
WHEN?
M-MIDNIGHT, CHRISTMAS EVE--!
WHY?
THE RAT--THE CONSIGLIERE! TH-THEY FINALLY FOUND HIM--!
HE TALKS FOR ALMOST SIX MINUTES.
BY THE TIME HE'S FINISHED, I HAVE MY PLAN OF ACTION PRETTY MUCH WORKED OUT.
GOOD.
PLEASE, DON'T--JUST DON'T PULL THE KNIFE OUT...
I WON'T PULL THE KNIFE OUT.
TH-THEN YOU'RE GONNA-- GONNA SHOOT ME, AREN'T YOU? OR STRANGLE ME WITH YOUR BARE HANDS... ?
NO.
S-SO... SO THAT'S IT...?
WHAT ABOUT THE KNIFE...?

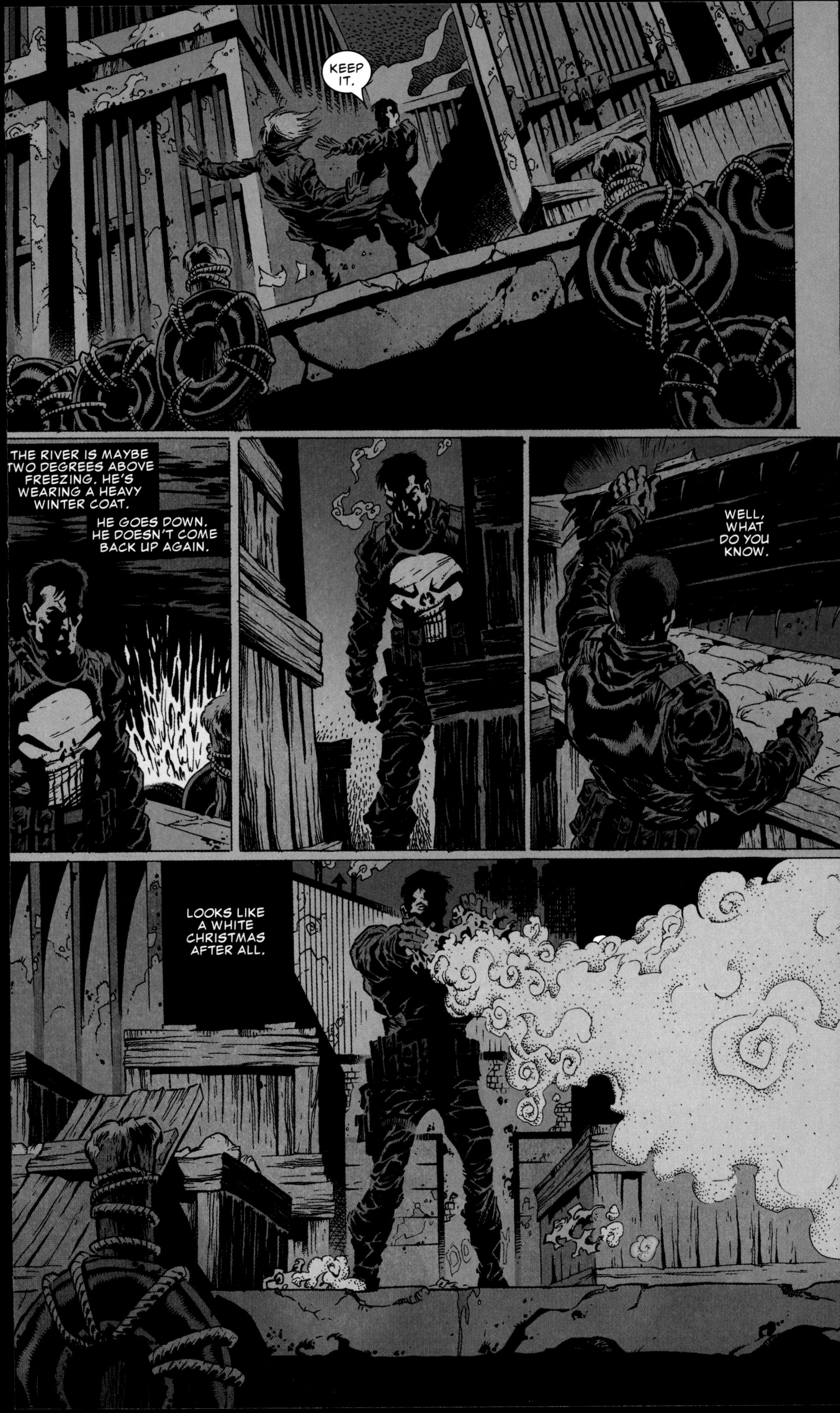
KEEP IT.
THE RIVER IS MAYBE TWO DEGREES ABOVE FREEZING. HE'S WEARING A HEAVY WINTER COAT.
HE GOES DOWN. HE DOESN'T COME BACK UP AGAIN.
WELL, WHAT DO YOU KNOW.
LOOKS LIKE A WHITE CHRISTMAS AFTER ALL.

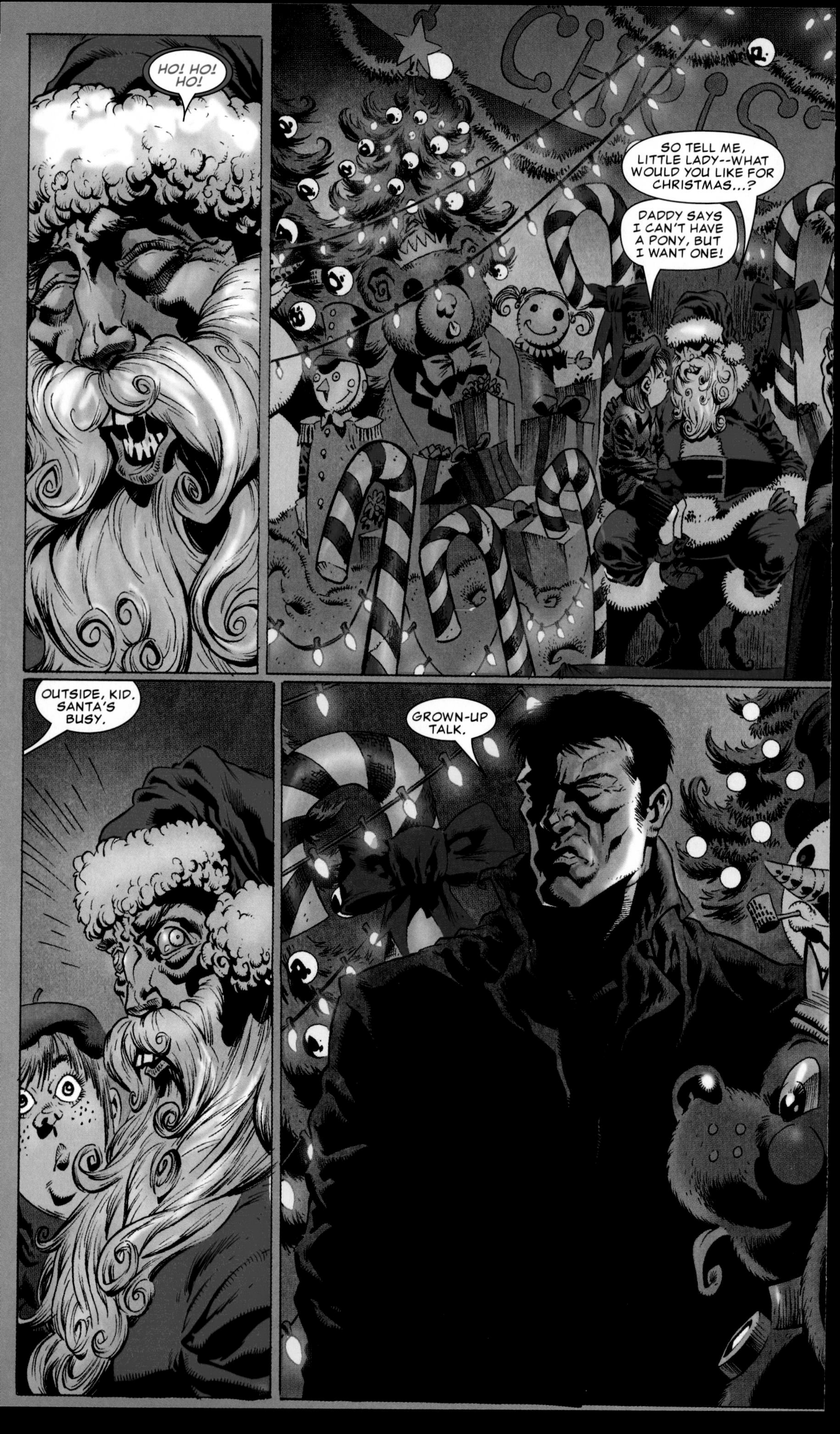
HO! HO! HO!
SO TELL ME, LITTLE LADY--WHAT WOULD YOU LIKE FOR CHRISTMAS...?
DADDY SAYS I CAN'T HAVE A PONY, BUT I WANT ONE!
OUTSIDE, KID. SANTA'S BUSY.
GROWN-UP TALK.

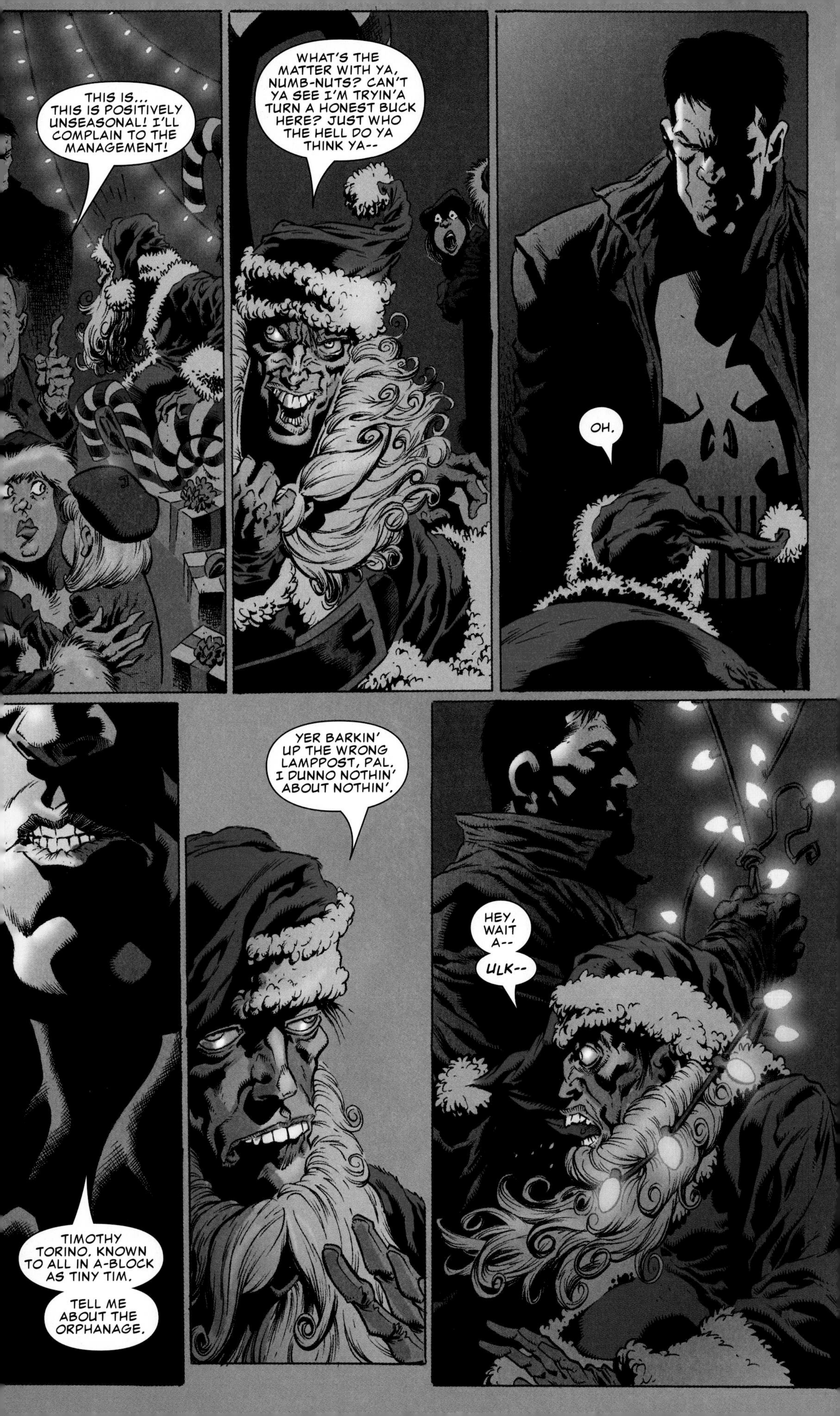
THIS IS... THIS IS POSITIVELY UNSEASONAL! I'LL COMPLAIN TO THE MANAGEMENT!
WHAT'S THE MATTER WITH YA, NUMB-NUTS? CAN'T YA SEE I'M TRYIN'A TURN A HONEST BUCK HERE? JUST WHO THE HELL DO YA THINK YA--
OH.
TIMOTHY TORINO. KNOWN TO ALL IN A-BLOCK AS TINY TIM.
TELL ME ABOUT THE ORPHANAGE.
YER BARKIN' UP THE WRONG LAMPPOST, PAL. I DUNNO NOTHIN' ABOUT NOTHIN'.
HEY, WAIT A--
ULK--

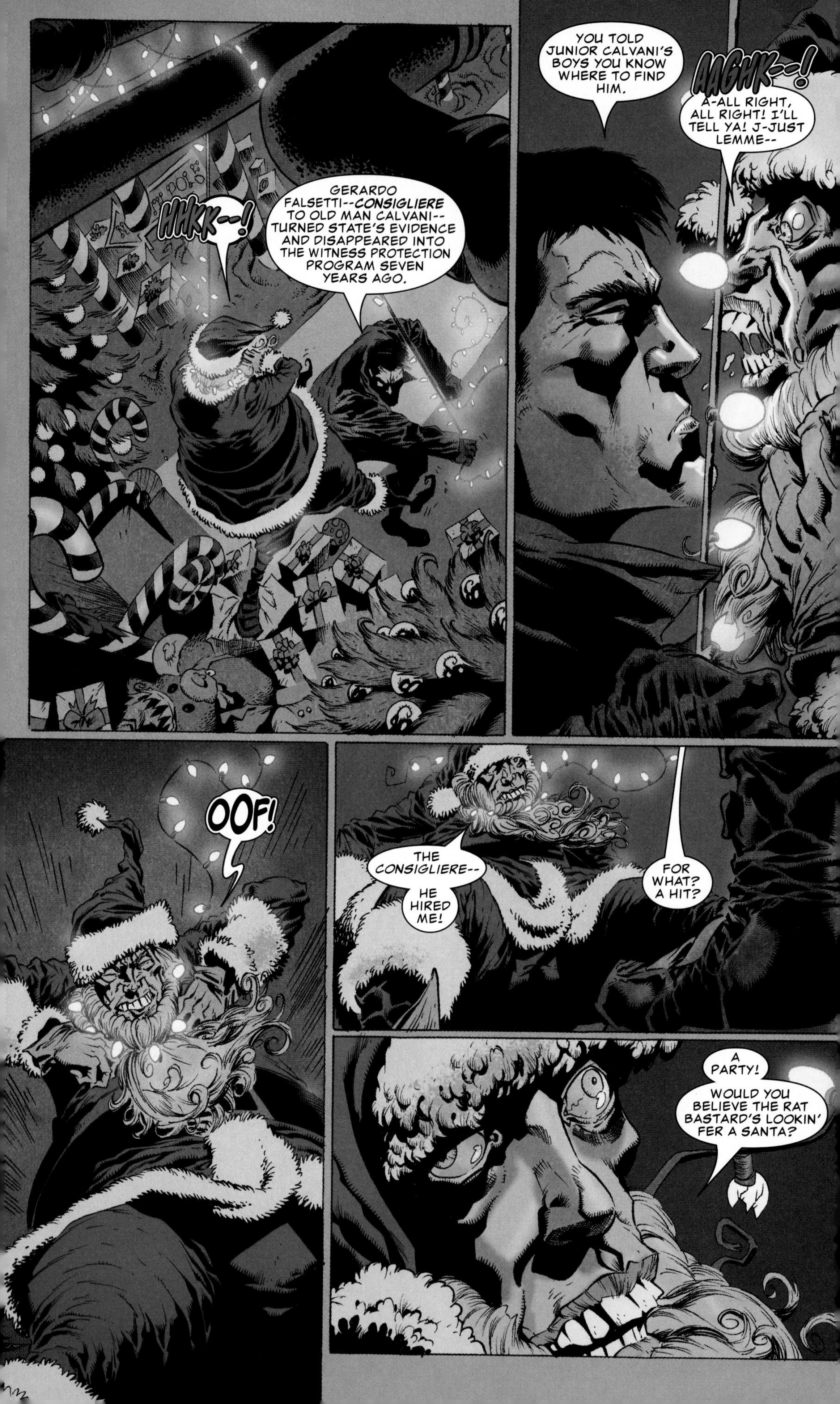
HHKK--!
GERARDO FALSETTI--CONSIGLIERE TO OLD MAN CALVANI--TURNED STATE'S EVIDENCE AND DISAPPEARED INTO THE WITNESS PROTECTION PROGRAM SEVEN YEARS AGO.
YOU TOLD JUNIOR CALVANI'S BOYS YOU KNOW WHERE TO FIND HIM.
AAGHK--!
A-ALL RIGHT, ALL RIGHT! I'LL TELL YA! J-JUST LEMME--
OOF!
THE CONSIGLIERE--
HE HIRED ME!
FOR WHAT? A HIT?
A PARTY!
WOULD YOU BELIEVE THE RAT BASTARD'S LOOKIN' FER A SANTA?

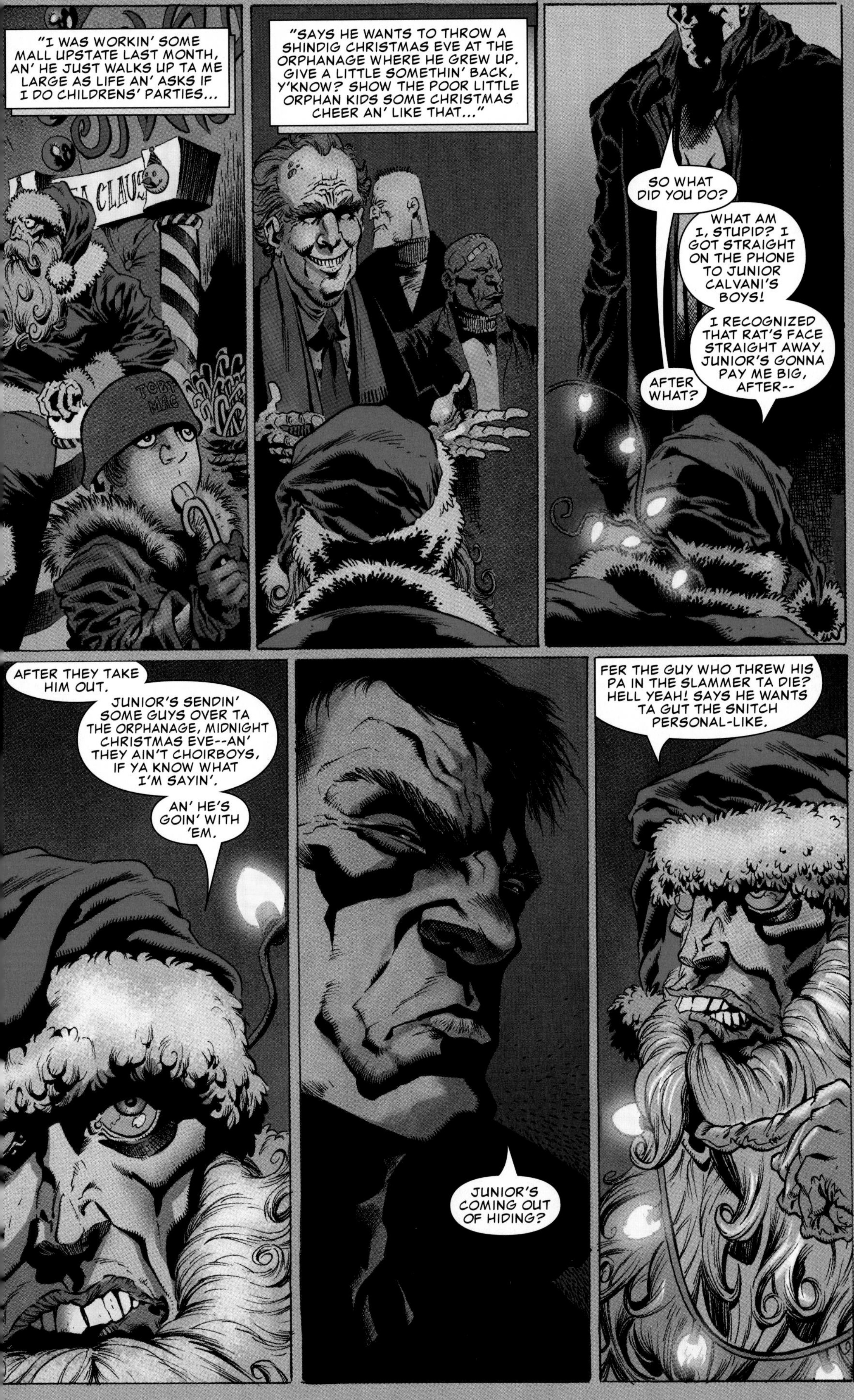
"I WAS WORKIN' SOME MALL UPSTATE LAST MONTH, AN' HE JUST WALKS UP TA ME LARGE AS LIFE AN' ASKS IF I DO CHILDRENS' PARTIES...
"SAYS HE WANTS TO THROW A SHINDIG CHRISTMAS EVE AT THE ORPHANAGE WHERE HE GREW UP. GIVE A LITTLE SOMETHIN' BACK, Y'KNOW? SHOW THE POOR LITTLE ORPHAN KIDS SOME CHRISTMAS CHEER AN' LIKE THAT..."
SO WHAT DID YOU DO?
WHAT AM I, STUPID? I GOT STRAIGHT ON THE PHONE TO JUNIOR CALVANI'S BOYS!
I RECOGNIZED THAT RAT'S FACE STRAIGHT AWAY. JUNIOR'S GONNA PAY ME BIG, AFTER--
AFTER WHAT?
AFTER THEY TAKE HIM OUT.
JUNIOR'S SENDIN' SOME GUYS OVER TA THE ORPHANAGE, MIDNIGHT CHRISTMAS EVE--AN' THEY AIN'T CHOIRBOYS, IF YA KNOW WHAT I'M SAYIN'.
AN' HE'S GOIN' WITH 'EM.
JUNIOR'S COMING OUT OF HIDING?
FER THE GUY WHO THREW HIS PA IN THE SLAMMER TA DIE? HELL YEAH! SAYS HE WANTS TA GUT THE SNITCH PERSONAL-LIKE.

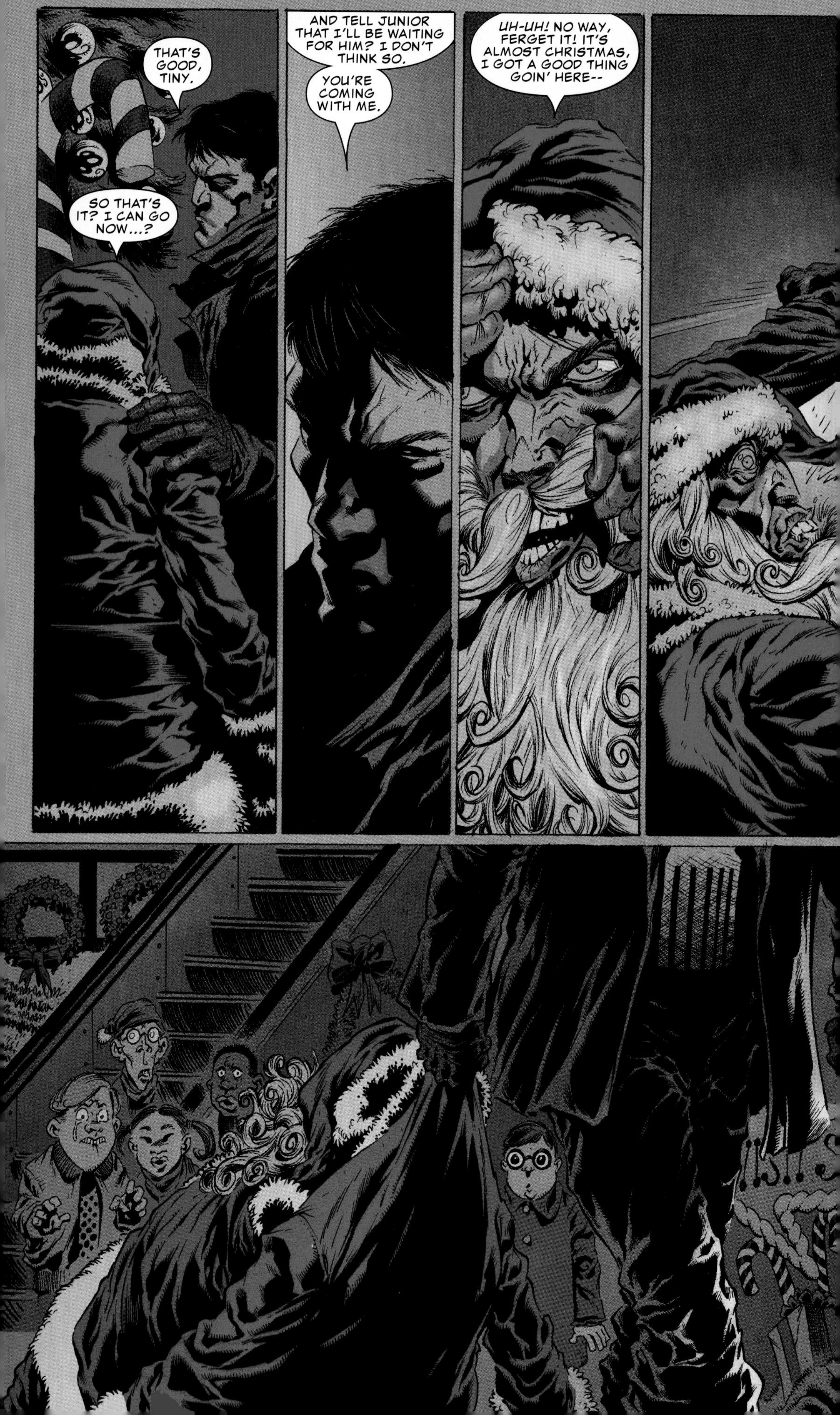
THAT'S GOOD, TINY.
SO THAT'S IT? I CAN GO NOW...?
AND TELL JUNIOR THAT I'LL BE WAITING FOR HIM? I DON'T THINK SO.
YOU'RE COMING WITH ME.
UH-UH! NO WAY, FERGET IT! IT'S ALMOST CHRISTMAS, I GOT A GOOD THING GOIN' HERE--

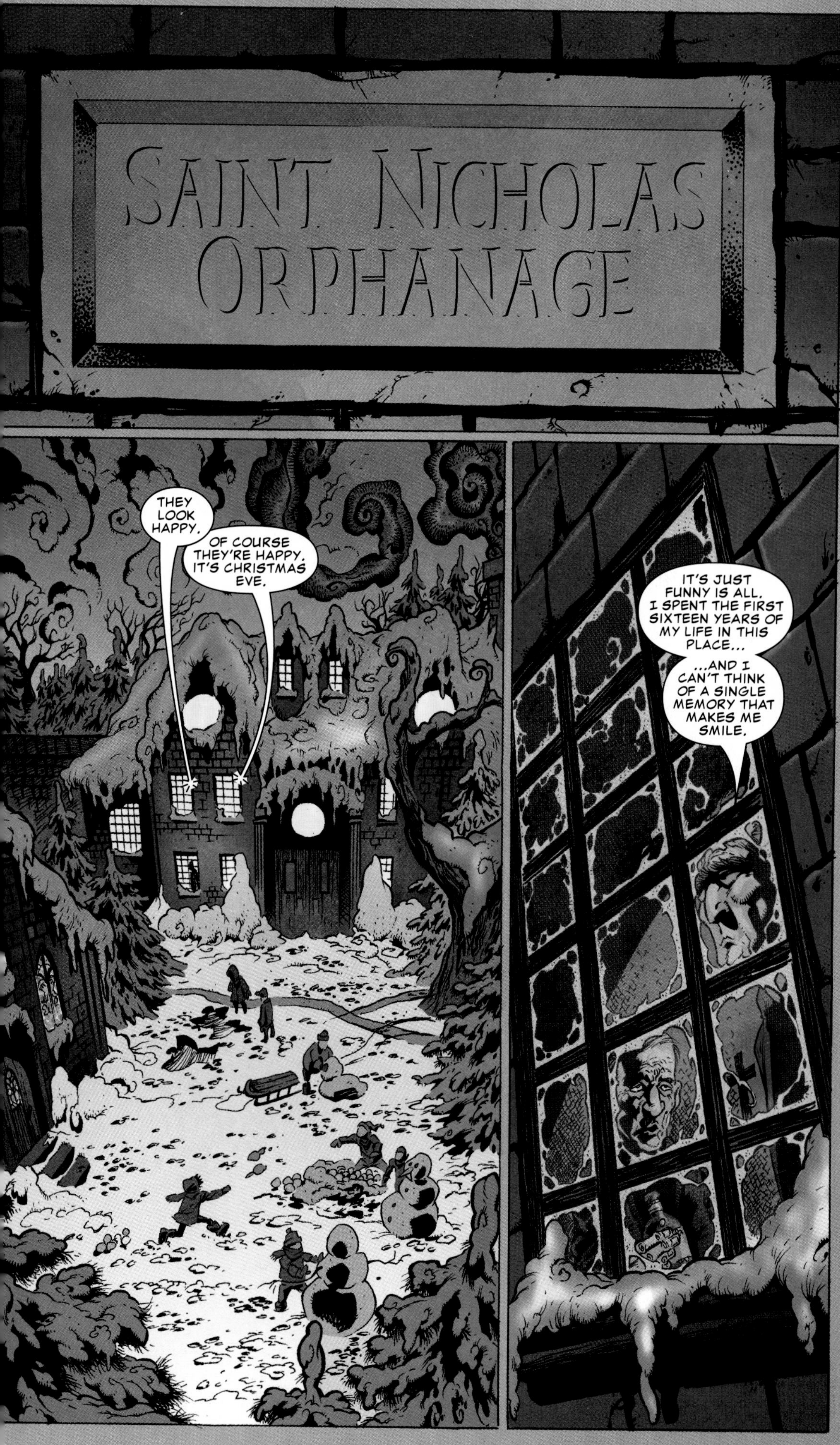
SAINT NICHOLAS ORPHANAGE
THEY LOOK HAPPY.
OF COURSE THEY'RE HAPPY. IT'S CHRISTMAS EVE.
IT'S JUST FUNNY IS ALL. I SPENT THE FIRST SIXTEEN YEARS OF MY LIFE IN THIS PLACE...
...AND I CAN'T THINK OF A SINGLE MEMORY THAT MAKES ME SMILE.

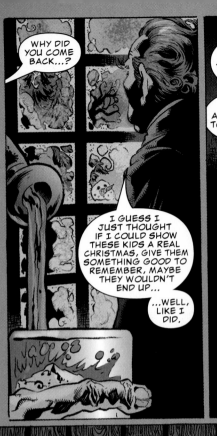

WHY DID YOU COME BACK...?

I GUESS I JUST THOUGHT IF I COULD SHOW THESE KIDS A REAL CHRISTMAS, GIVE THEM SOMETHING GOOD TO REMEMBER, MAYBE THEY WOULDN'T END UP...

...WELL, LIKE I DID.

YOU MADE SOME BAD CHOICES IN LIFE, IT'S TRUE, BUT YOU TURNED YOUR BACK ON WICKEDNESS, GERARDO.

YOU ARE AN EXAMPLE TO US ALL, THAT IT'S NEVER TOO LATE TO CHANGE YOUR WAYS.

HEH.

YOU MAKE IT SOUND LIKE I HAD A CHOICE.

NEVERTHELESS, YOU DID THE RIGHT THING WHEN YOU TURNED STATE'S EVIDENCE. GOD HAS FORGIVEN YOU YOUR SINS.

IT AIN'T GOD I'M WORRIED ABOUT.

I BETRAYED MY OWN PEOPLE. CLOSEST THING TO A REAL FAMILY I EVER HAD...

THEN PERHAPS YOU NEED TO FORGIVE YOURSELF. TELL ME, WHEN DID YOU LAST CONFESS...?

RIGHT ABOUT THE TIME THE FEDS KICKED IN MY FRONT DOOR AND OFFERED ME A DEAL.

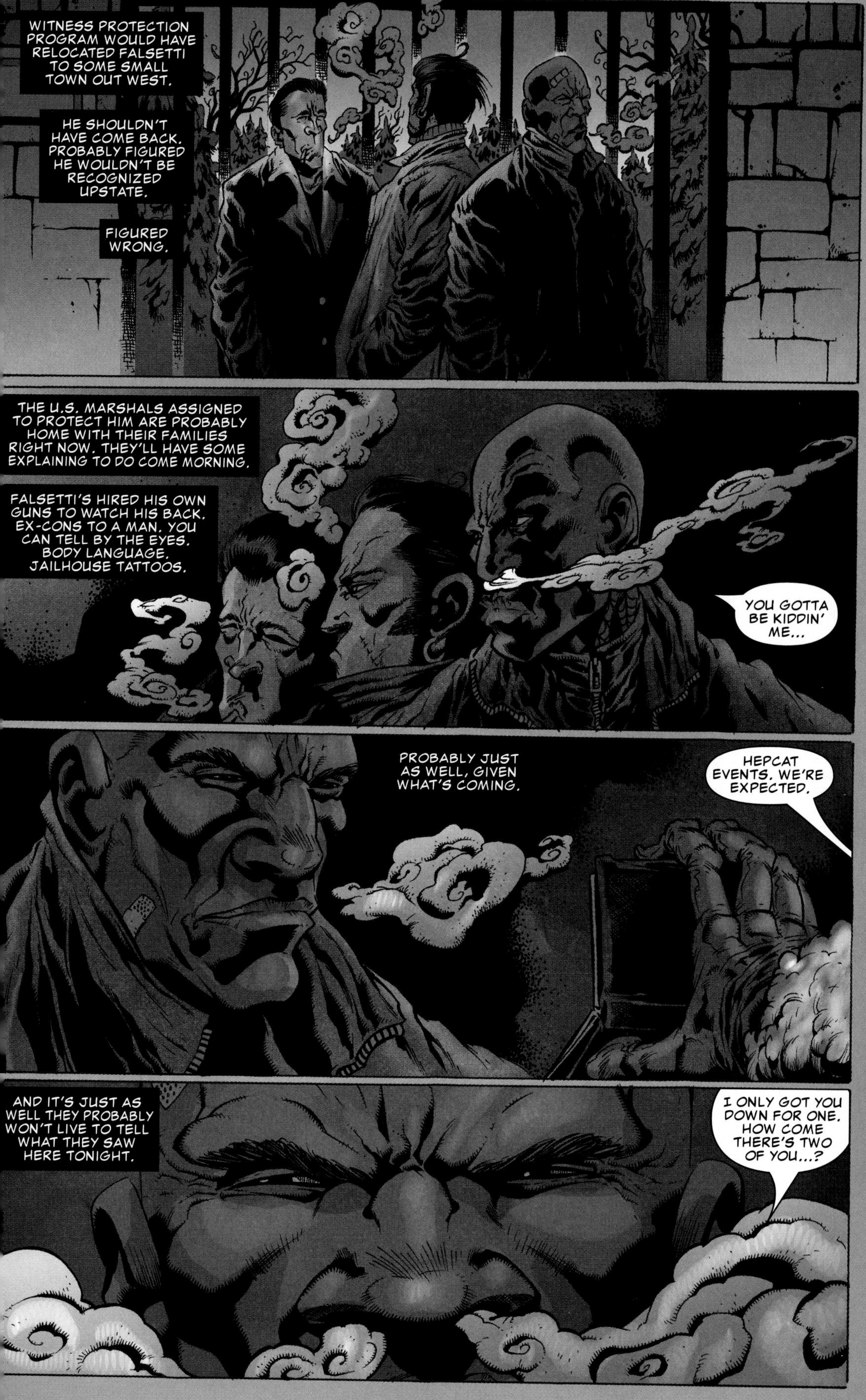
WITNESS PROTECTION PROGRAM WOULD HAVE RELOCATED FALSETTI TO SOME SMALL TOWN OUT WEST.
HE SHOULDN'T HAVE COME BACK. PROBABLY FIGURED HE WOULDN'T BE RECOGNIZED UPSTATE.
FIGURED WRONG.
THE U.S. MARSHALS ASSIGNED TO PROTECT HIM ARE PROBABLY HOME WITH THEIR FAMILIES RIGHT NOW. THEY'LL HAVE SOME EXPLAINING TO DO COME MORNING.
FALSETTI'S HIRED HIS OWN GUNS TO WATCH HIS BACK. EX-CONS TO A MAN. YOU CAN TELL BY THE EYES. BODY LANGUAGE. JAILHOUSE TATTOOS.
YOU GOTTA BE KIDDIN' ME...
PROBABLY JUST AS WELL, GIVEN WHAT'S COMING.
HEPCAT EVENTS. WE'RE EXPECTED.
AND IT'S JUST AS WELL THEY PROBABLY WON'T LIVE TO TELL WHAT THEY SAW HERE TONIGHT.
I ONLY GOT YOU DOWN FOR ONE. HOW COME THERE'S TWO OF YOU...?

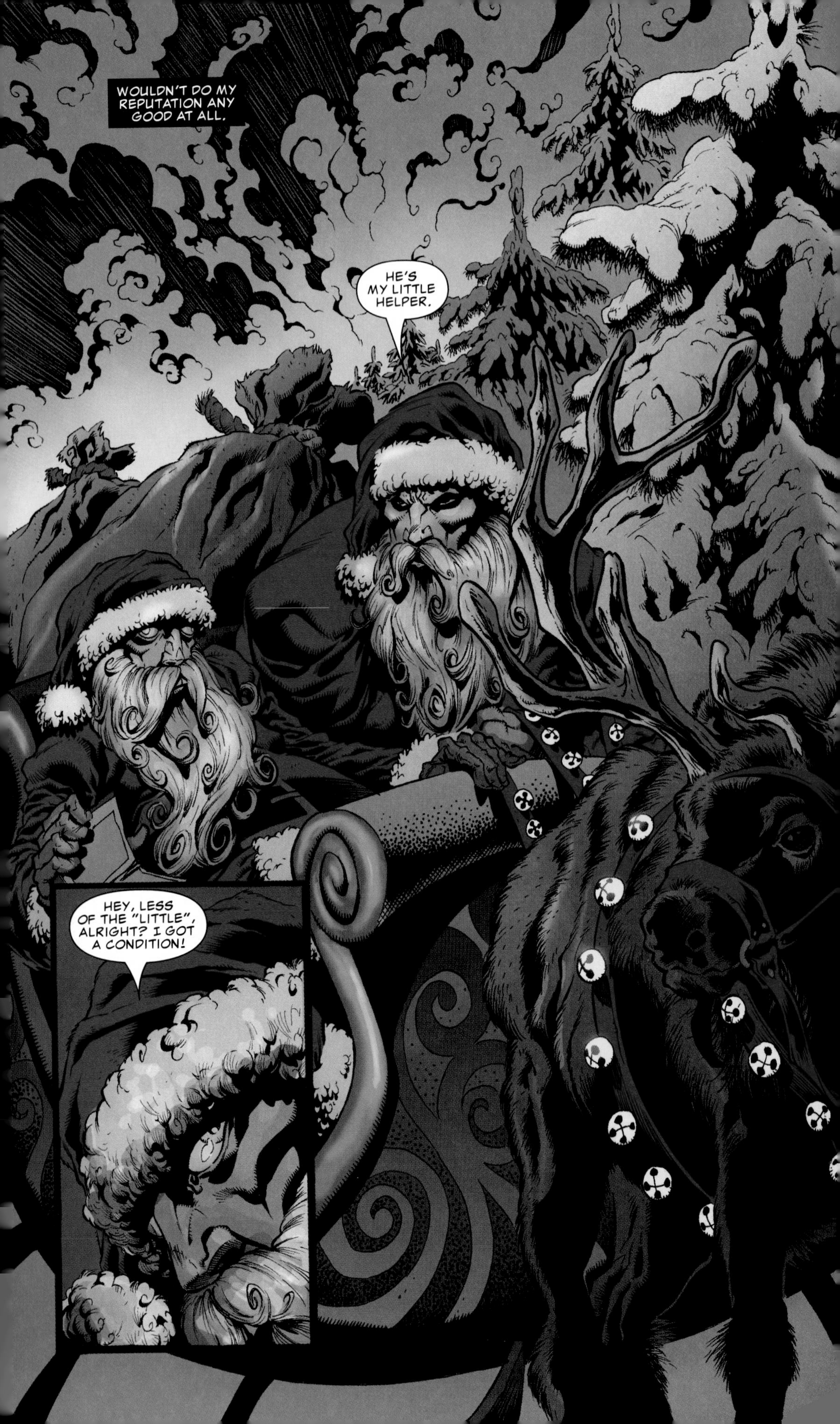
WOULDN'T DO MY REPUTATION ANY GOOD AT ALL.
HE'S MY LITTLE HELPER.
HEY, LESS OF THE "LITTLE", ALRIGHT? I GOT A CONDITION!

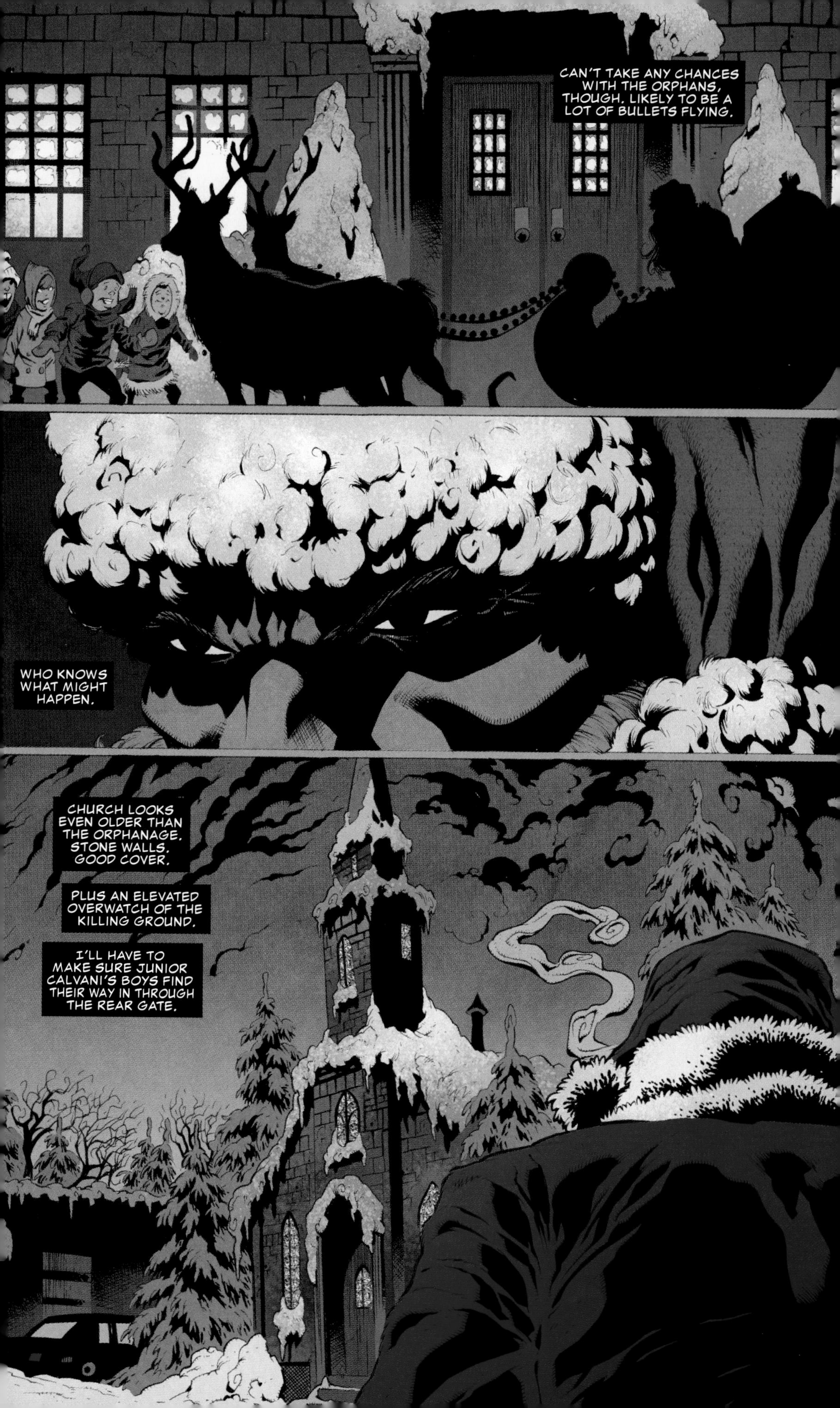
CAN'T TAKE ANY CHANCES WITH THE ORPHANS, THOUGH. LIKELY TO BE A LOT OF BULLETS FLYING.
WHO KNOWS WHAT MIGHT HAPPEN.
CHURCH LOOKS EVEN OLDER THAN THE ORPHANAGE. STONE WALLS. GOOD COVER.
PLUS AN ELEVATED OVERWATCH OF THE KILLING GROUND.
I'LL HAVE TO MAKE SURE JUNIOR CALVANI'S BOYS FIND THEIR WAY IN THROUGH THE REAR GATE.

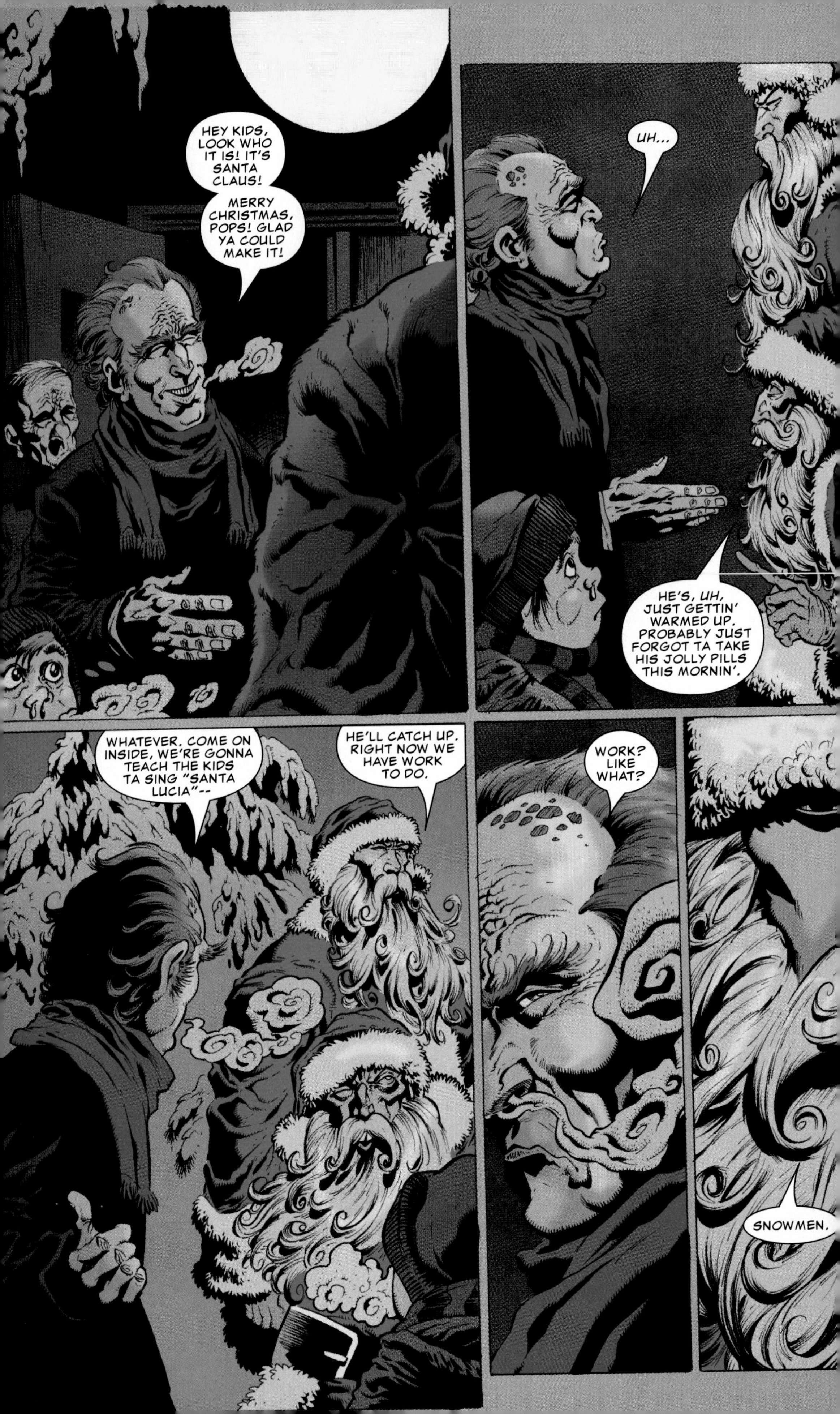
HEY KIDS, LOOK WHO IT IS! IT'S SANTA CLAUS!
MERRY CHRISTMAS, POPS! GLAD YA COULD MAKE IT!
UH...
HE'S, UH, JUST GETTIN' WARMED UP. PROBABLY JUST FORGOT TA TAKE HIS JOLLY PILLS THIS MORNIN'.
WHATEVER. COME ON INSIDE, WE'RE GONNA TEACH THE KIDS TA SING "SANTA LUCIA"--
HE'LL CATCH UP. RIGHT NOW WE HAVE WORK TO DO.
WORK? LIKE WHAT?
SNOWMEN.

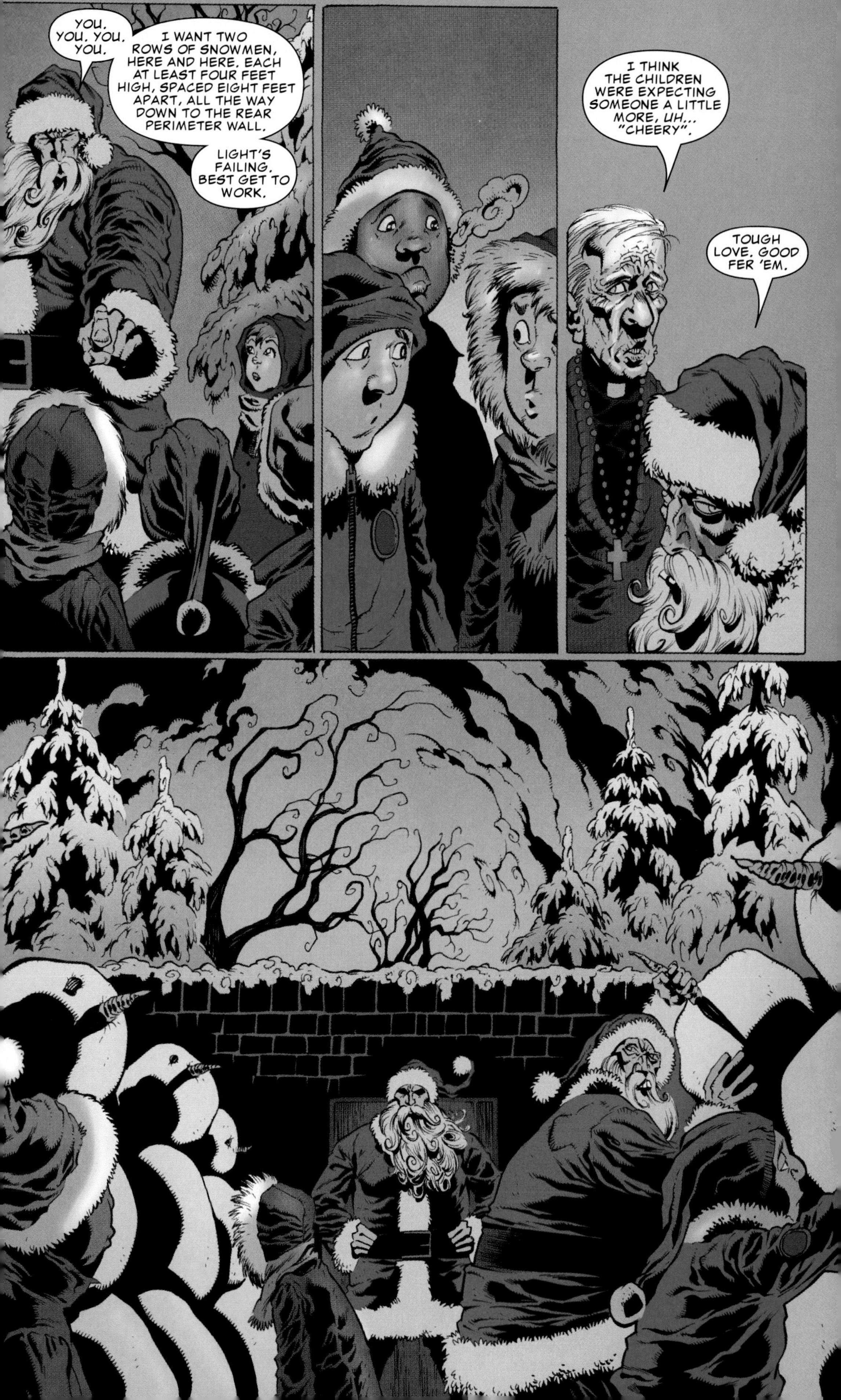
YOU. YOU. YOU. YOU.
I WANT TWO ROWS OF SNOWMEN, HERE AND HERE. EACH AT LEAST FOUR FEET HIGH, SPACED EIGHT FEET APART, ALL THE WAY DOWN TO THE REAR PERIMETER WALL.
LIGHT'S FAILING. BEST GET TO WORK.
I THINK THE CHILDREN WERE EXPECTING SOMEONE A LITTLE MORE, UH... "CHEERY".
TOUGH LOVE. GOOD FER 'EM.

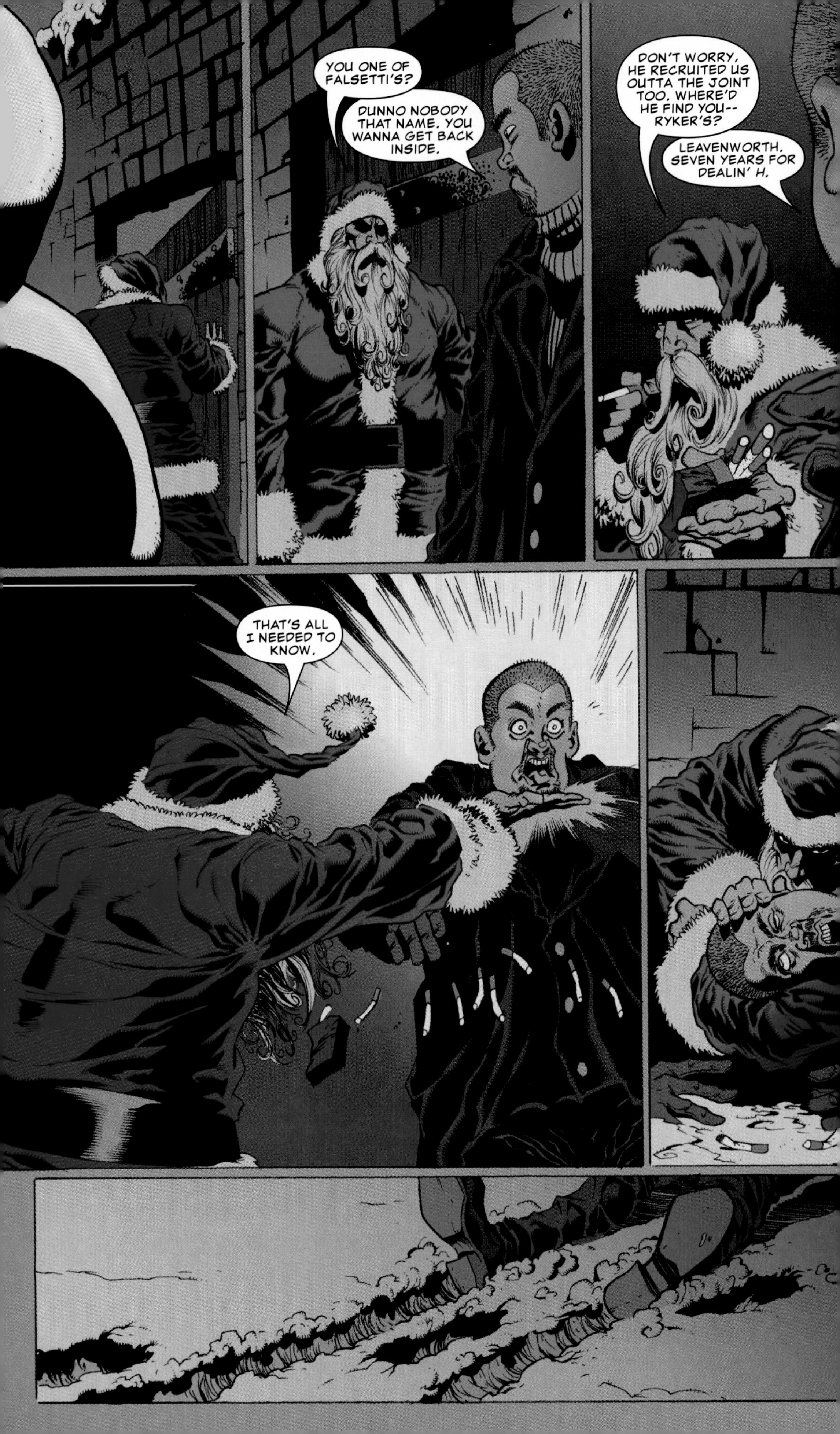
YOU ONE OF FALSETTI'S?
DUNNO NOBODY THAT NAME. YOU WANNA GET BACK INSIDE.
DON'T WORRY, HE RECRUITED US OUTTA THE JOINT TOO. WHERE'D HE FIND YOU-- RYKER'S?
LEAVENWORTH. SEVEN YEARS FOR DEALIN' H.
THAT'S ALL I NEEDED TO KNOW.

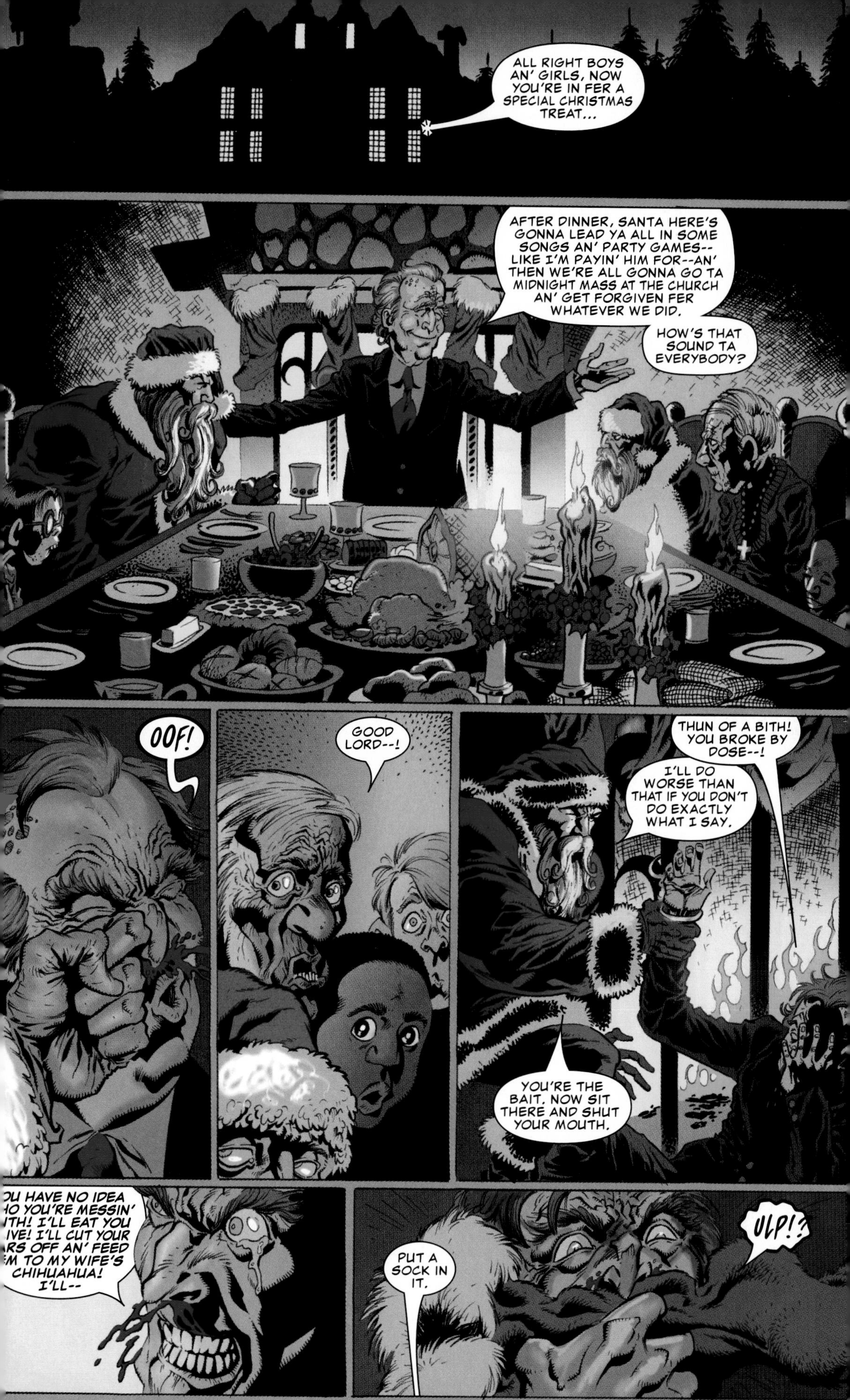
ALL RIGHT BOYS AN' GIRLS, NOW YOU'RE IN FER A SPECIAL CHRISTMAS TREAT...
AFTER DINNER, SANTA HERE'S GONNA LEAD YA ALL IN SOME SONGS AN' PARTY GAMES-- LIKE I'M PAYIN' HIM FOR--AN' THEN WE'RE ALL GONNA GO TA MIDNIGHT MASS AT THE CHURCH AN' GET FORGIVEN FER WHATEVER WE DID.
HOW'S THAT SOUND TA EVERYBODY?
OOF!
GOOD LORD--!
THUN OF A BITH! YOU BROKE BY DOSE--!
I'LL DO WORSE THAN THAT IF YOU DON'T DO EXACTLY WHAT I SAY.
YOU'RE THE BAIT. NOW SIT THERE AND SHUT YOUR MOUTH.
OU HAVE NO IDEA HO YOU'RE MESSIN' ITH! I'LL EAT YOU IVE! I'LL CUT YOUR ARS OFF AN' FEED EM TO MY WIFE'S CHIHUAHUA! I'LL--
PUT A SOCK IN IT.
ULP!?

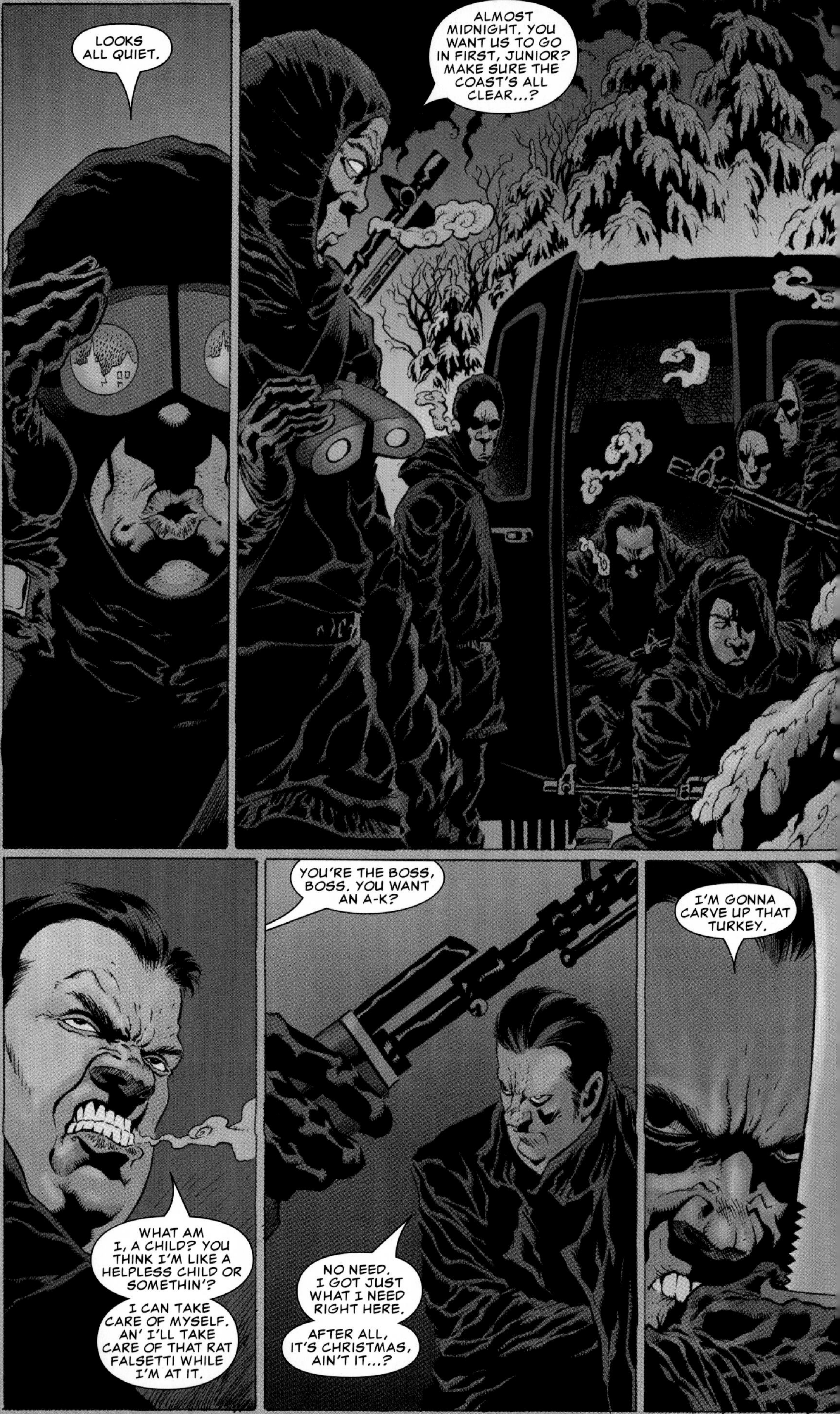
LOOKS ALL QUIET.
ALMOST MIDNIGHT. YOU WANT US TO GO IN FIRST, JUNIOR? MAKE SURE THE COAST'S ALL CLEAR...?
WHAT AM I, A CHILD? YOU THINK I'M LIKE A HELPLESS CHILD OR SOMETHIN'?
I CAN TAKE CARE OF MYSELF. AN' I'LL TAKE CARE OF THAT RAT FALSETTI WHILE I'M AT IT.
YOU'RE THE BOSS, BOSS. YOU WANT AN A-K?
NO NEED. I GOT JUST WHAT I NEED RIGHT HERE.
AFTER ALL, IT'S CHRISTMAS, AIN'T IT...?
I'M GONNA CARVE UP THAT TURKEY.

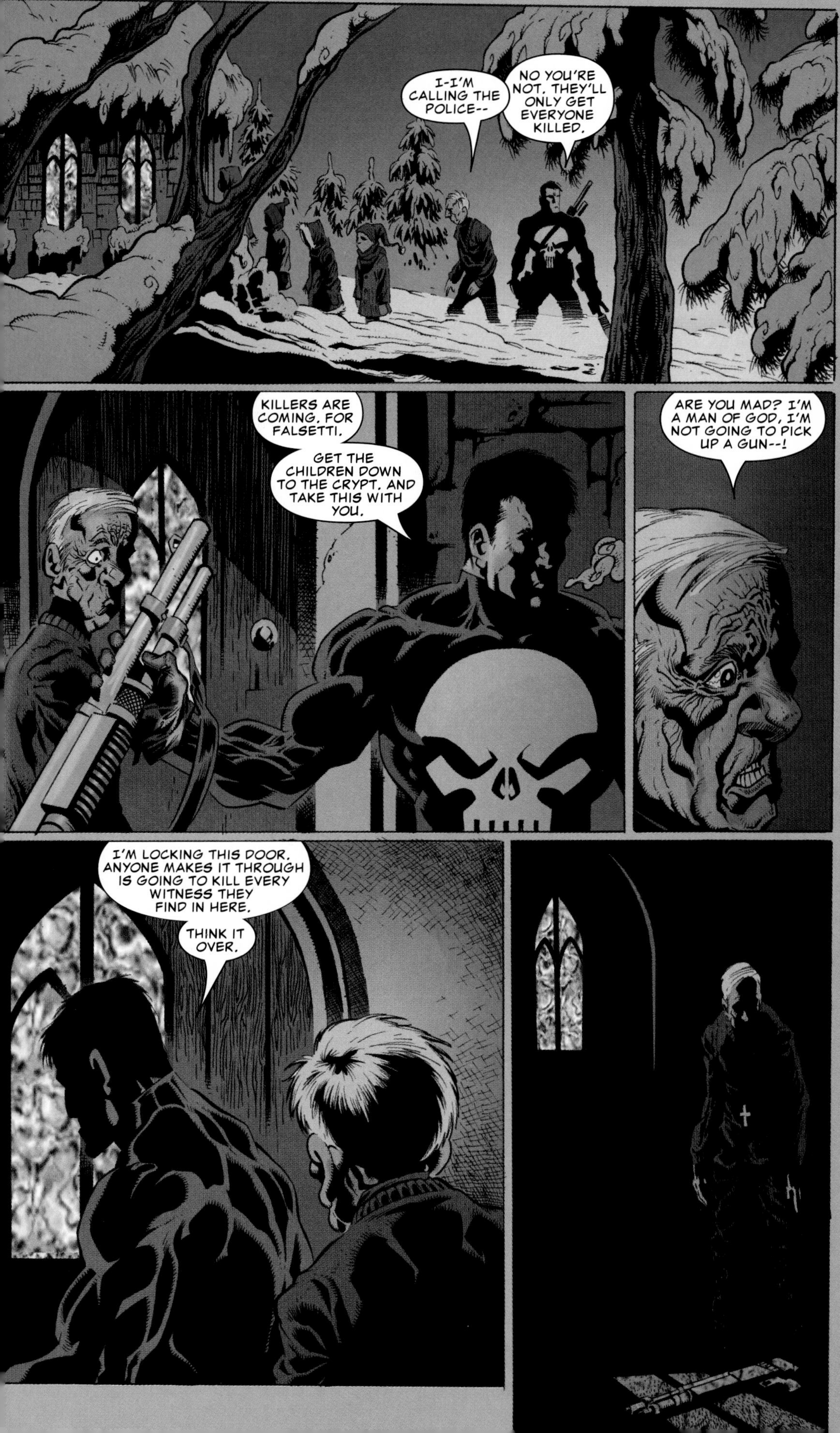

I-I'M CALLING THE POLICE--
NO YOU'RE NOT. THEY'LL ONLY GET EVERYONE KILLED.
KILLERS ARE COMING. FOR FALSETTI.
GET THE CHILDREN DOWN TO THE CRYPT. AND TAKE THIS WITH YOU.
ARE YOU MAD? I'M A MAN OF GOD. I'M NOT GOING TO PICK UP A GUN--!
I'M LOCKING THIS DOOR. ANYONE MAKES IT THROUGH IS GOING TO KILL EVERY WITNESS THEY FIND IN HERE.
THINK IT OVER.

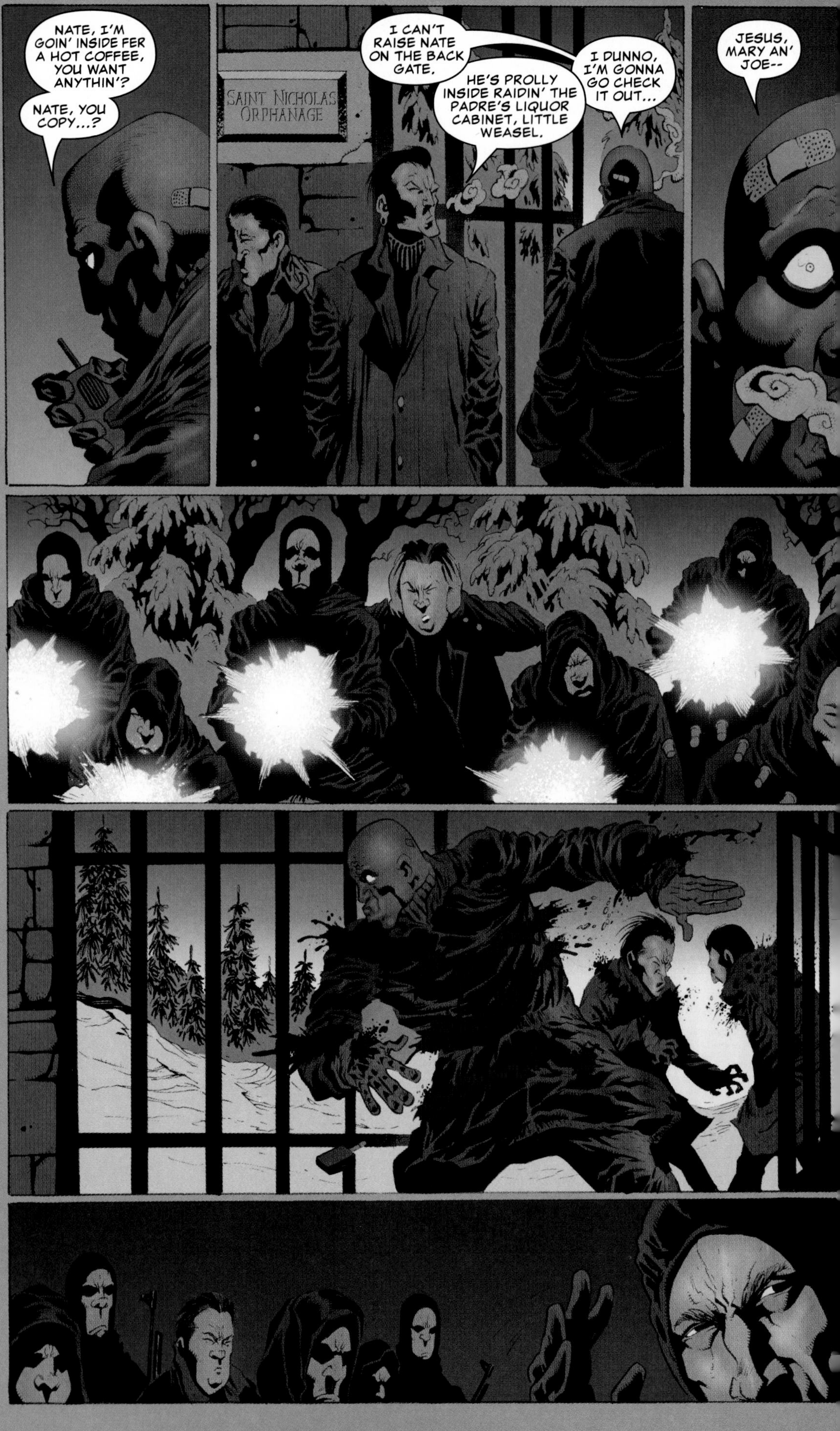
NATE, I'M GOIN' INSIDE FER A HOT COFFEE, YOU WANT ANYTHIN'?
NATE, YOU COPY...?
SAINT NICHOLAS ORPHANAGE
I CAN'T RAISE NATE ON THE BACK GATE.
HE'S PROLLY INSIDE RAIDIN' THE PADRE'S LIQUOR CABINET, LITTLE WEASEL.
I DUNNO, I'M GONNA GO CHECK IT OUT...
JESUS, MARY AN' JOE--

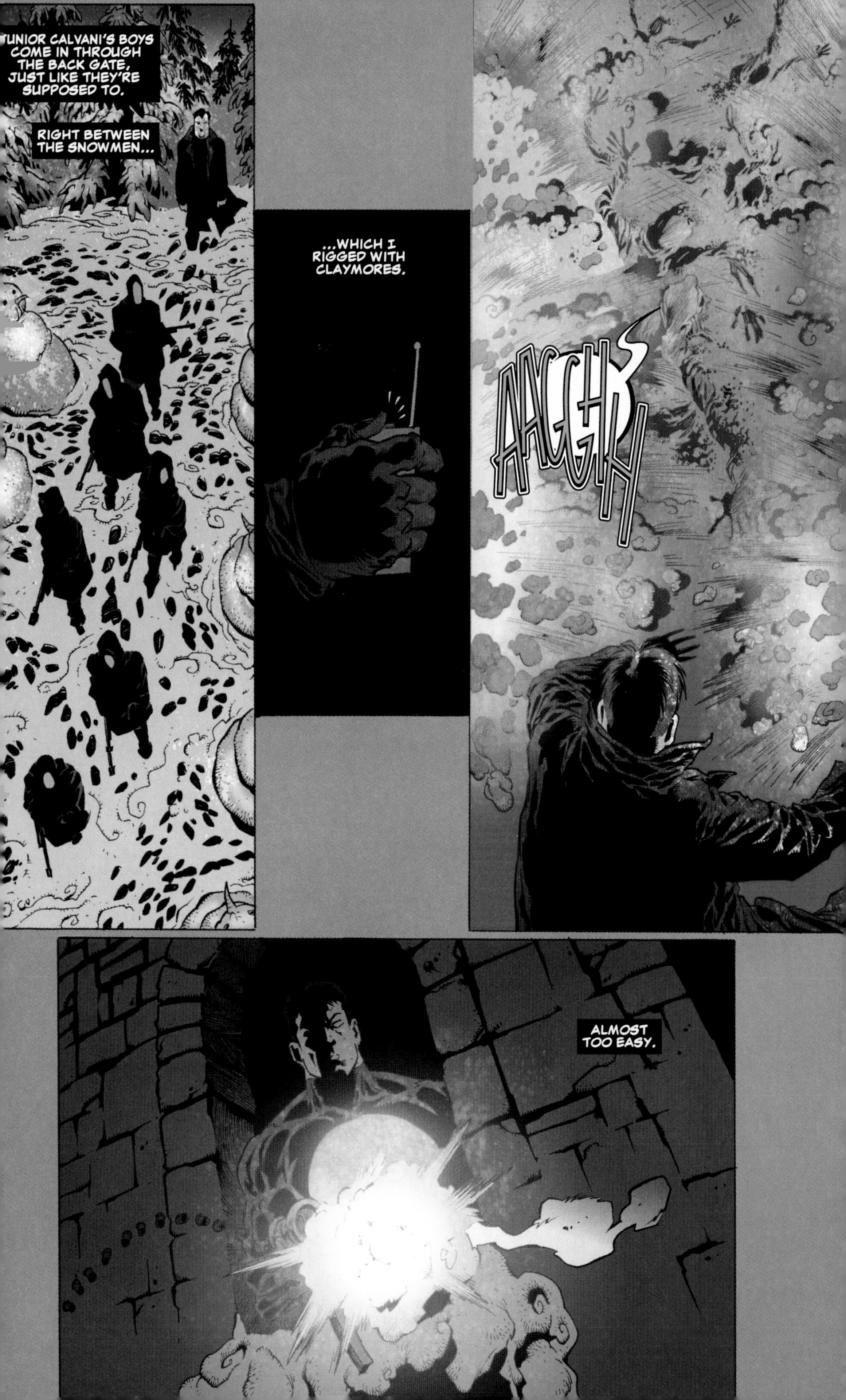
JUNIOR CALVANI'S BOYS COME IN THROUGH THE BACK GATE, JUST LIKE THEY'RE SUPPOSED TO.
RIGHT BETWEEN THE SNOWMEN...
...WHICH I RIGGED WITH CLAYMORES.
AAGGHH
ALMOST TOO EASY.

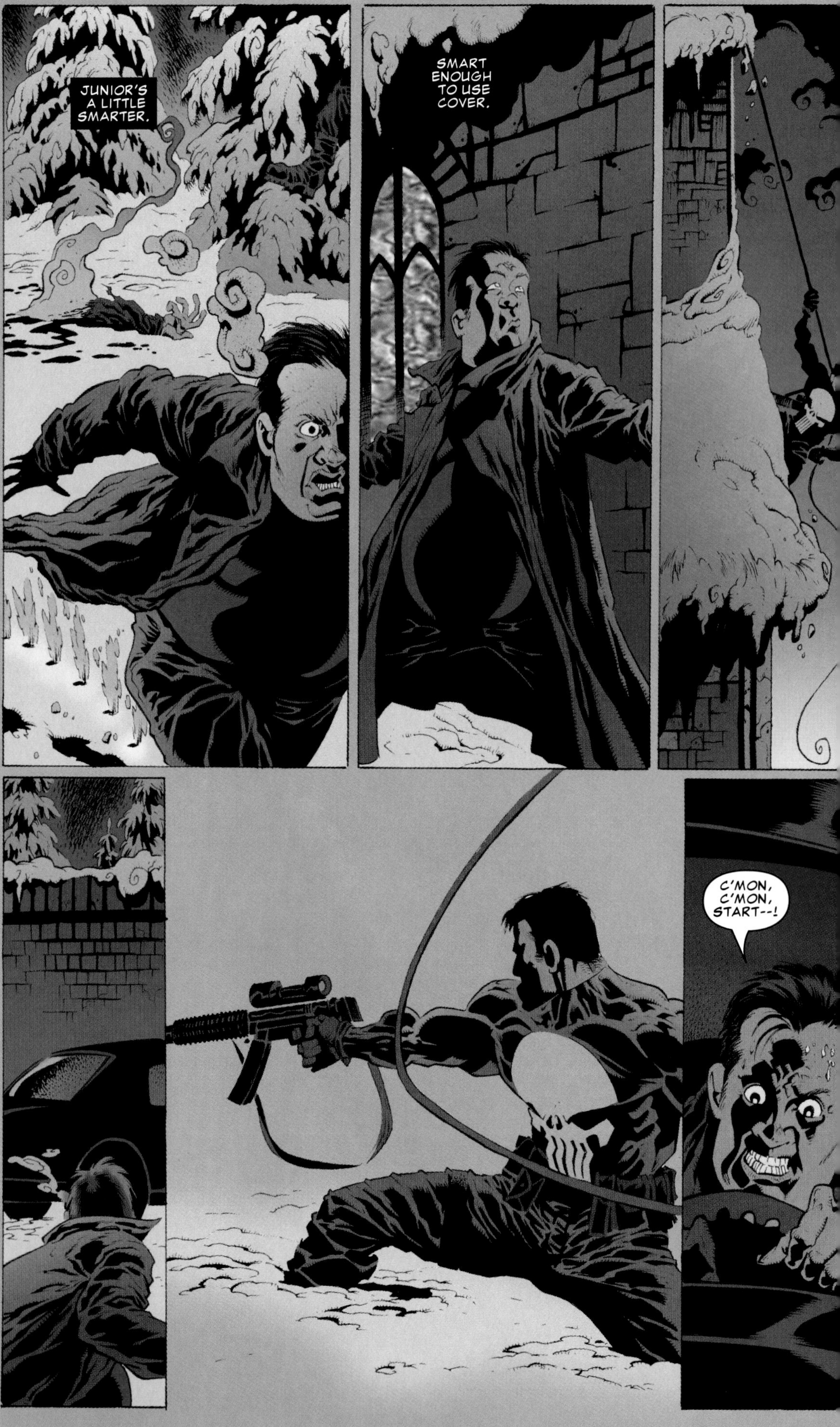
JUNIOR'S A LITTLE SMARTER.
SMART ENOUGH TO USE COVER.
C'MON, C'MON, START--!

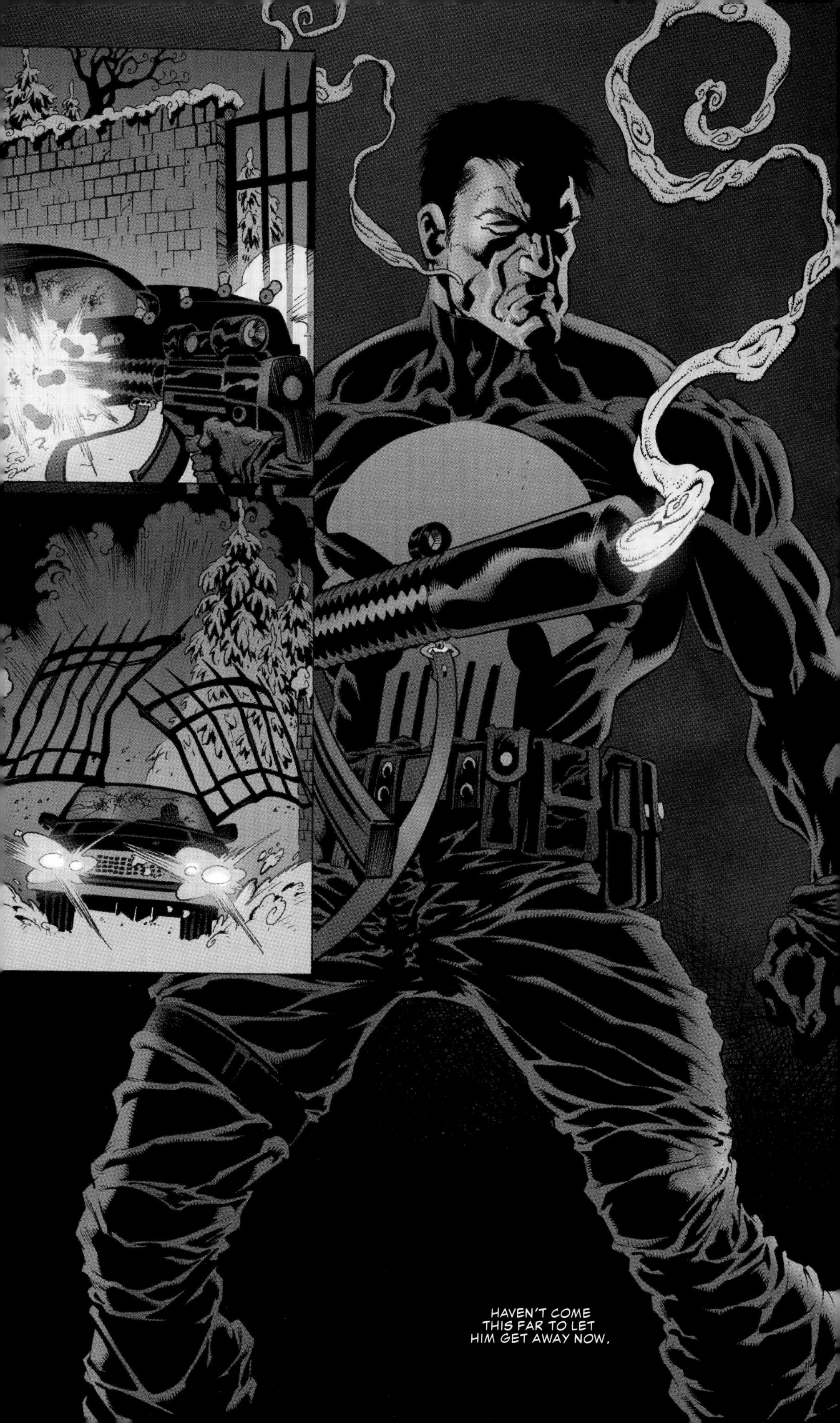
HAVEN'T COME THIS FAR TO LET HIM GET AWAY NOW.

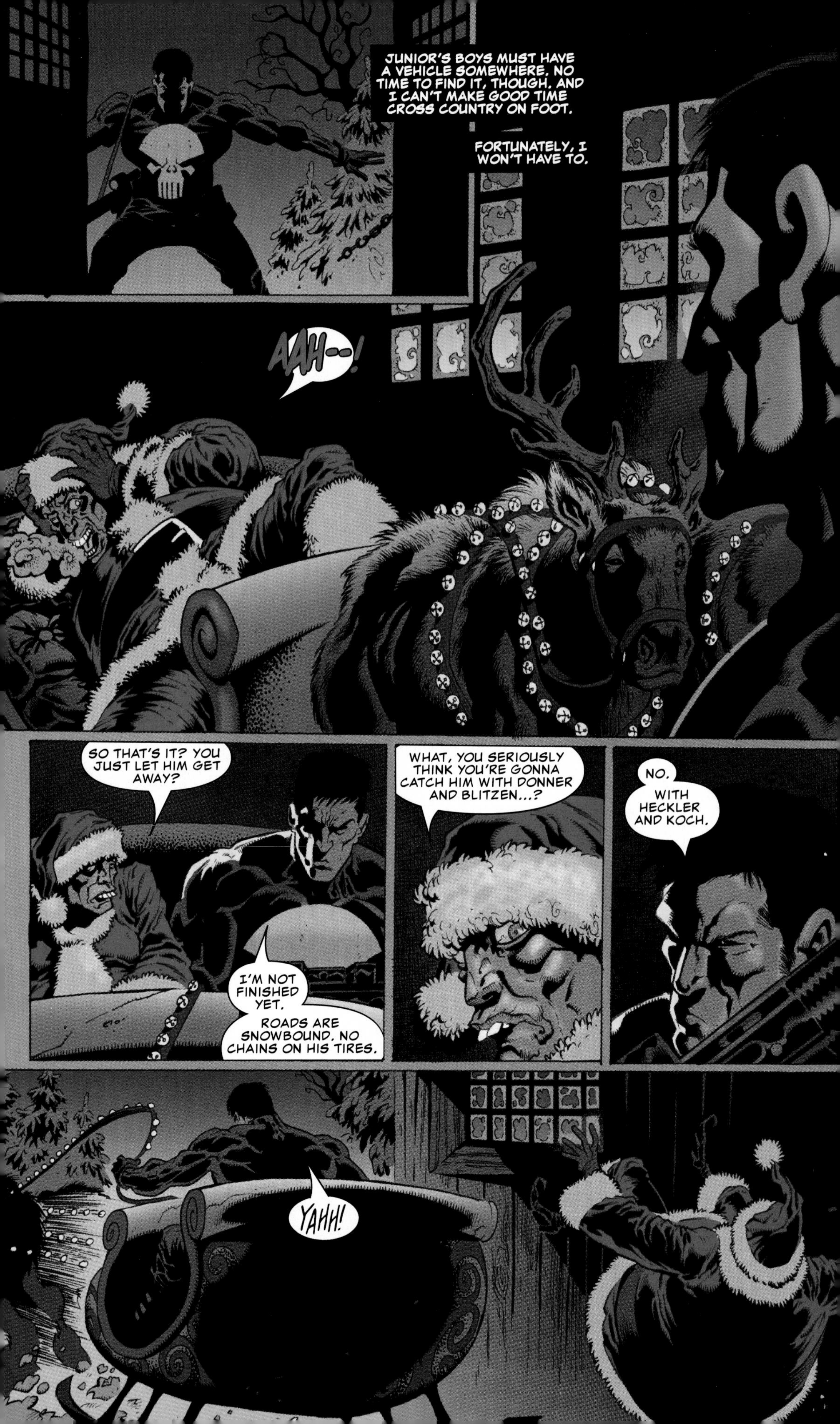
JUNIOR'S BOYS MUST HAVE A VEHICLE SOMEWHERE. NO TIME TO FIND IT, THOUGH. AND I CAN'T MAKE GOOD TIME CROSS COUNTRY ON FOOT.
FORTUNATELY, I WON'T HAVE TO.
AAH--!
SO THAT'S IT? YOU JUST LET HIM GET AWAY?
I'M NOT FINISHED YET.
ROADS ARE SNOWBOUND. NO CHAINS ON HIS TIRES.
WHAT, YOU SERIOUSLY THINK YOU'RE GONNA CATCH HIM WITH DONNER AND BLITZEN...?
NO.
WITH HECKLER AND KOCH.
YAHH!

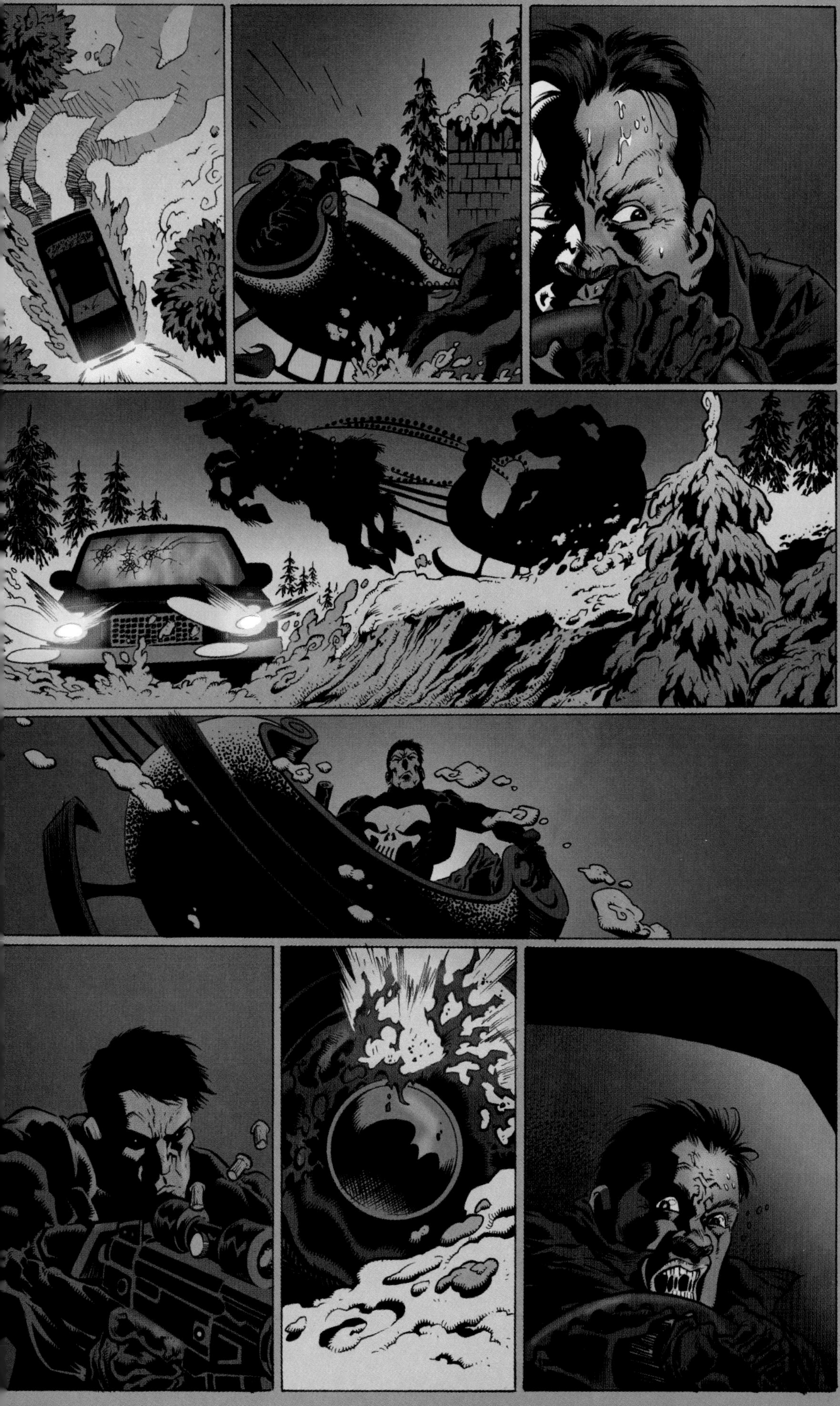

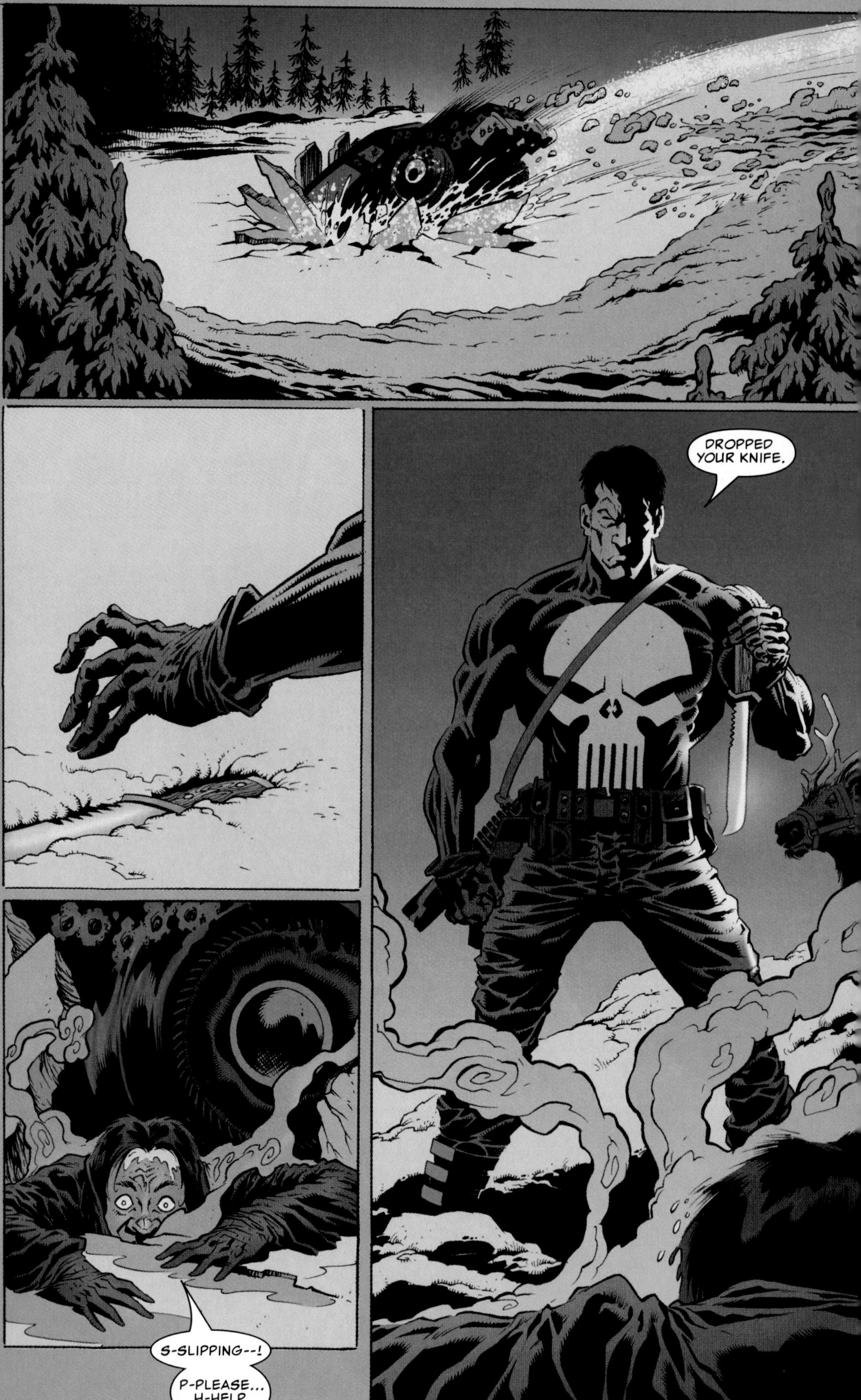

DROPPED YOUR KNIFE.
S-SLIPPING--!
P-PLEASE... H-HELP ME...

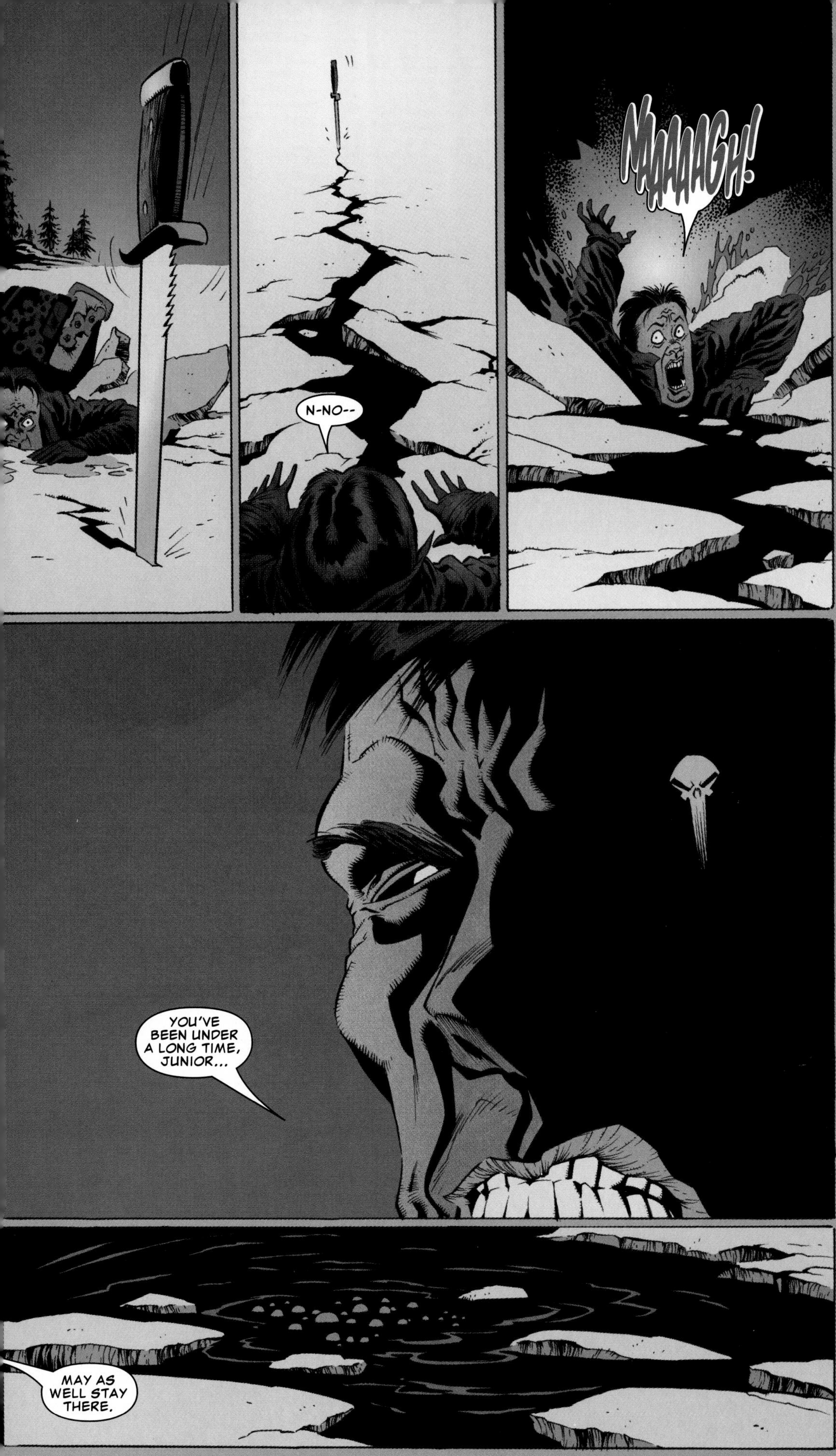
N-NO--
NAAAAAGH!
YOU'VE BEEN UNDER A LONG TIME, JUNIOR...
MAY AS WELL STAY THERE.

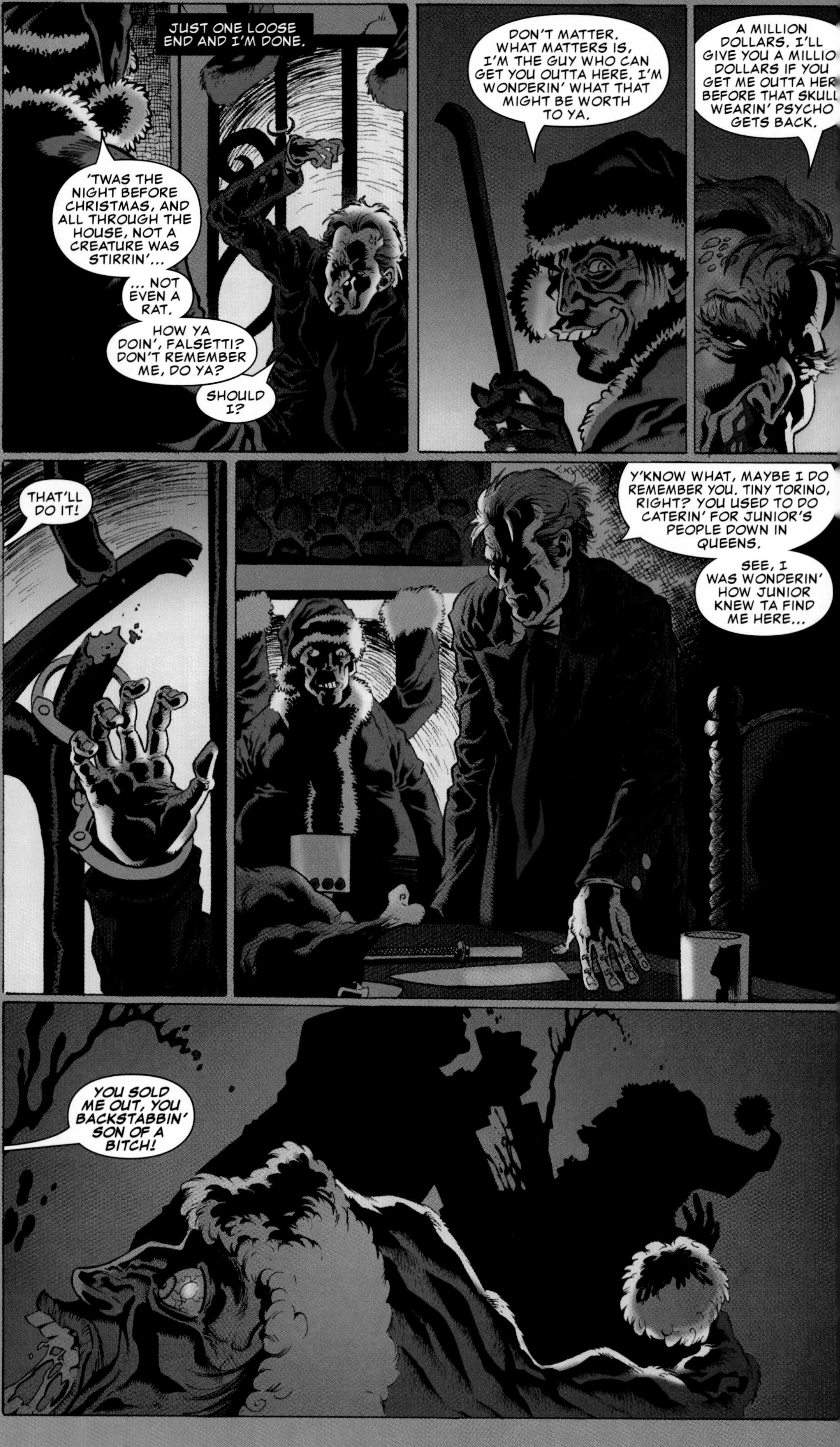
JUST ONE LOOSE END AND I'M DONE.
'TWAS THE NIGHT BEFORE CHRISTMAS, AND ALL THROUGH THE HOUSE, NOT A CREATURE WAS STIRRIN'...
... NOT EVEN A RAT.
HOW YA DOIN', FALSETTI? DON'T REMEMBER ME, DO YA?
SHOULD I?
DON'T MATTER. WHAT MATTERS IS, I'M THE GUY WHO CAN GET YOU OUTTA HERE. I'M WONDERIN' WHAT THAT MIGHT BE WORTH TO YA.
A MILLION DOLLARS. I'LL GIVE YOU A MILLIO DOLLARS IF YOU GET ME OUTTA HER BEFORE THAT SKULL WEARIN' PSYCHO GETS BACK.
THAT'LL DO IT!
Y'KNOW WHAT, MAYBE I DO REMEMBER YOU. TINY TORINO, RIGHT? YOU USED TO DO CATERIN' FOR JUNIOR'S PEOPLE DOWN IN QUEENS.
SEE, I WAS WONDERIN' HOW JUNIOR KNEW TA FIND ME HERE...
YOU SOLD ME OUT, YOU BACKSTABBIN' SON OF A BITCH!

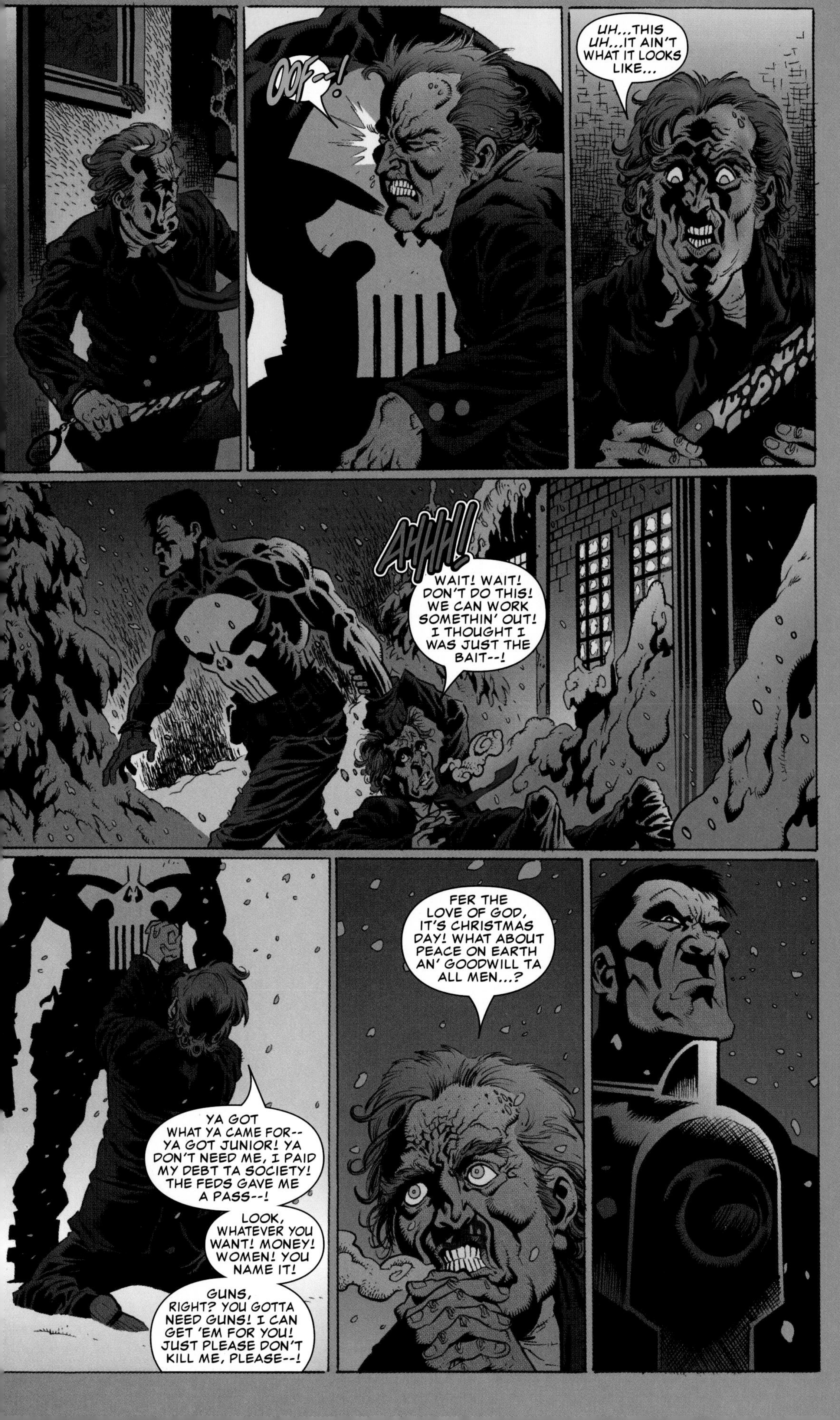
OOF--!
UH...THIS UH...IT AIN'T WHAT IT LOOKS LIKE...
AHHH!
WAIT! WAIT! DON'T DO THIS! WE CAN WORK SOMETHIN' OUT! I THOUGHT I WAS JUST THE BAIT--!
YA GOT WHAT YA CAME FOR-- YA GOT JUNIOR! YA DON'T NEED ME, I PAID MY DEBT TA SOCIETY! THE FEDS GAVE ME A PASS--!
LOOK, WHATEVER YOU WANT! MONEY! WOMEN! YOU NAME IT!
GUNS, RIGHT? YOU GOTTA NEED GUNS! I CAN GET 'EM FOR YOU! JUST PLEASE DON'T KILL ME, PLEASE--!
FER THE LOVE OF GOD, IT'S CHRISTMAS DAY! WHAT ABOUT PEACE ON EARTH AN' GOODWILL TA ALL MEN...?

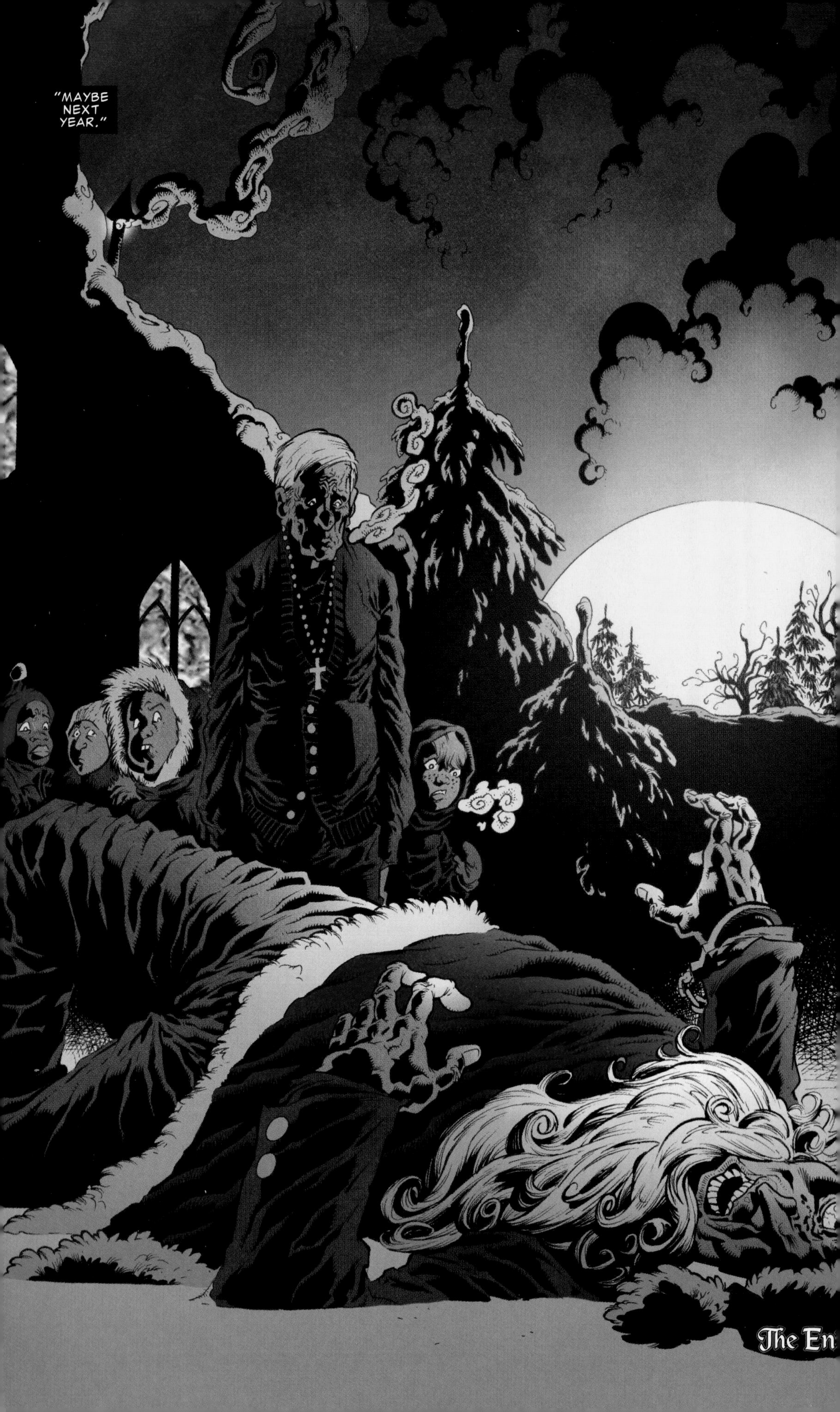
"MAYBE NEXT YEAR."
The En

nisher: Silent Night Cover Concepts by Mike Deodato

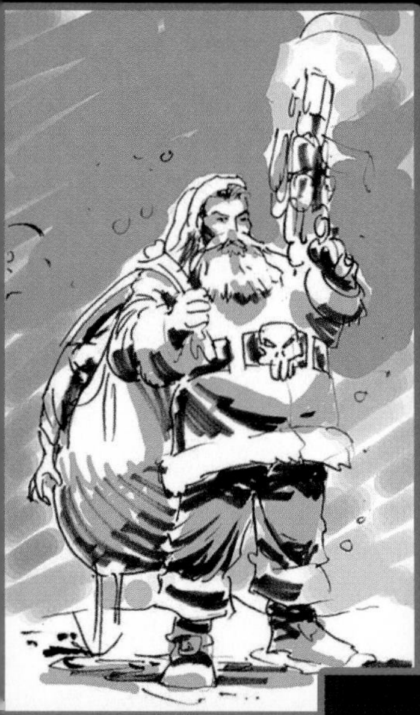

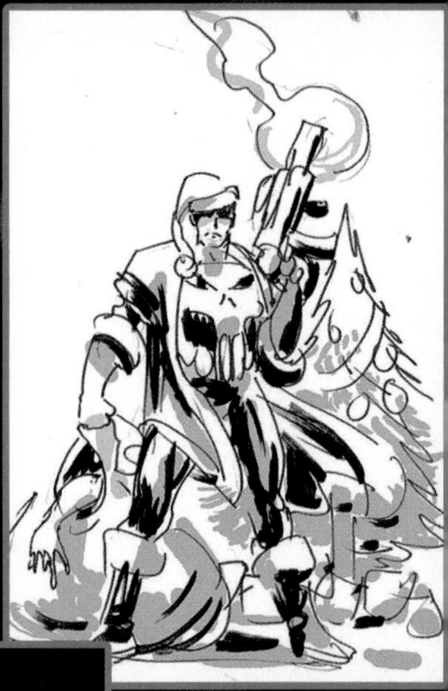

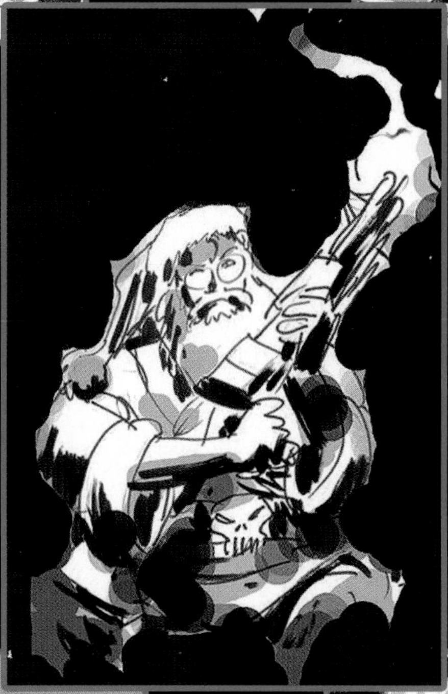

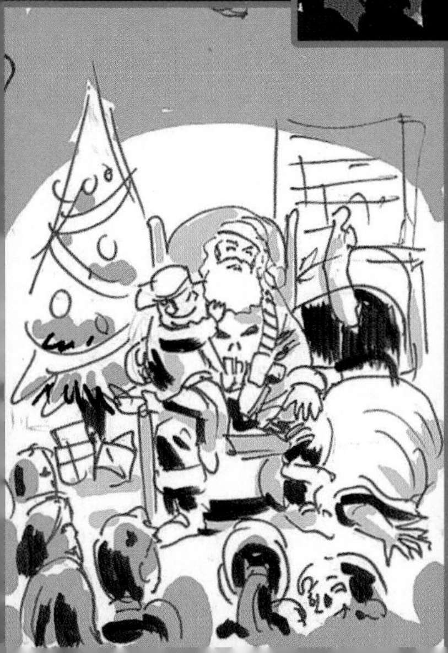

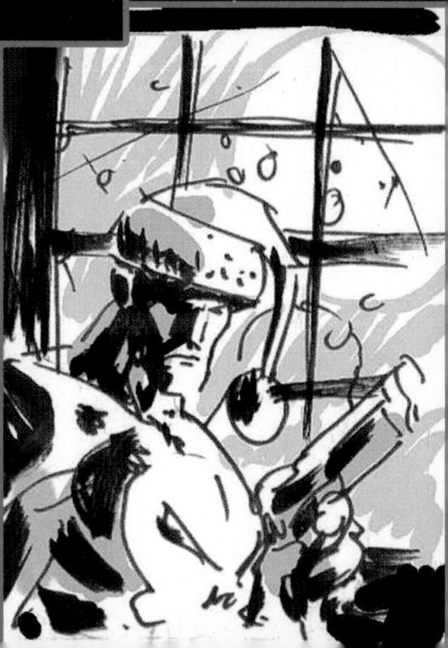

Punisher: Silent Night Cover Inks by Mike Deodato Jr.

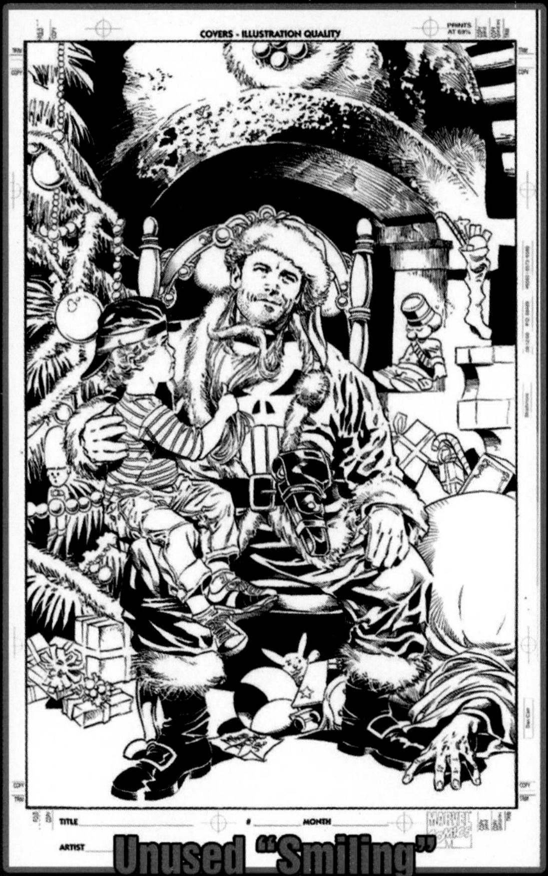

COVERS - ILLUSTRATION QUALITY
PRINTS AT 69%
TITLE
#
MONTH
ARTIST
MARVEL COMICS

Unused "Smiling"

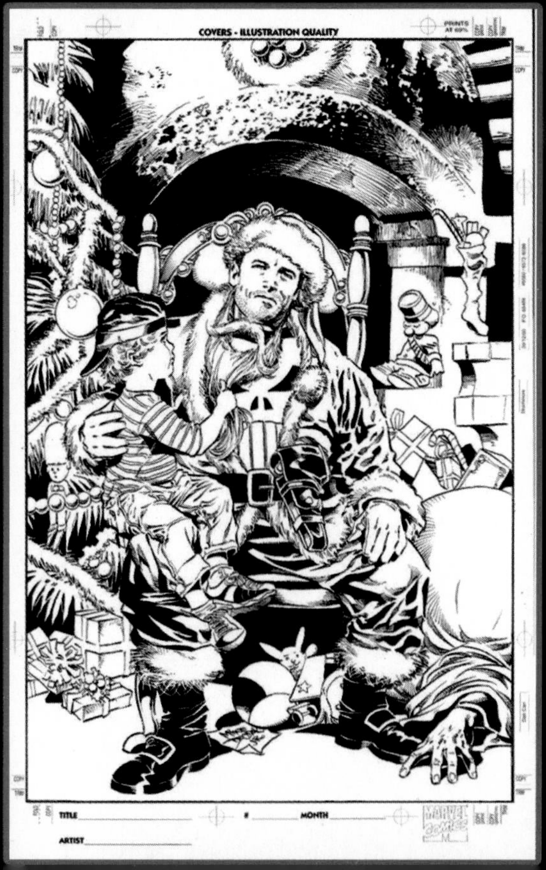

COVERS - ILLUSTRATION QUALITY
PRINTS AT 69%
TITLE
#
MONTH
ARTIST
MARVEL COMICS